# A gregory TREASURY 2



Created, written, drawn and lettered by

**Marc Hempel**

secret lovers

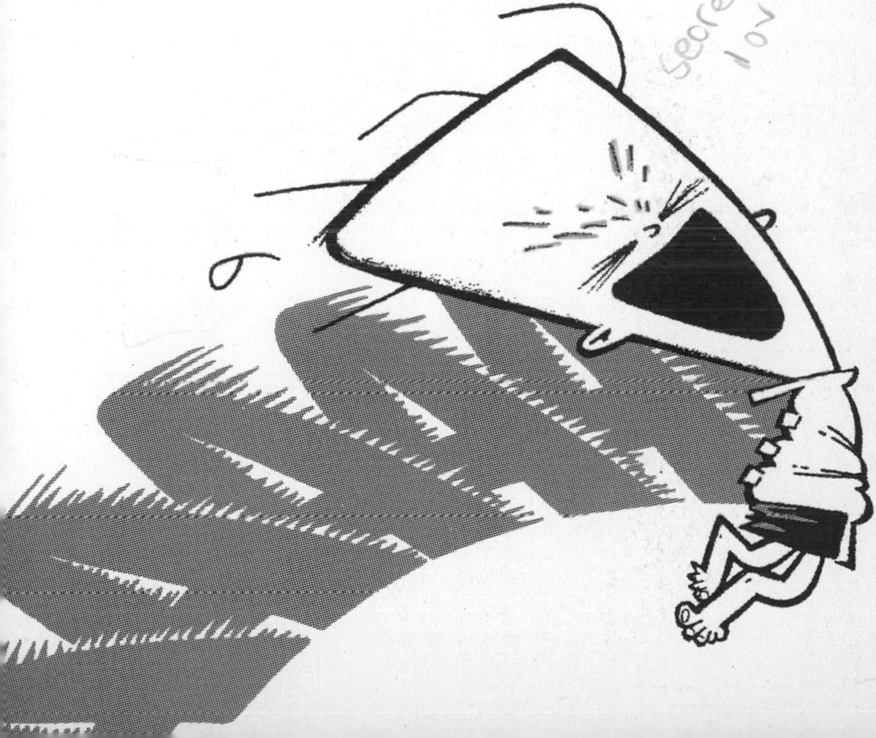

*AG*
*HEM*

**A GREGORY TREASURY VOL. 2**
Published by DC Comics. Cover, introduction and compilation
copyright © 2004 DC Comics. All Rights Reserved.

Originally published in single magazine form as GREGORY III and
GREGORY IV: FAT BOY. Copyright © 1993 Marc Hempel. All Rights Reserved.
All characters, their distinctive likenesses and related elements featured
in this publication are trademarks of DC Comics. The stories, characters and
incidents featured in this publication are entirely fictional. DC Comics
does not read or accept unsolicited submissions of ideas, stories or artwork.

DC Comics, 1700 Broadway, New York, NY 10019
A Warner Bros. Entertainment Company
Printed in Canada. First Printing.
ISBN: 1-4012-0301-9

Cover illustration by Marc Hempel.
Publication design by Peter Hamboussi.

# CONTENTS



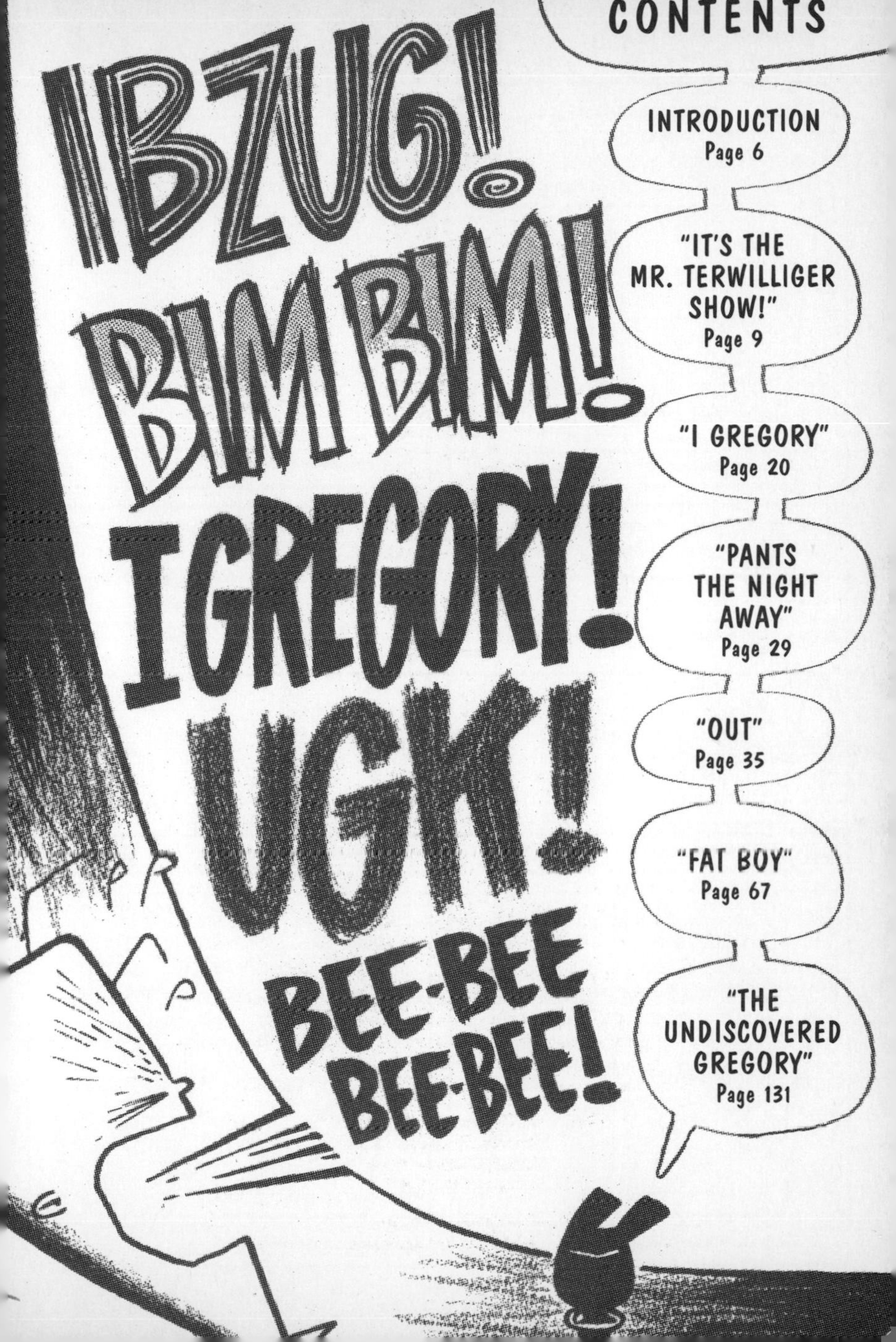

BZUG!
BIM BIM!
I GREGORY!
UGK!
BEE-BEE BEE-BEE!

# GREGORY: 2150 A.D.!

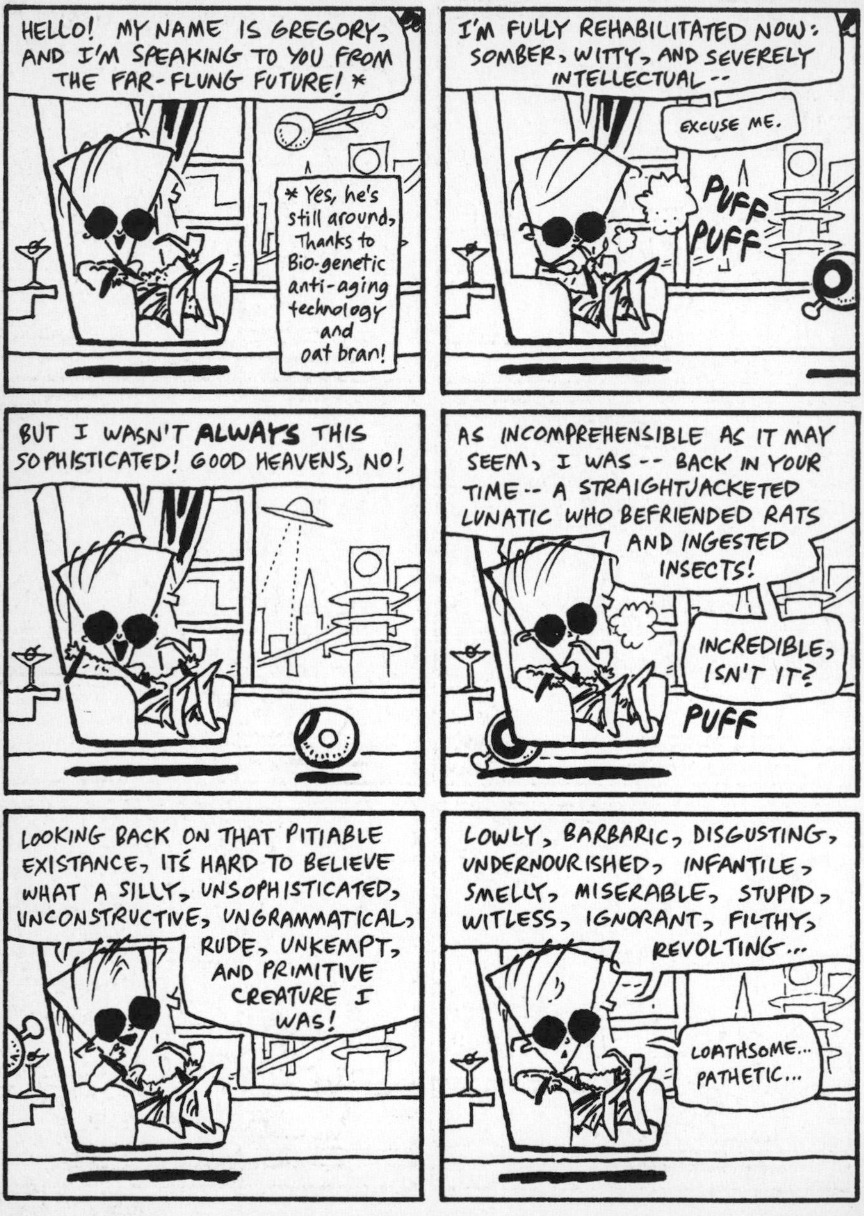

HELLO! MY NAME IS GREGORY, AND I'M SPEAKING TO YOU FROM THE FAR-FLUNG FUTURE! *
* Yes, he's still around, Thanks to Bio-genetic anti-aging technology and oat bran!
I'M FULLY REHABILITATED NOW: SOMBER, WITTY, AND SEVERELY INTELLECTUAL --
EXCUSE ME.
PUFF PUFF
BUT I WASN'T **ALWAYS** THIS SOPHISTICATED! GOOD HEAVENS, NO!
AS INCOMPREHENSIBLE AS IT MAY SEEM, I WAS -- BACK IN YOUR TIME -- A STRAIGHTJACKETED LUNATIC WHO BEFRIENDED RATS AND INGESTED INSECTS!
INCREDIBLE, ISN'T IT?
PUFF
LOOKING BACK ON THAT PITIABLE EXISTANCE, ITS HARD TO BELIEVE WHAT A SILLY, UNSOPHISTICATED, UNCONSTRUCTIVE, UNGRAMMATICAL, RUDE, UNKEMPT, AND PRIMITIVE CREATURE I WAS!
LOWLY, BARBARIC, DISGUSTING, UNDERNOURISHED, INFANTILE, SMELLY, MISERABLE, STUPID, WITLESS, IGNORANT, FILTHY, REVOLTING...
LOATHSOME... PATHETIC...

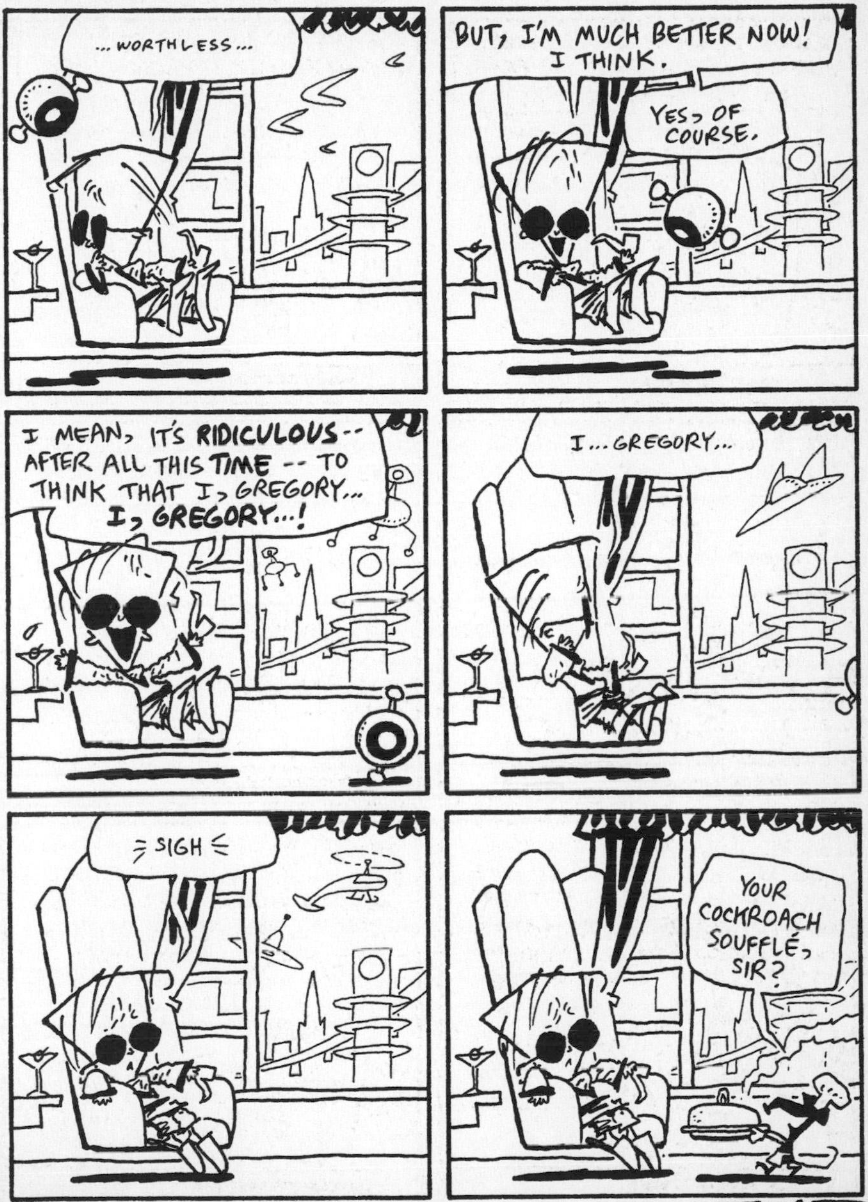
...WORTHLESS...
BUT, I'M MUCH BETTER NOW! I THINK.
YES, OF COURSE.
I MEAN, IT'S **RIDICULOUS** -- AFTER ALL THIS **TIME** -- TO THINK THAT I, GREGORY... **I, GREGORY...!**
I... GREGORY...
≡ SIGH ≡
YOUR COCKROACH SOUFFLÉ, SIR?
END

# INTRODUCTION

**Ah, Gregory!** It was my first book-length solo endeavor — a joyous primal scream of highly personal humor that I first unleashed upon unsuspecting comics readers in 1989. *Gregory* was the wrong thing at the wrong time, and yet it seemed so right. More importantly, if I didn't get this stuff out, I probably would've ended up in a straightjacket myself! But more on that later.

It all started back in 1986: I had sold a short, 3-page strip — "It's Spring!" — to Fantagraphics for publication in their humor magazine *Honk!*. The story was almost identical to the version that appears in *A Gregory Treasury Volume 1* (and was meant to be analogous to the experience of shut-in cartoonists). It featured a prototypical Gregory-type character, though of a much more gangly physique. In the meantime, however, I was toiling away on Comico's *Jonny Quest* comic — for the most part contributing solid yet somewhat stilted pencils that Mark Wheatley would ink. Well, it started out as a fun gig — both Mark and I were fans of the TV series — but after several months the novelty began to wear off; I grew to dislike the work and became generally stressed out. I started to miss deadlines, and, more important, I missed being truly creative. At the time, I had so much pent-up anger and frustration that I began to experience severe stomach problems — a reprise of the stress-related symptoms that I had first experienced during the run of First Comics' *Mars* that Mark and I had worked on a few years earlier. Several doctor visits and barium milkshakes later, no physical problem was ever diagnosed. Nevertheless, I was a mess. Something had to get out, and it wasn't just the contents of my stomach!

Fortunately for me, however, that funny little "It's Spring!" story kept haunting me. I had inadvertently created something highly personal and satisfying, and I wanted its lovable, infantile character to live on in zany new misadventures!!! After my illness had momentarily subsided — and realizing that I had more on my hands than a mere one-off gag — I easily came up with several more story ideas. I also redesigned the main character, now named Gregory (because it sounded right), so that he appeared shorter, cuddlier, and more childlike. I then submitted some of this new material (including "The Show," printed for the first time in this volume) to several prospective publishers. One book publisher loved it, but declined; Fantagraphics offered to publish, but didn't pay an advance against royalties (hey — I had some bills!). Fortunately, DC Comics had just started up its Piranha Press imprint, and editor Mark Nevelow wanted the property as well. So, to make a long story short, DC paid an advance, I wrote and drew 120 pages, and *Gregory* went on to sell 25,000 copies in two printings — as well as earn critical acclaim and a couple of award nominations.

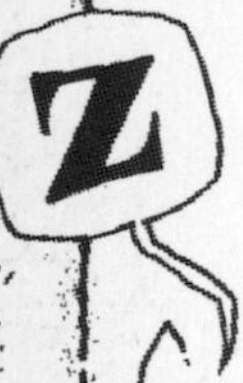
Z

Conceptually, *Gregory* was a repository for all my pent-up fears and insecurities, though tempered with a good deal of childlike joy and abandon; it was a manic explosion of crudely expressive art, character humor and god-awful puns. The book, if not exactly a parabolic telling of the story of my life, was at least a darkly humorous expression of some of the emotions that had been building up

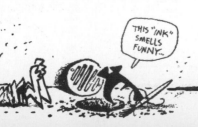

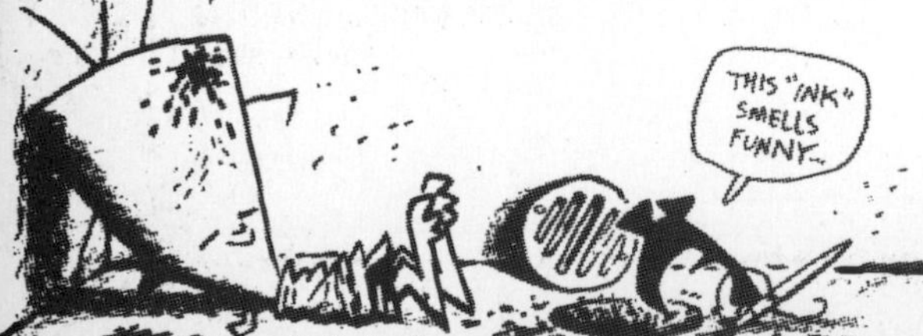
THIS "INK" SMELLS FUNNY

inside me. If the pint-sized protagonist represented my "inner child" — eager to openly love and express joy — his straightjacket was a metaphor for fear, for feelings of powerlessness. The characters were all honest expressions of various aspects of my personality, and the stories and humor flowed very easily from my manic mind. At some point I realized that Gregory needed a friend (and the book needed a character who actually talked!), so the rat named Herman Vermin was born: an obsessive, insecure yin to Gregory's innocent yang. Wendell materialized when I realized that Herman needed someone even smaller to boss around. Hal Roach was merely a bad pun.

After Mark Wheatley and I created *Breathtaker* (also for DC), I returned to do three more *Gregory* books for Piranha Press, now working with editor Margaret Clark. For me, the most personal and autobiographical of the original *Gregory* volumes was *Gregory IV: Fat Boy*, which constitutes the final chapter of the book you are holding. A lot of Rusty's family life, pressures, experiences and emotions mirrored my own from that stage of my life. Visually, I based him on a couple of childhood friends that I identified with (as I wasn't overweight as a kid). By the way, the amusing "upham!" incident was real (though not the word); a younger cousin was... um... responsible.

So, you may ask (and many have), will I ever create new adventures for Gregory? Well, probably not — but who knows? At some point in the early nineties, Gregory ideas gave way to *Tug & Buster* ideas (my later humor series), and I moved on. But cartoonists never forget their children, so the possibility is always there. Gregory — the character and the series — occupy a very special place in my heart. Fortunately for those of you who are "champing at the bit" for more *Gregory* material, several rare or previously unpublished pieces are included at the end of this very book!

In conclusion, I'd like to thank all the wonderful people who helped make *Gregory* possible: Mark Nevelow, Margaret Clark and everyone at DC Comics; Bob Chapman at Graphitti Designs (for all the cool toys); Drew Ogier, prop master for *Roseanne*, who worked a T-shirt and poster into the sitcom (check the reruns!); the late, great Walt Kelly (whose classic comic strip *Pogo* was a major influence); and the even later and also great Charles Schulz (another personal hero, and one who just didn't understand *Gregory* but sent a nice letter). Thanks also to Mike Myers, who — in apparent tribute — actually worked my last name into a "Wayne's World" skit on *Saturday Night Live*! But my most heartfelt thanks go to all those longtime *Gregory* fans and supporters who might be buying these new volumes to replace dog-eared or lent-out-and-never-returned original copies. And to those new readers who are experiencing this mayhem for the first time, I hope you get a few laughs out of this unlikely, loony labor of love.

**"IB ZUG!"**

— Marc Hempel
Baltimore, Maryland
February 2004

# gregory

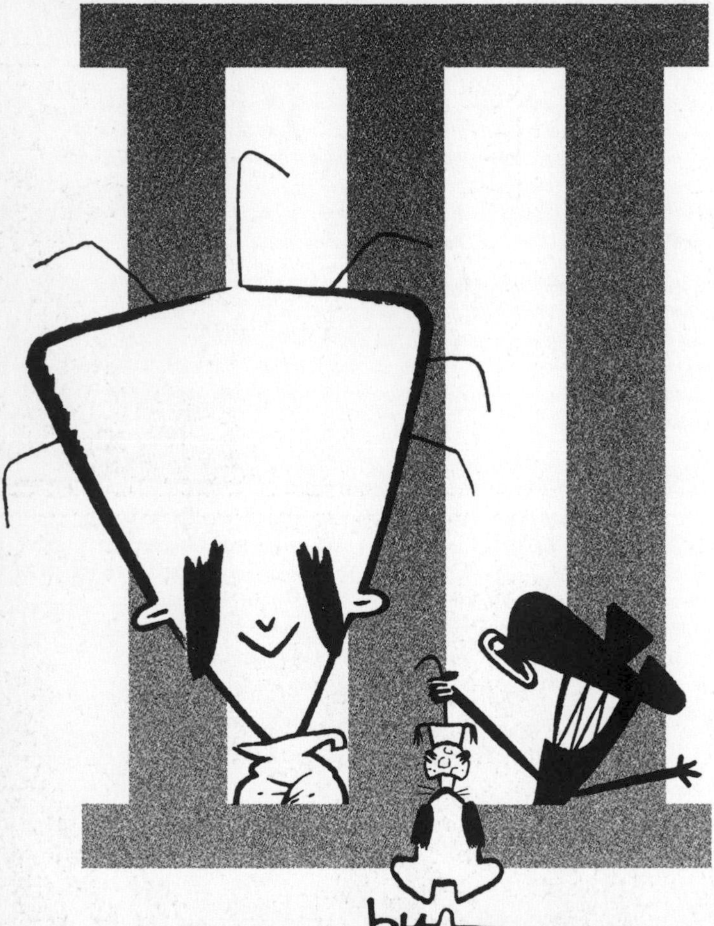
Hello,

by Marc Hempel

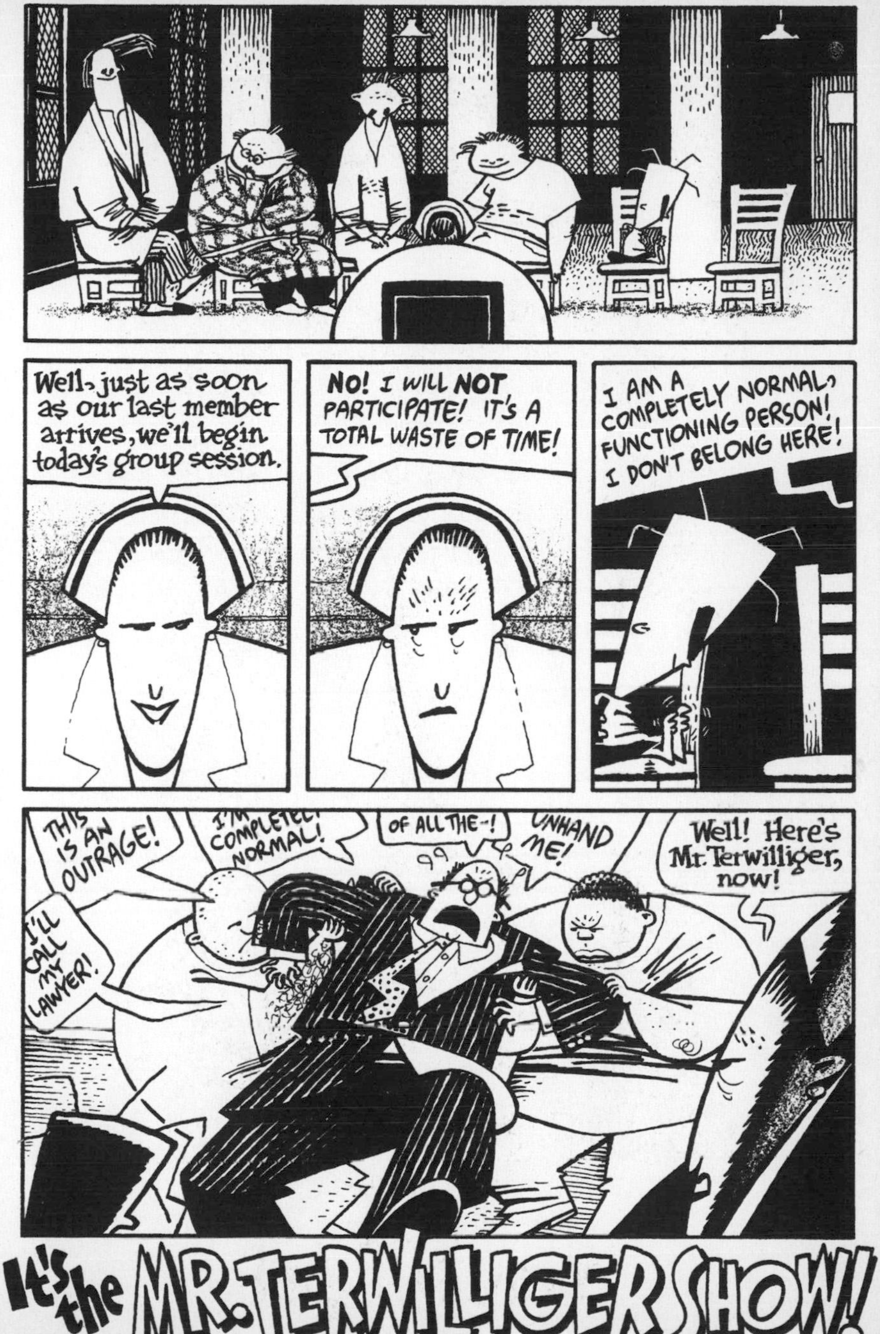
Well, just as soon as our last member arrives, we'll begin today's group session.
NO! I WILL NOT PARTICIPATE! IT'S A TOTAL WASTE OF TIME!
I AM A COMPLETELY NORMAL, FUNCTIONING PERSON! I DON'T BELONG HERE!
THIS IS AN OUTRAGE!
I'LL CALL MY LAWYER!
OF ALL THE--!
UNHAND ME!
Well! Here's Mr. Terwilliger, now!
It's the MR. TERWILLIGER SHOW!

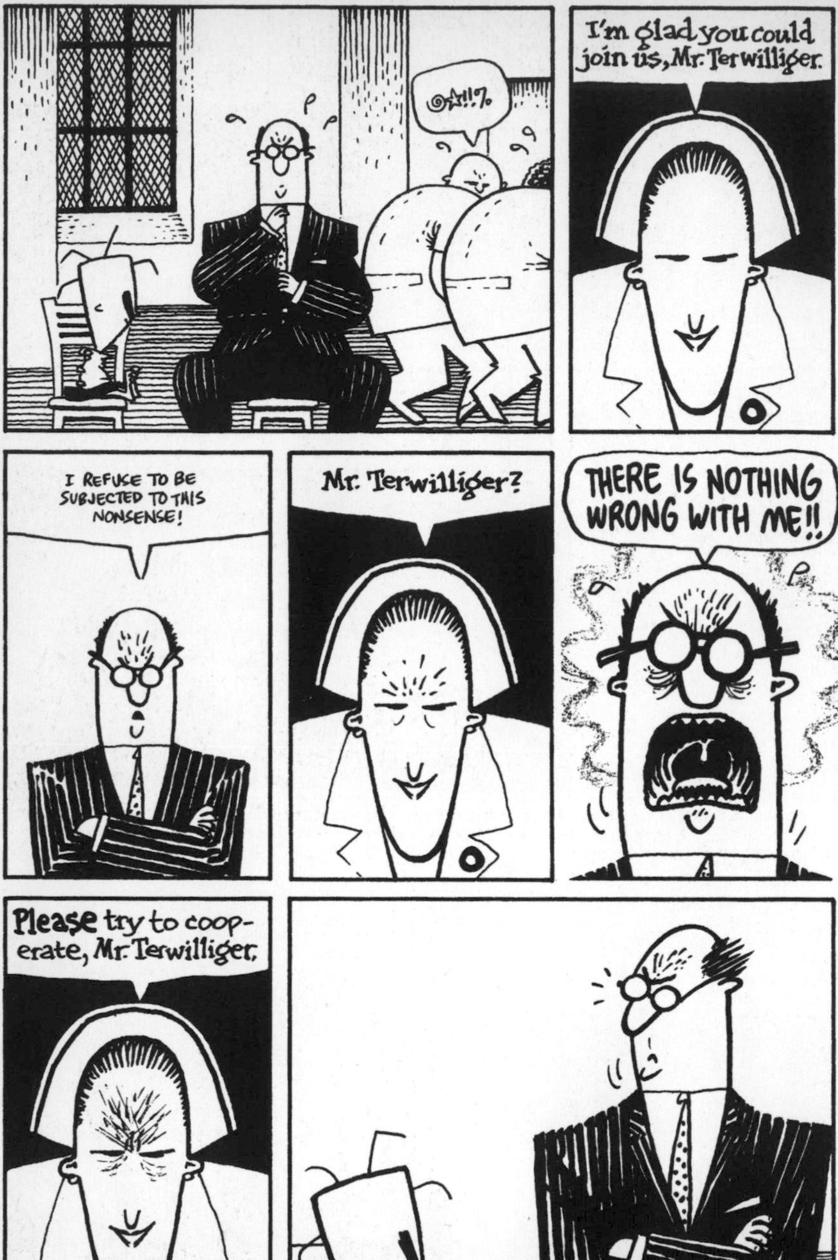

I'm glad you could join us, Mr. Terwilliger.
I REFUSE TO BE SUBJECTED TO THIS NONSENSE!
Mr. Terwilliger?
THERE IS NOTHING WRONG WITH ME!!
Please try to cooperate, Mr. Terwilliger.

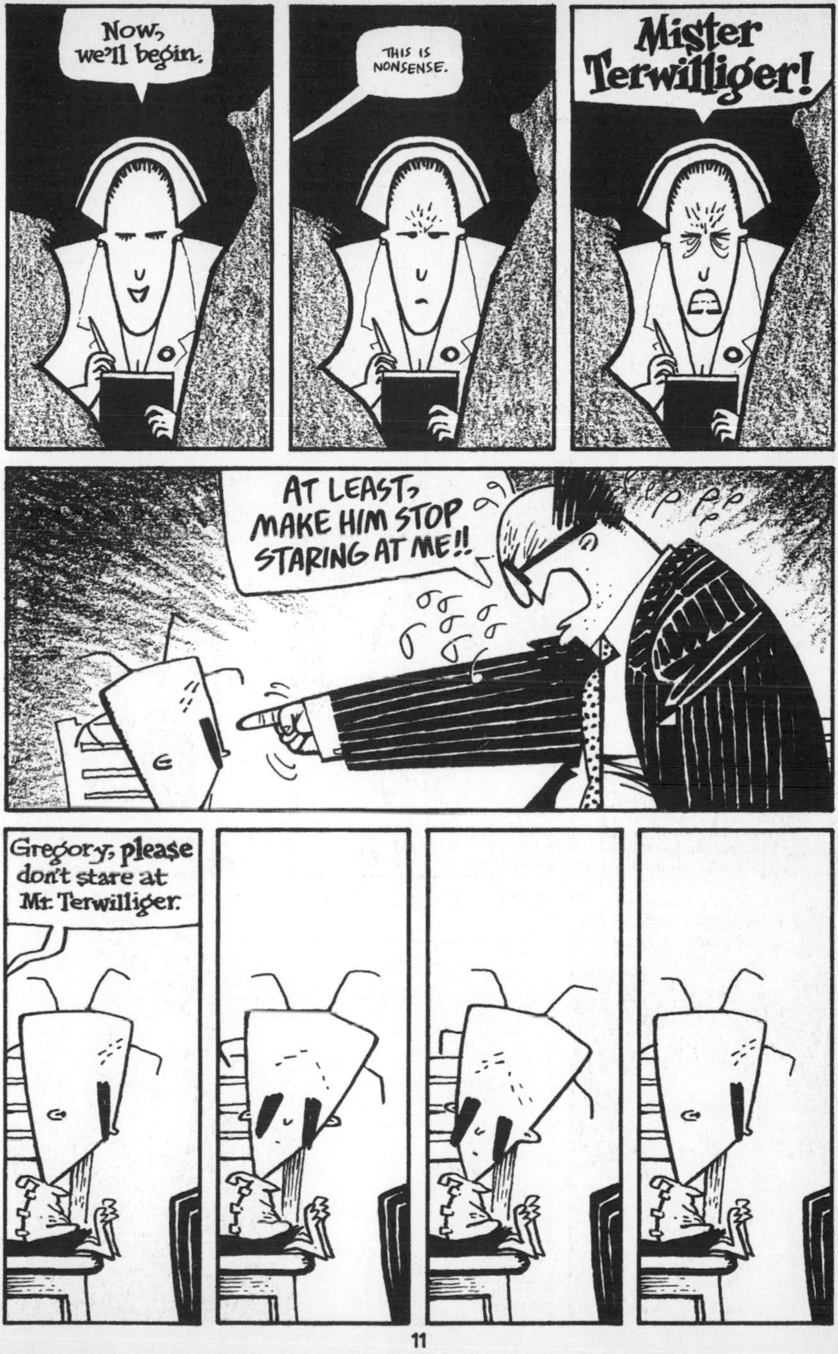
Now, we'll begin.
THIS IS NONSENSE.
Mister Terwilliger!
AT LEAST, MAKE HIM STOP STARING AT ME!!
Gregory, please don't stare at Mr. Terwilliger.

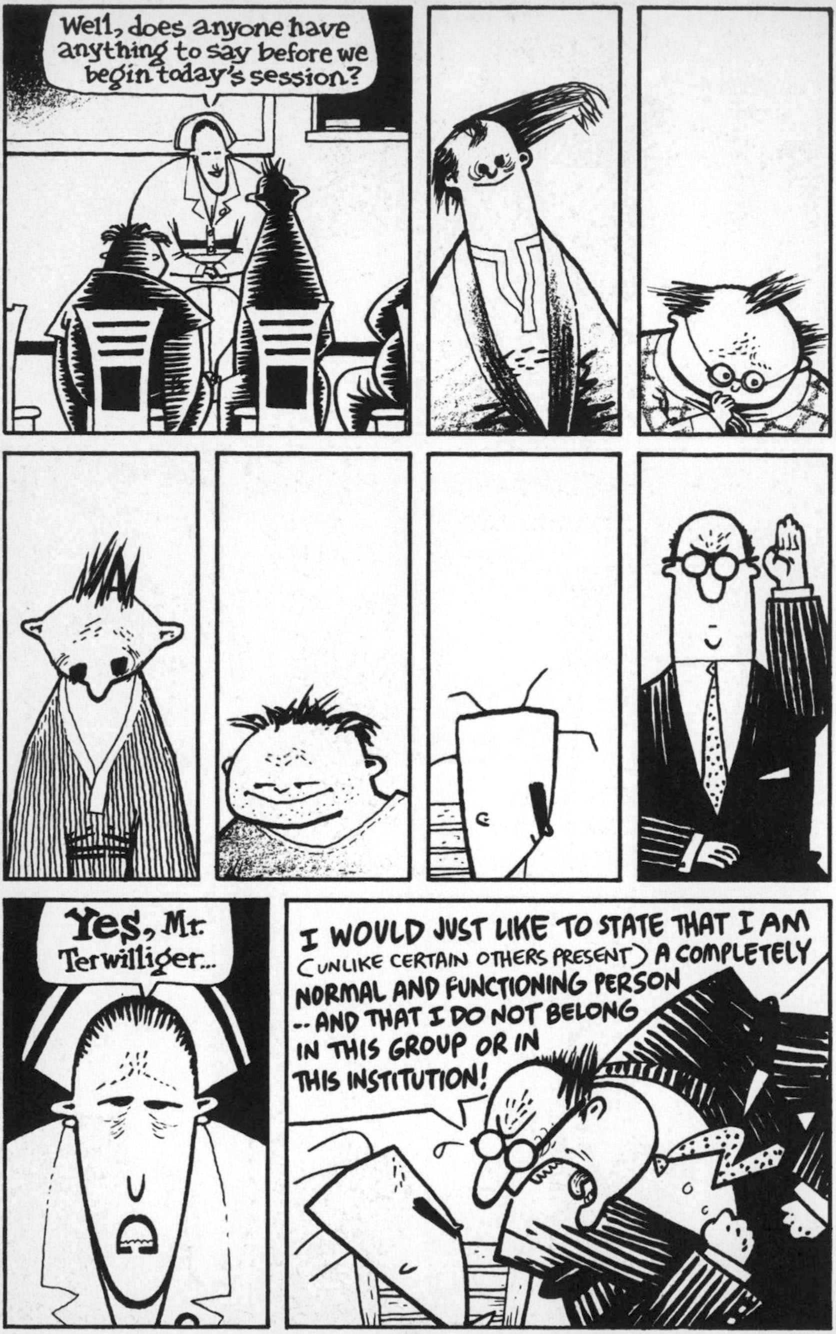
Well, does anyone have anything to say before we begin today's session?
Yes, Mr. Terwilliger...
I WOULD JUST LIKE TO STATE THAT I AM (UNLIKE CERTAIN OTHERS PRESENT) A COMPLETELY NORMAL AND FUNCTIONING PERSON -- AND THAT I DO NOT BELONG IN THIS GROUP OR IN THIS INSTITUTION!

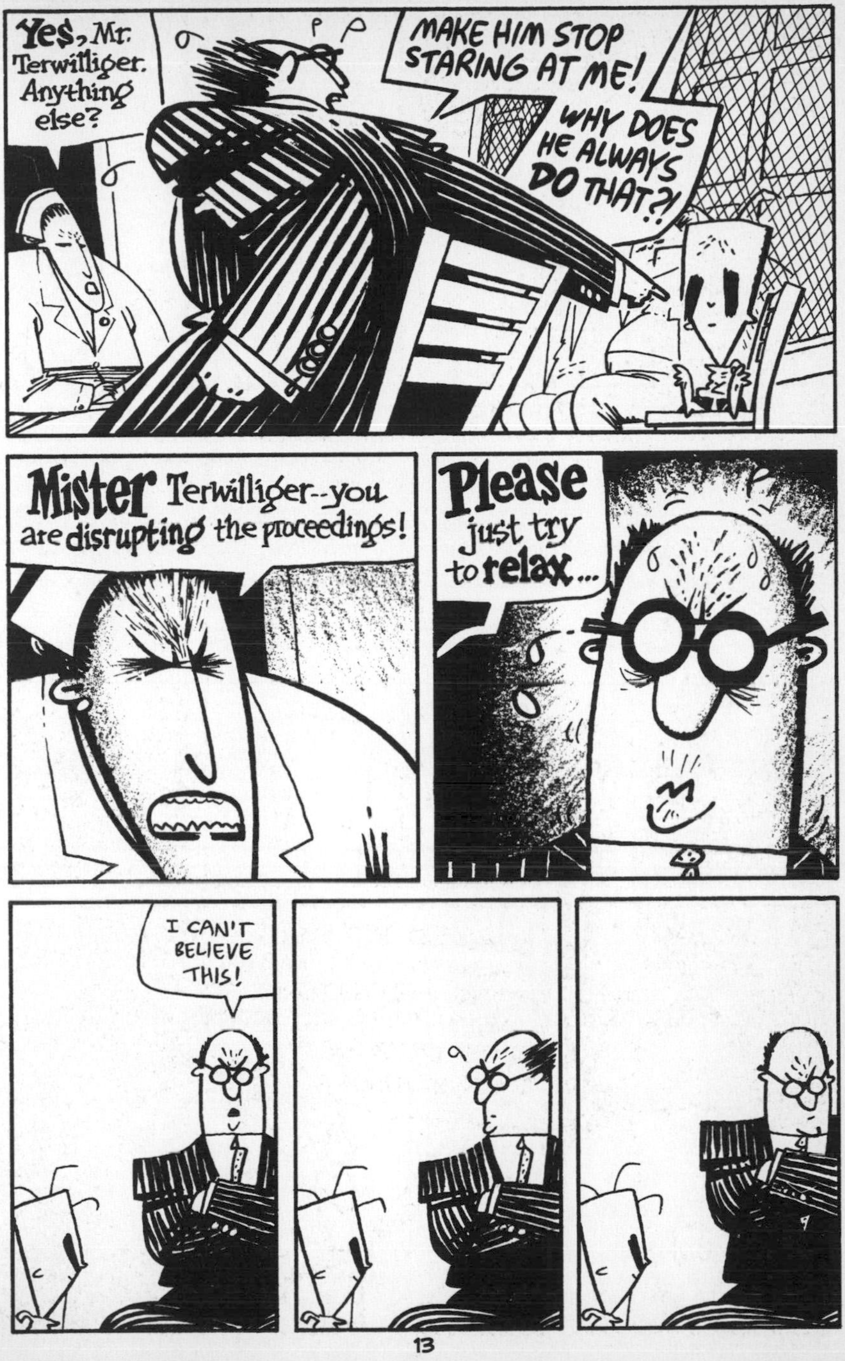
Yes, Mr. Terwilliger. Anything else?
MAKE HIM STOP STARING AT ME!
WHY DOES HE ALWAYS DO THAT?!
Mister Terwilliger--you are disrupting the proceedings!
Please just try to relax...
I CAN'T BELIEVE THIS!

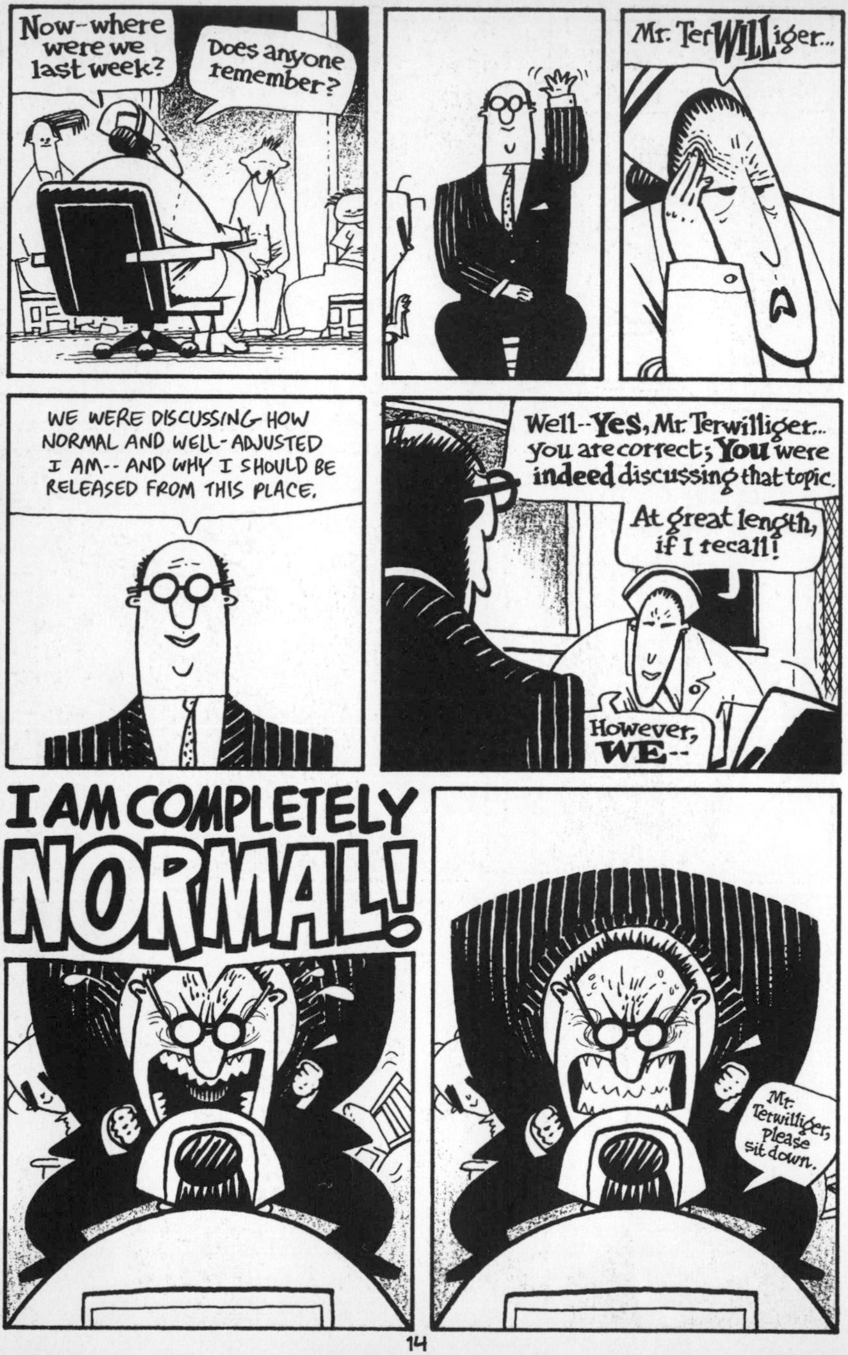
Now-where were we last week?
Does anyone remember?
Mr. TerWILLiger...
WE WERE DISCUSSING HOW NORMAL AND WELL-ADJUSTED I AM-- AND WHY I SHOULD BE RELEASED FROM THIS PLACE.
Well--Yes, Mr. Terwilliger... you are correct; You were indeed discussing that topic.
At great length, if I recall!
However, WE--
I AM COMPLETELY NORMAL!
Mr. Terwilliger, Please sit down.

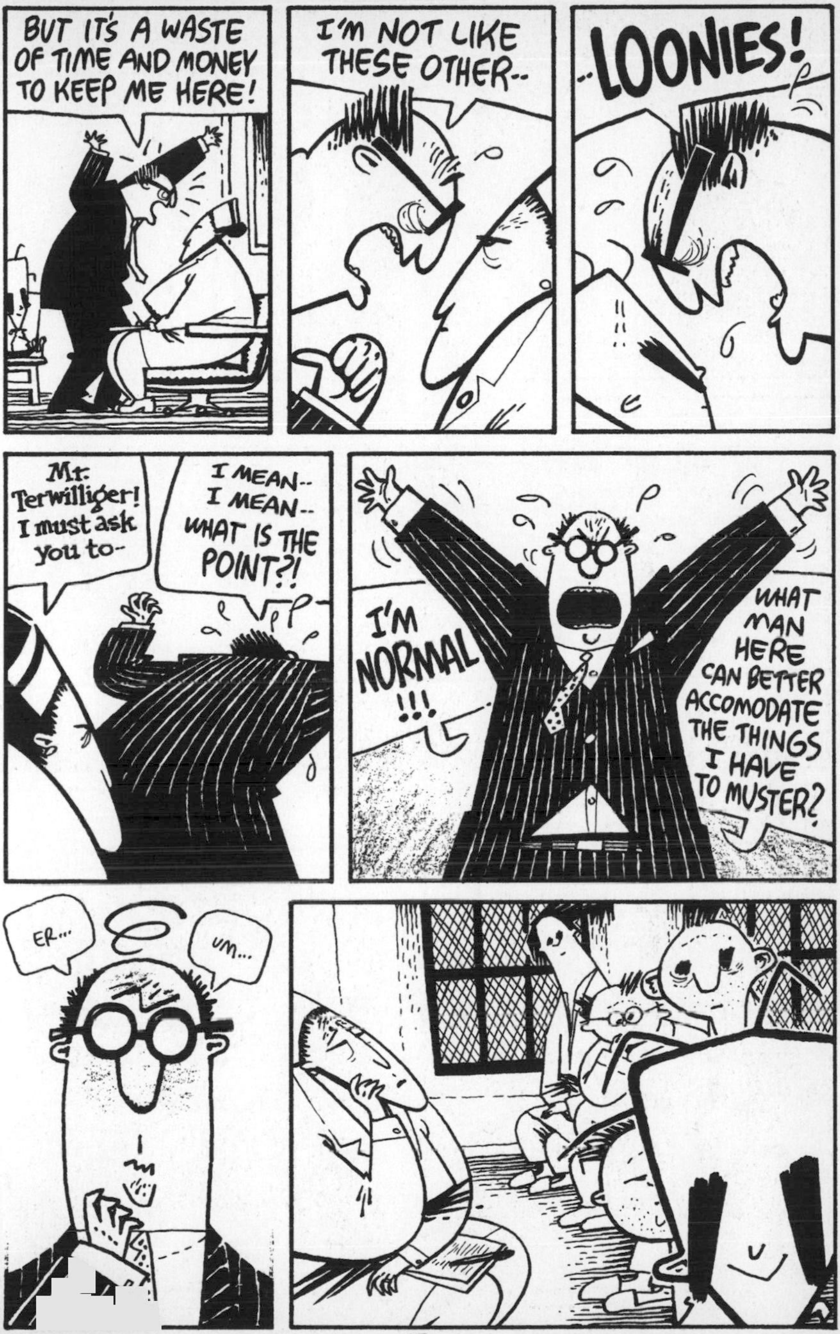
BUT IT'S A WASTE OF TIME AND MONEY TO KEEP ME HERE!
I'M NOT LIKE THESE OTHER--
--LOONIES!
Mr. Terwilliger! I must ask you to-
I MEAN-- I MEAN-- WHAT IS THE POINT?!
I'M NORMAL!!!
WHAT MAN HERE CAN BETTER ACCOMODATE THE THINGS I HAVE TO MUSTER?
ER...
UM...

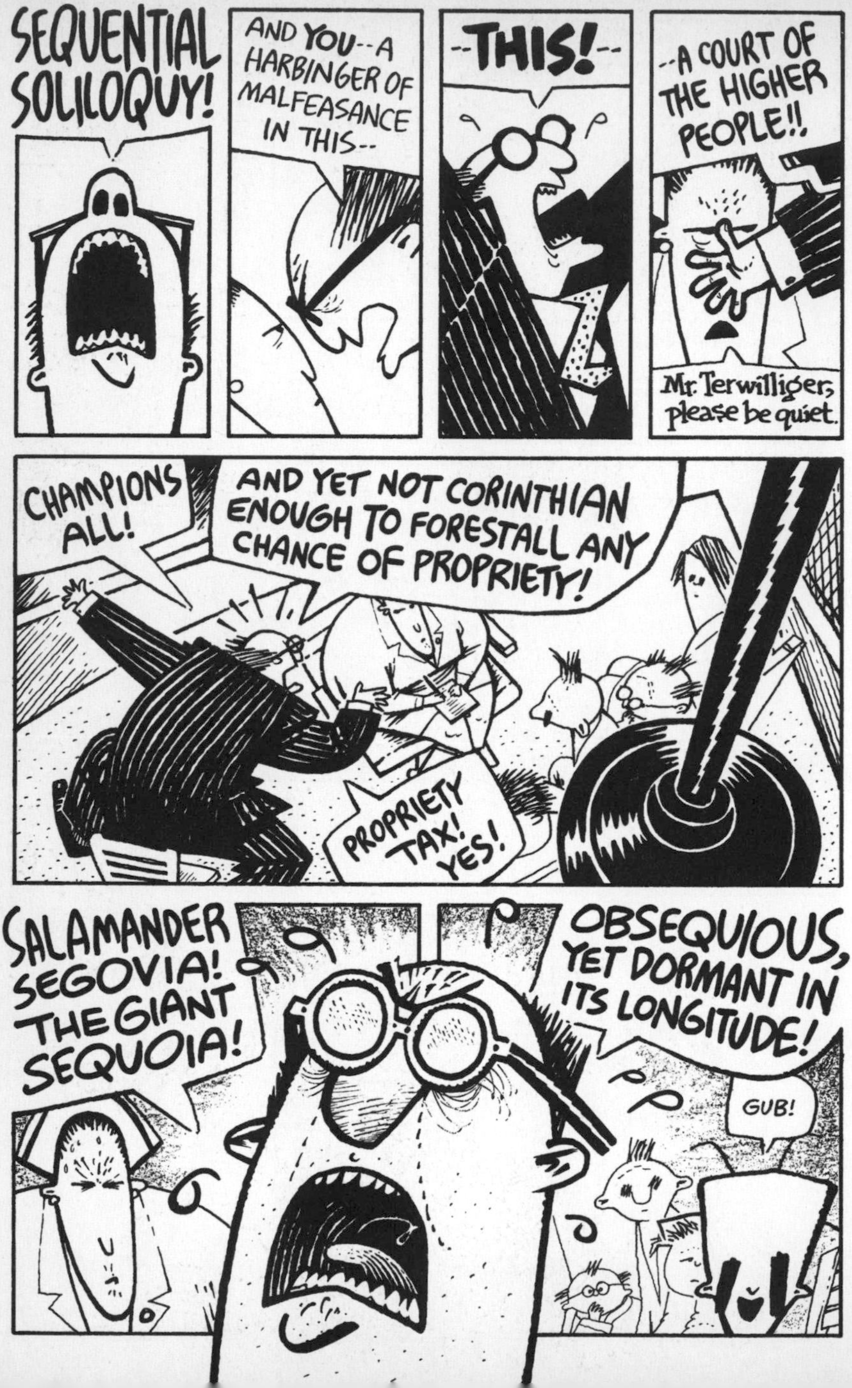
SEQUENTIAL SOLILOQUY!
AND YOU--A HARBINGER OF MALFEASANCE IN THIS--
--THIS!--
--A COURT OF THE HIGHER PEOPLE!!
Mr. Terwilliger, please be quiet.
CHAMPIONS ALL!
AND YET NOT CORINTHIAN ENOUGH TO FORESTALL ANY CHANCE OF PROPRIETY!
PROPRIETY TAX! YES!
SALAMANDER SEGOVIA! THE GIANT SEQUOIA!
OBSEQUIOUS, YET DORMANT IN ITS LONGITUDE!
GUB!

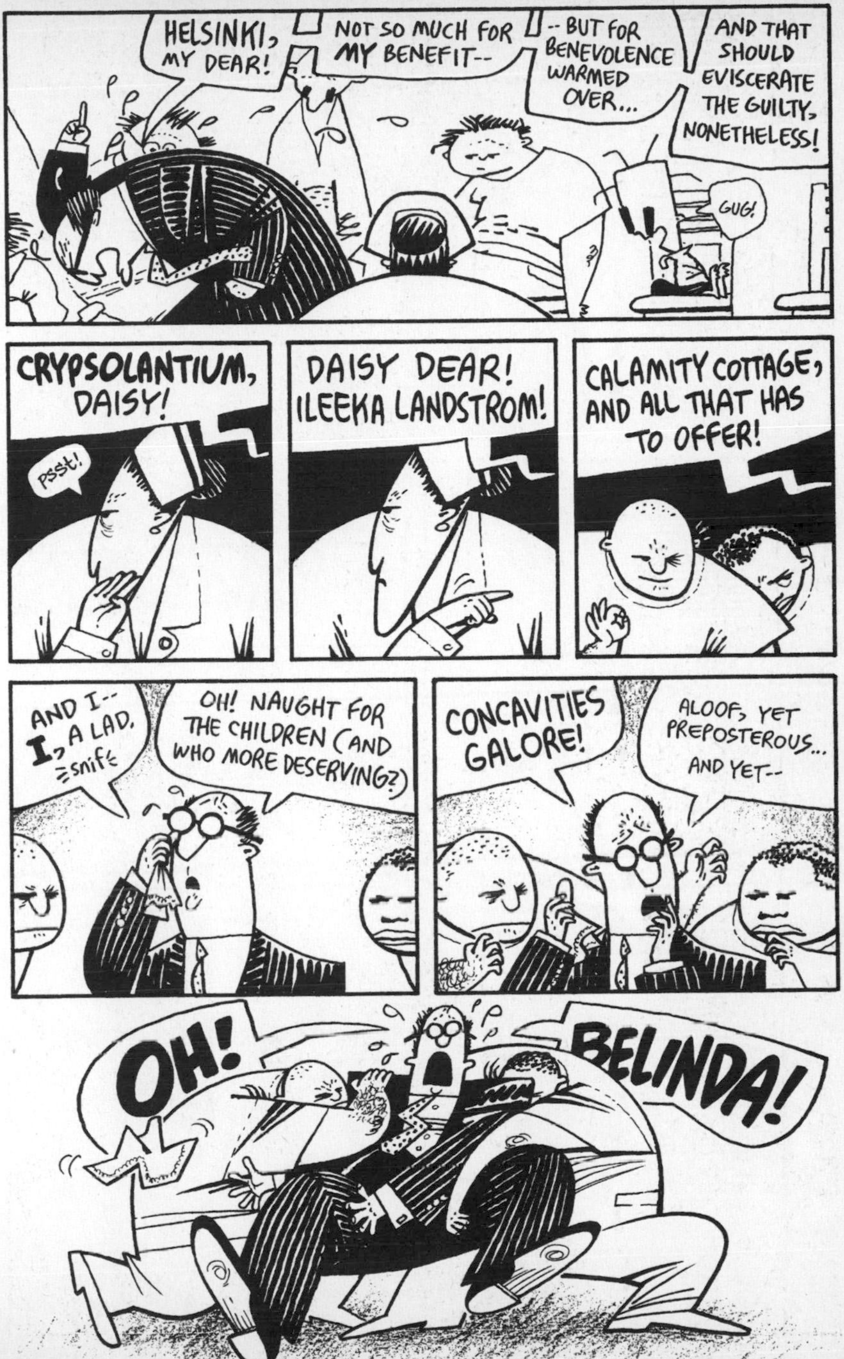

HELSINKI, MY DEAR!
NOT SO MUCH FOR MY BENEFIT--
-- BUT FOR BENEVOLENCE WARMED OVER...
AND THAT SHOULD EVISCERATE THE GUILTY, NONETHELESS!
GUG!
CRYPSOLANTIUM, DAISY!
psst!
DAISY DEAR! ILEEKA LANDSTROM!
CALAMITY COTTAGE, AND ALL THAT HAS TO OFFER!
AND I-- I, A LAD.
snif
OH! NAUGHT FOR THE CHILDREN (AND WHO MORE DESERVING?)
CONCAVITIES GALORE!
ALOOF, YET PREPOSTEROUS...
AND YET--
OH!
BELINDA!

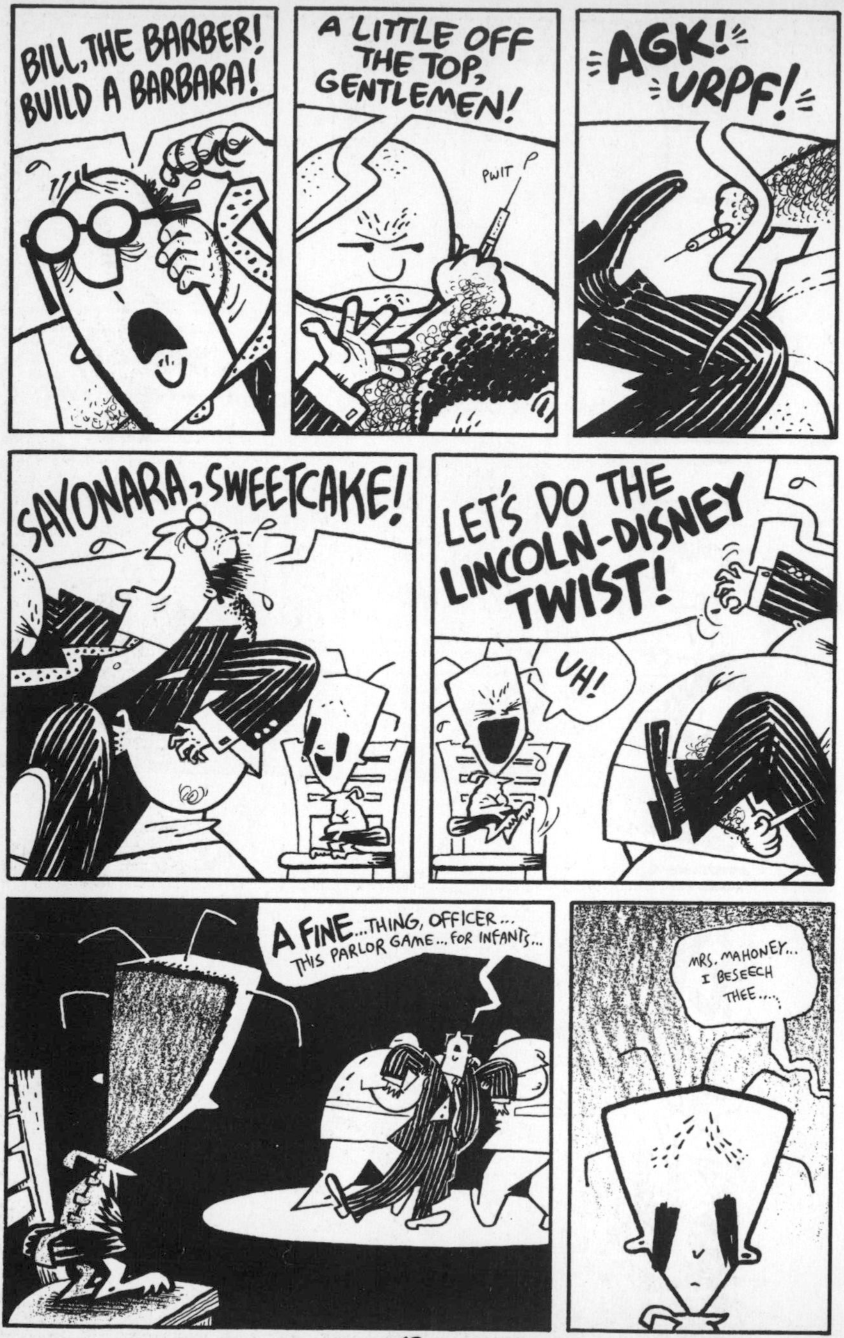

BILL, THE BARBER! BUILD A BARBARA!
A LITTLE OFF THE TOP, GENTLEMEN!
PWIT
AGK! URPF!
SAYONARA, SWEETCAKE!
LET'S DO THE LINCOLN-DISNEY TWIST!
UH!
A FINE...THING, OFFICER... THIS PARLOR GAME...FOR INFANTS...
MRS. MAHONEY... I BESEECH THEE....

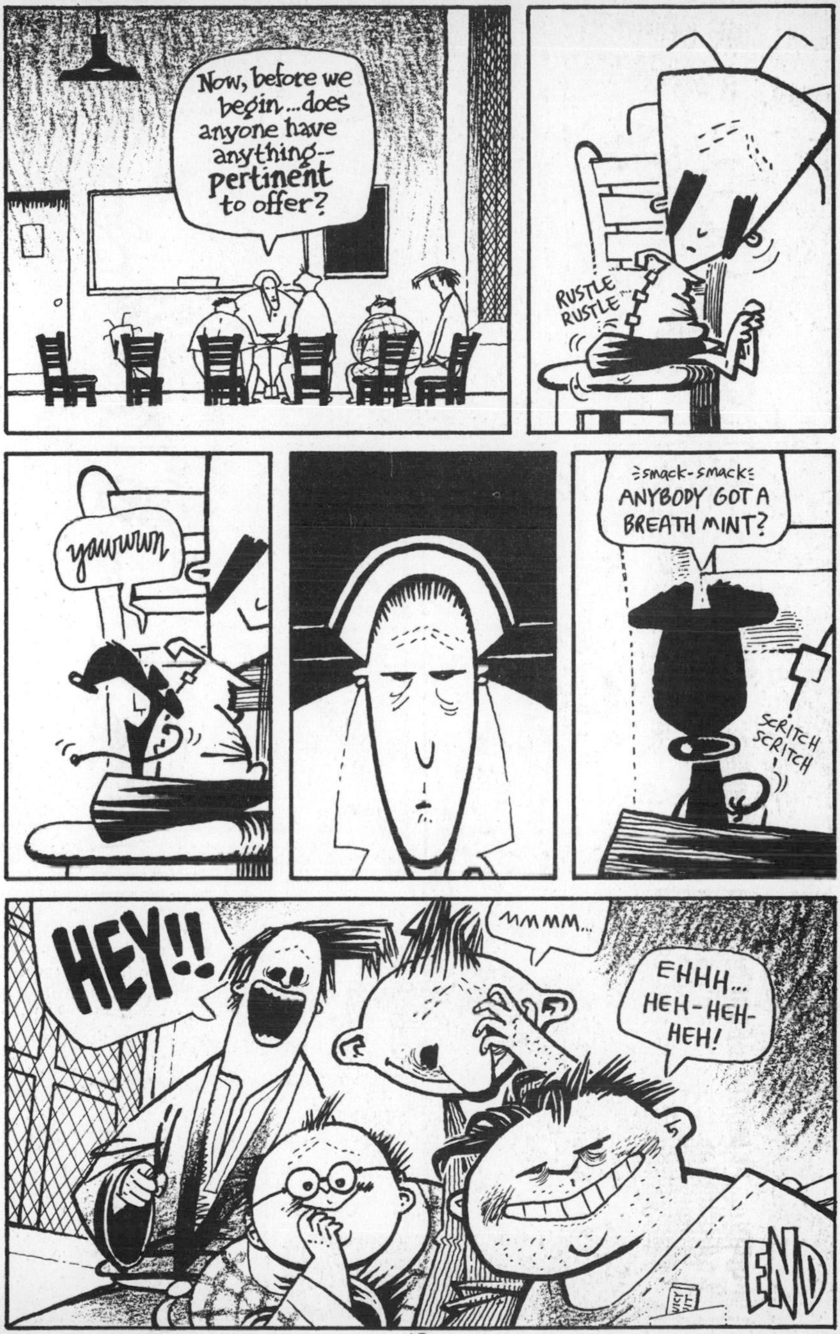

Now, before we begin...does anyone have anything-- pertinent to offer?
RUSTLE RUSTLE
yawwwn
smack-smack
ANYBODY GOT A BREATH MINT?
SCRITCH SCRITCH
HEY!!
MMMM...
EHHH... HEH-HEH-HEH!
END

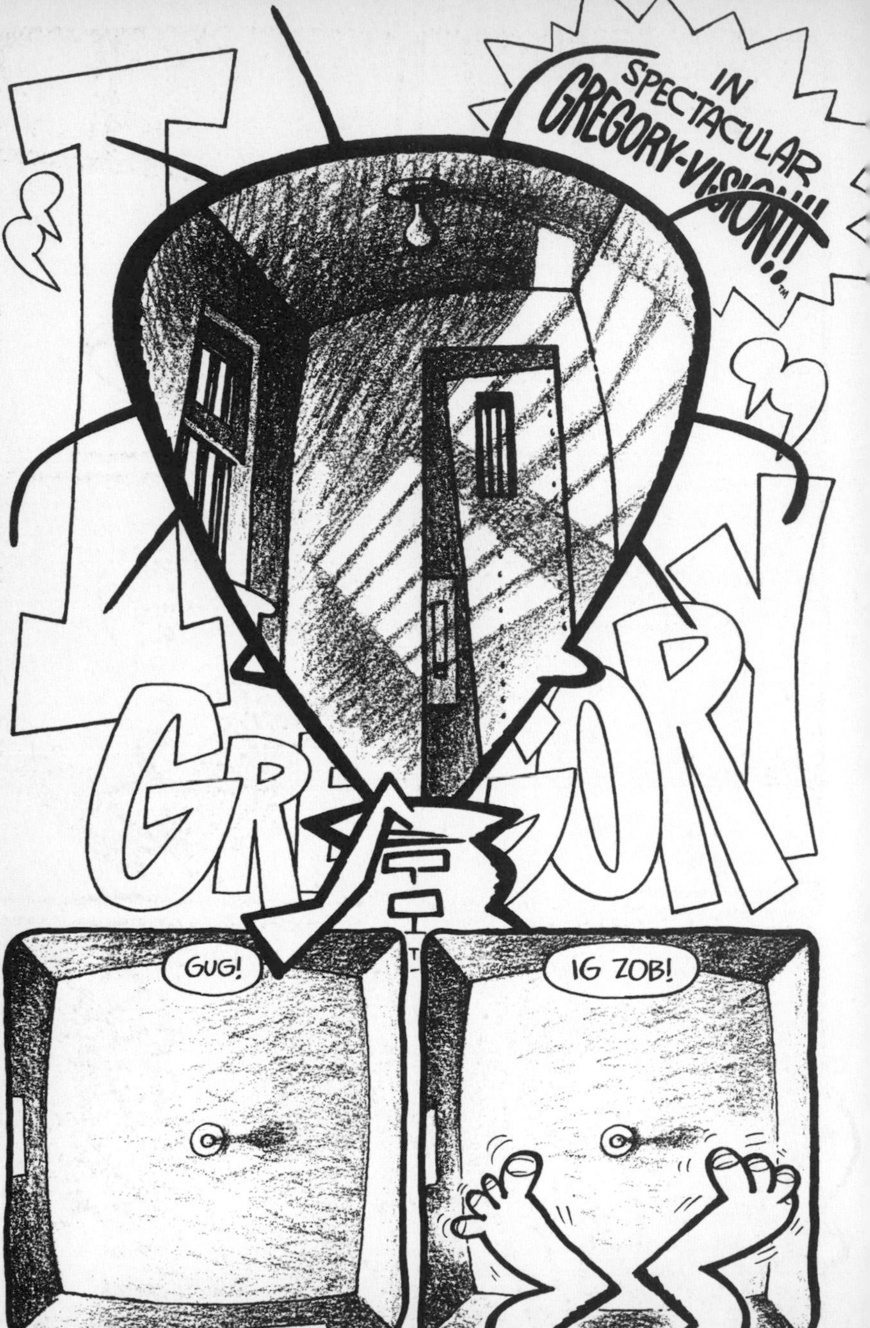
IN SPECTACULAR GREGORY-VISION!!!™
GREGORY
GUG!
IG ZOB!

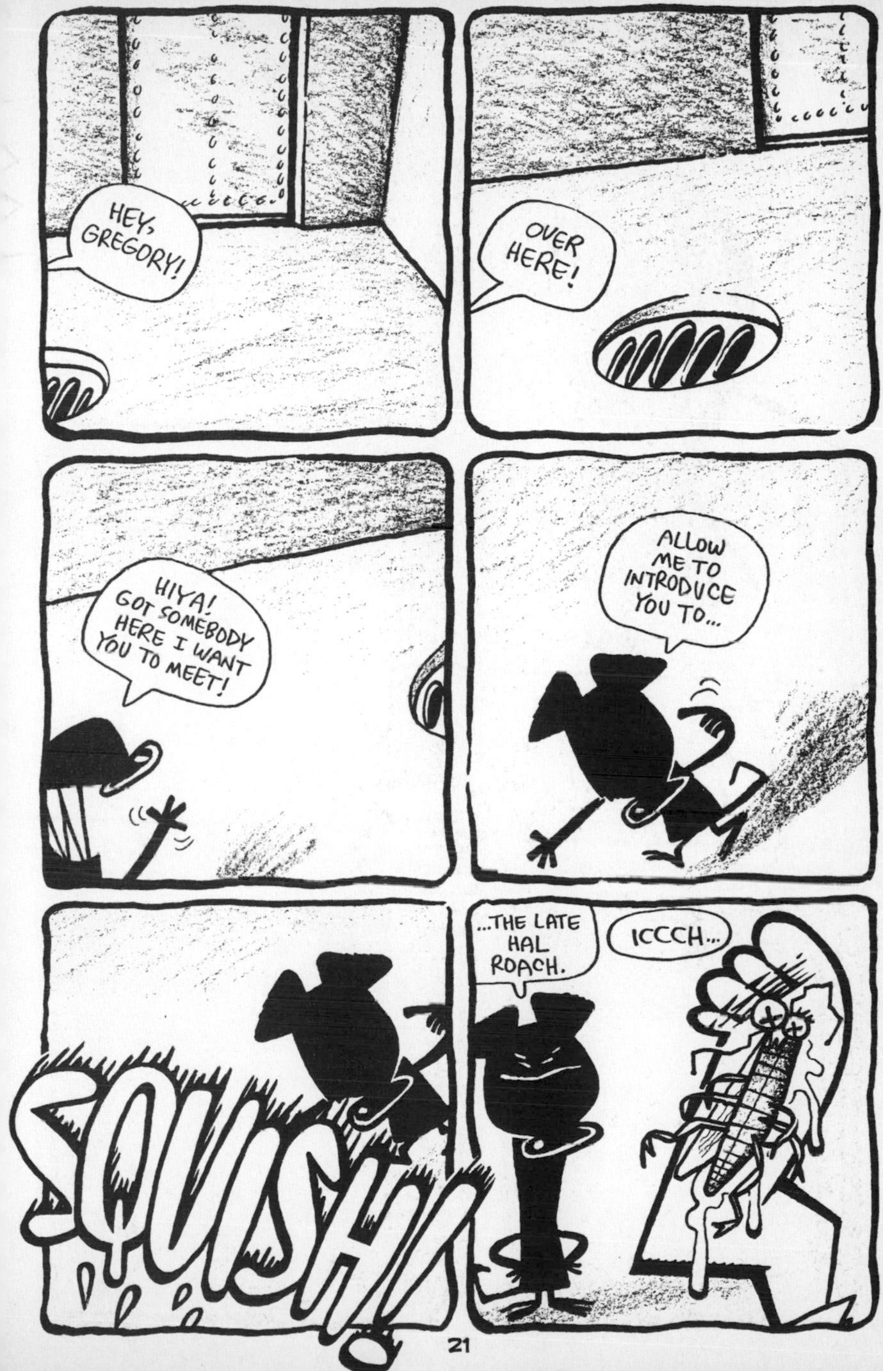
HEY, GREGORY!
OVER HERE!
HIYA! GOT SOMEBODY HERE I WANT YOU TO MEET!
ALLOW ME TO INTRODUCE YOU TO...
SQUISH!!
...THE LATE HAL ROACH.
ICCCH...

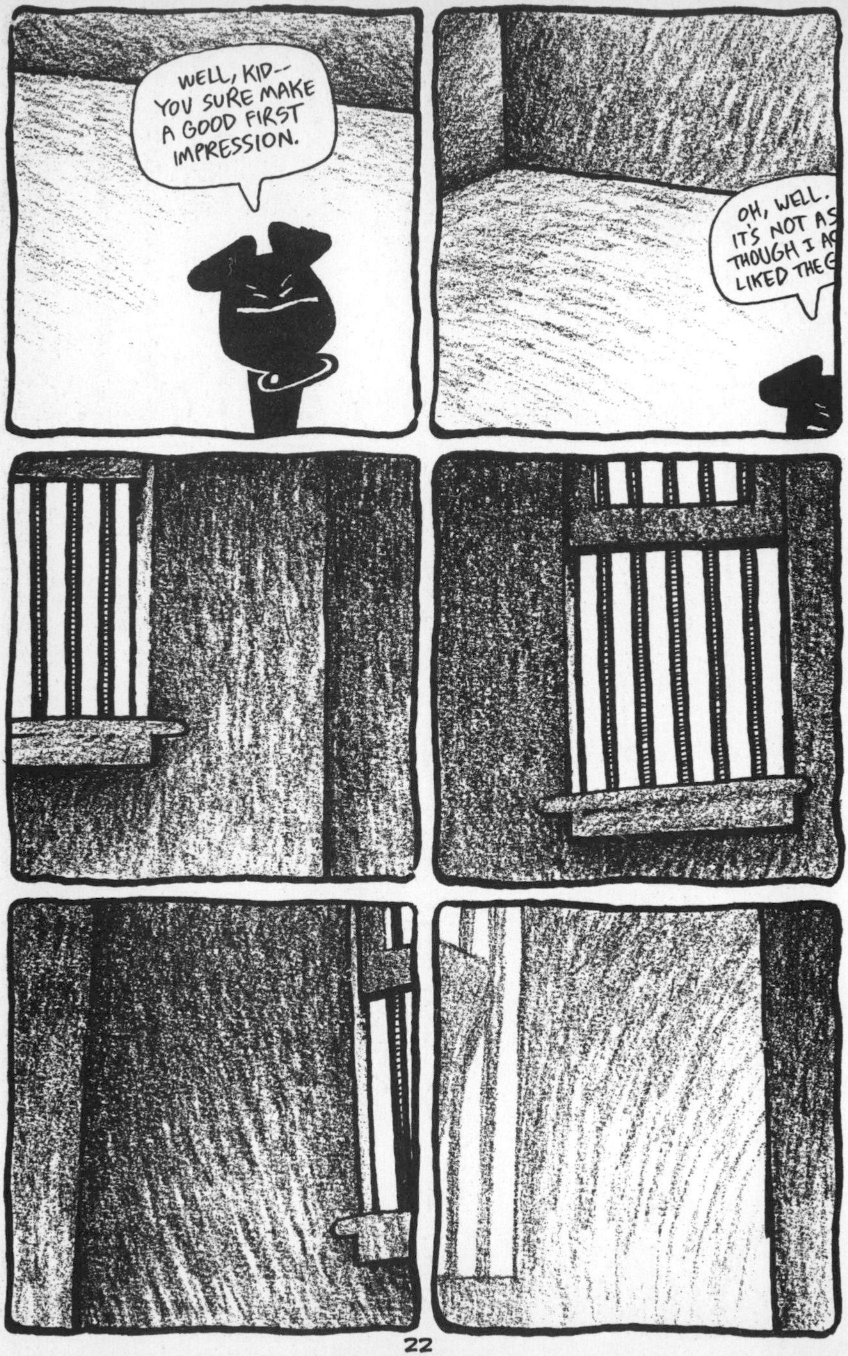
WELL, KID-- YOU SURE MAKE A GOOD FIRST IMPRESSION.
OH, WELL. IT'S NOT AS THOUGH I AC LIKED THE G

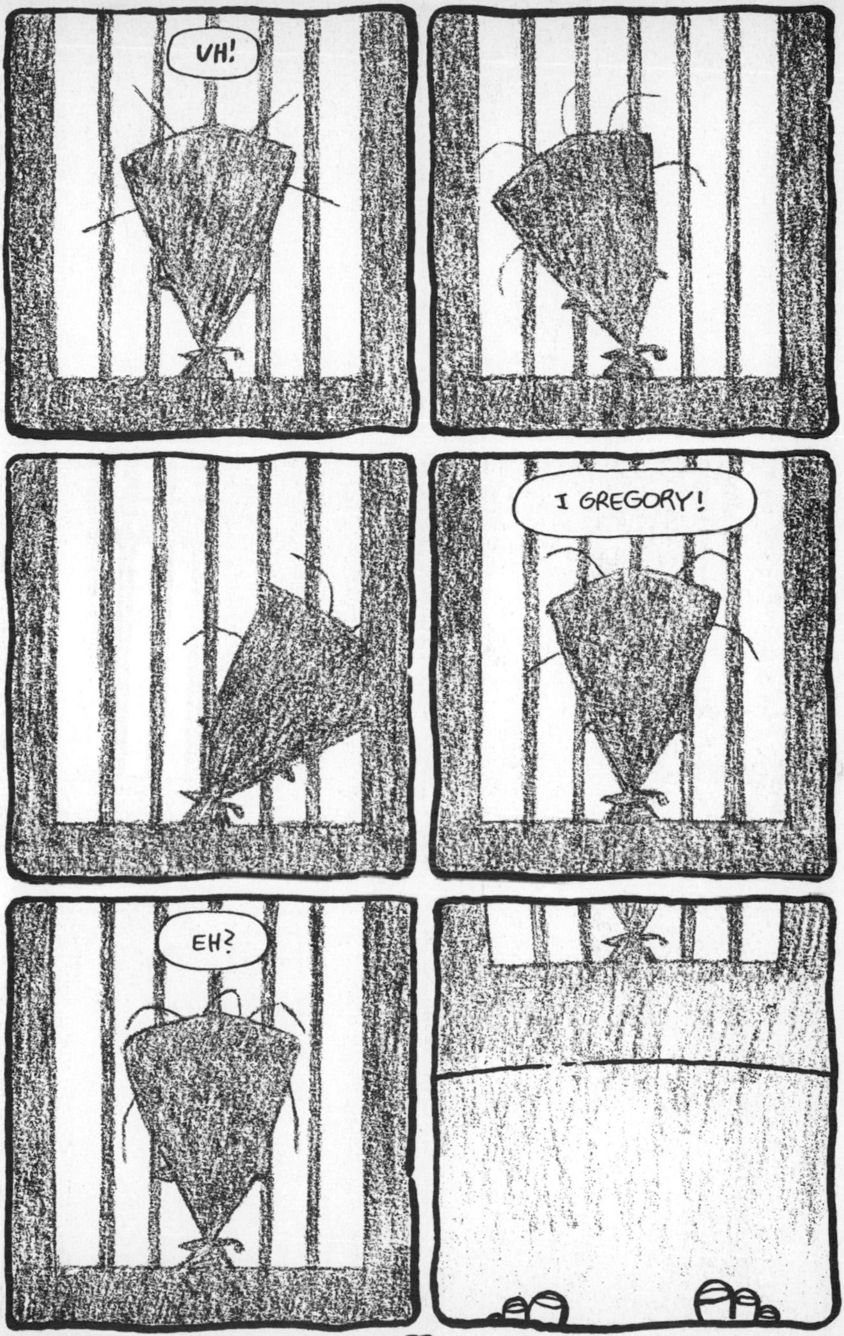
UH!
I GREGORY!
EH?

UH!
uhhh...
MMMM...
...MMNNM...
I...
I GREGORY!

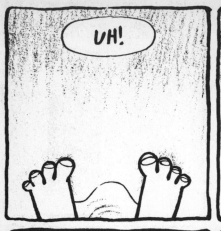

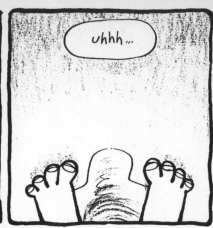

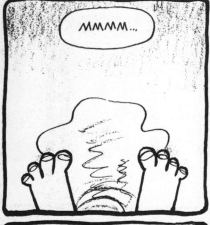

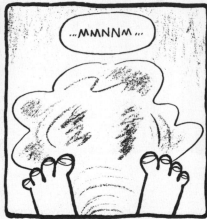

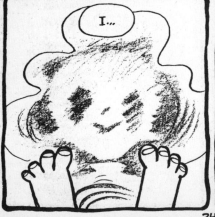

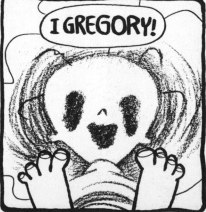

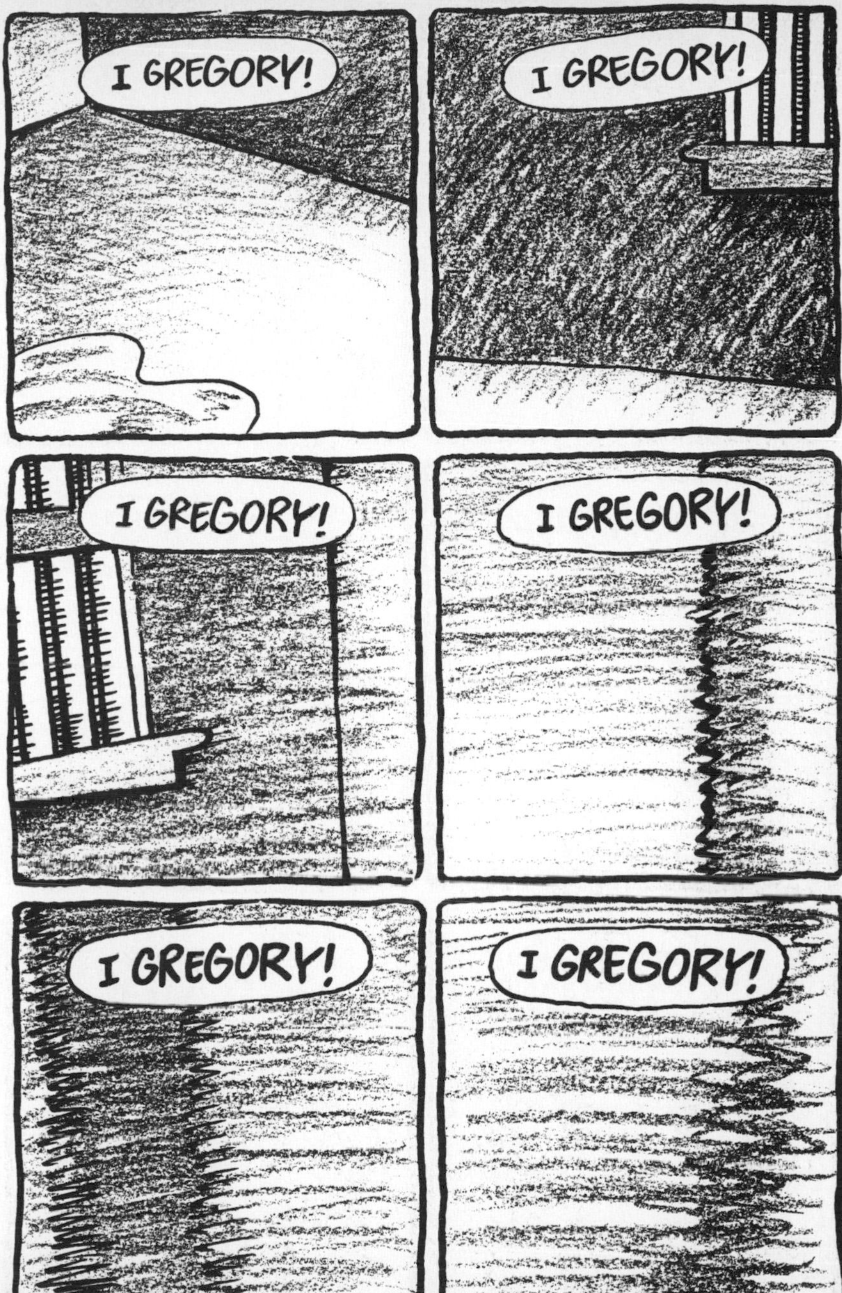
I GREGORY!
I GREGORY!
I GREGORY!
I GREGORY!
I GREGORY!
I GREGORY!

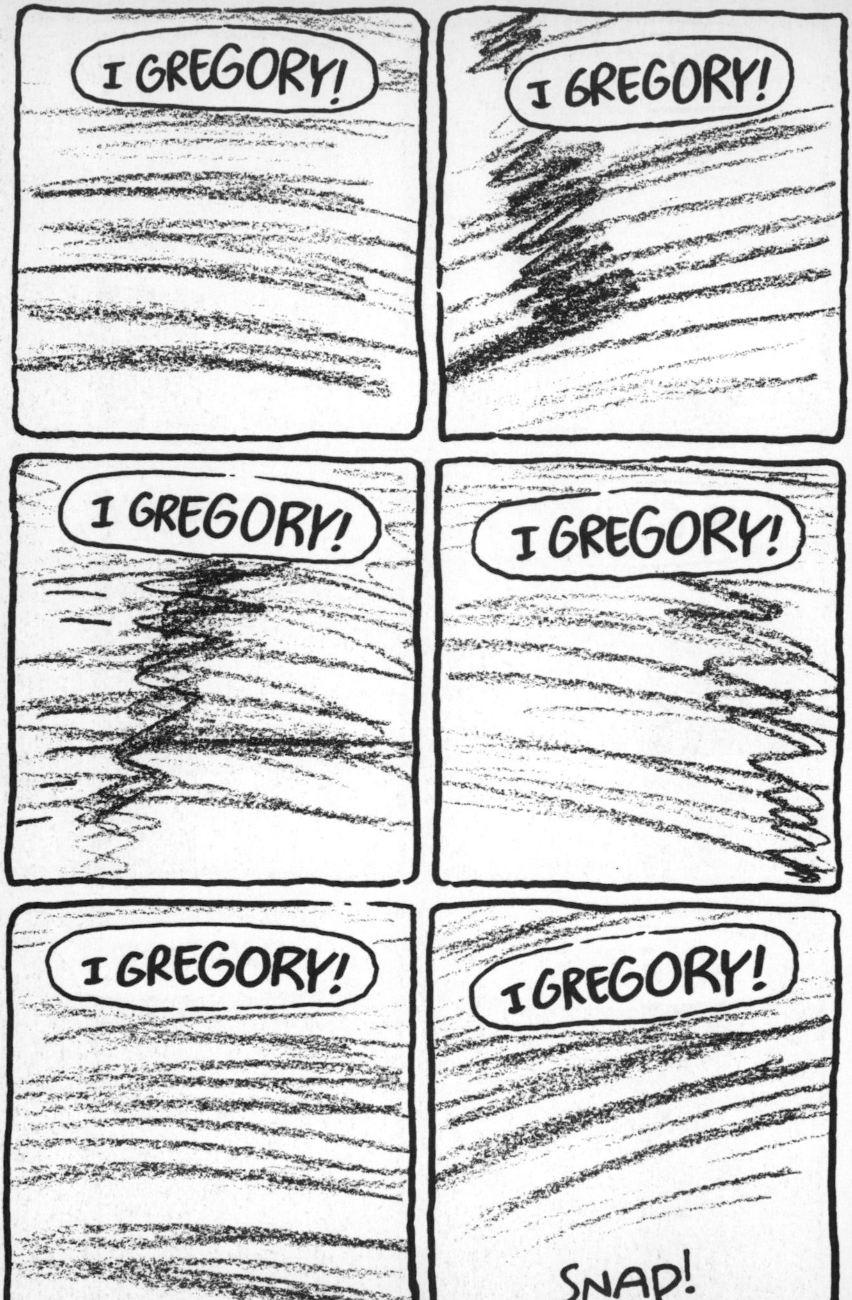
I GREGORY!
I GREGORY!
I GREGORY!
I GREGORY!
I GREGORY!
I GREGORY!
SNAP!

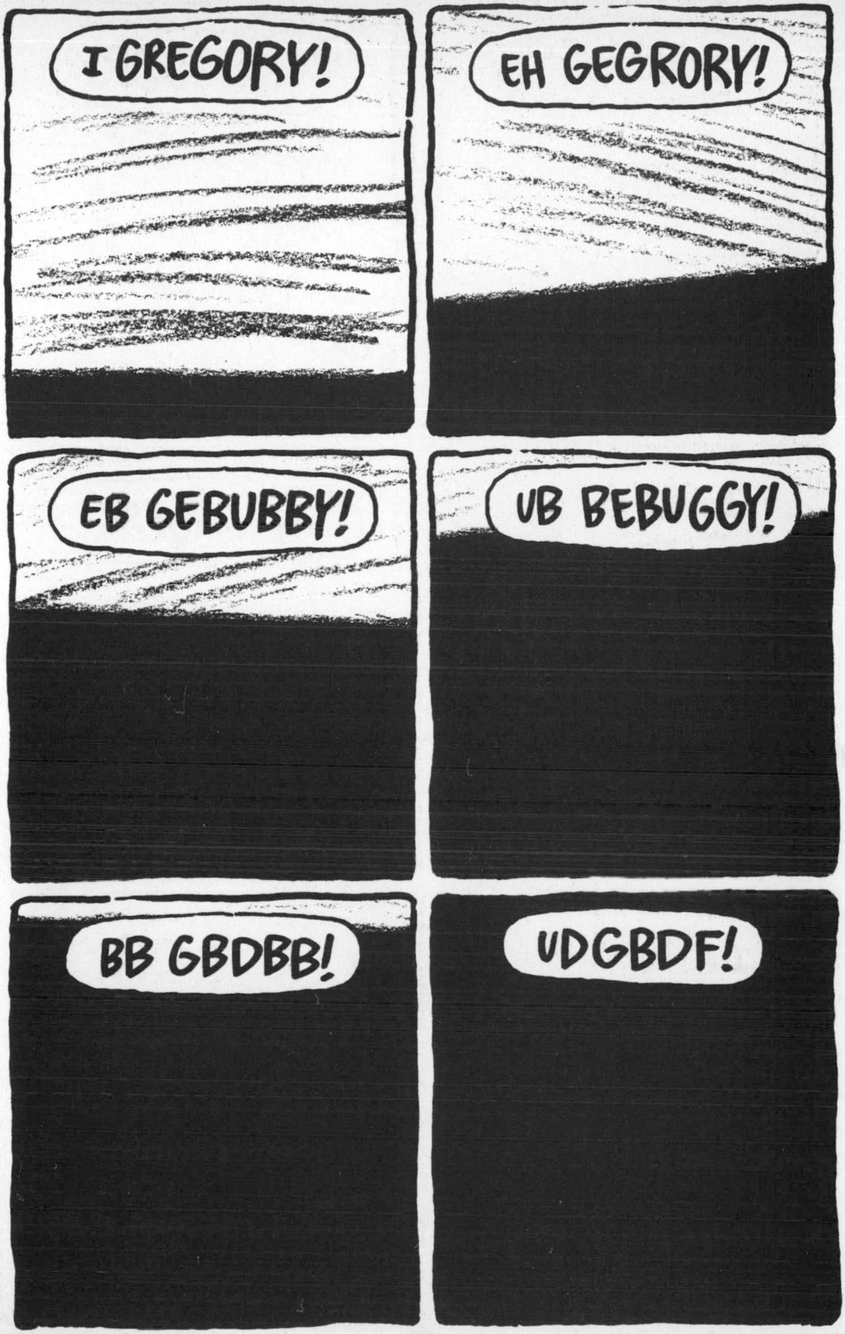

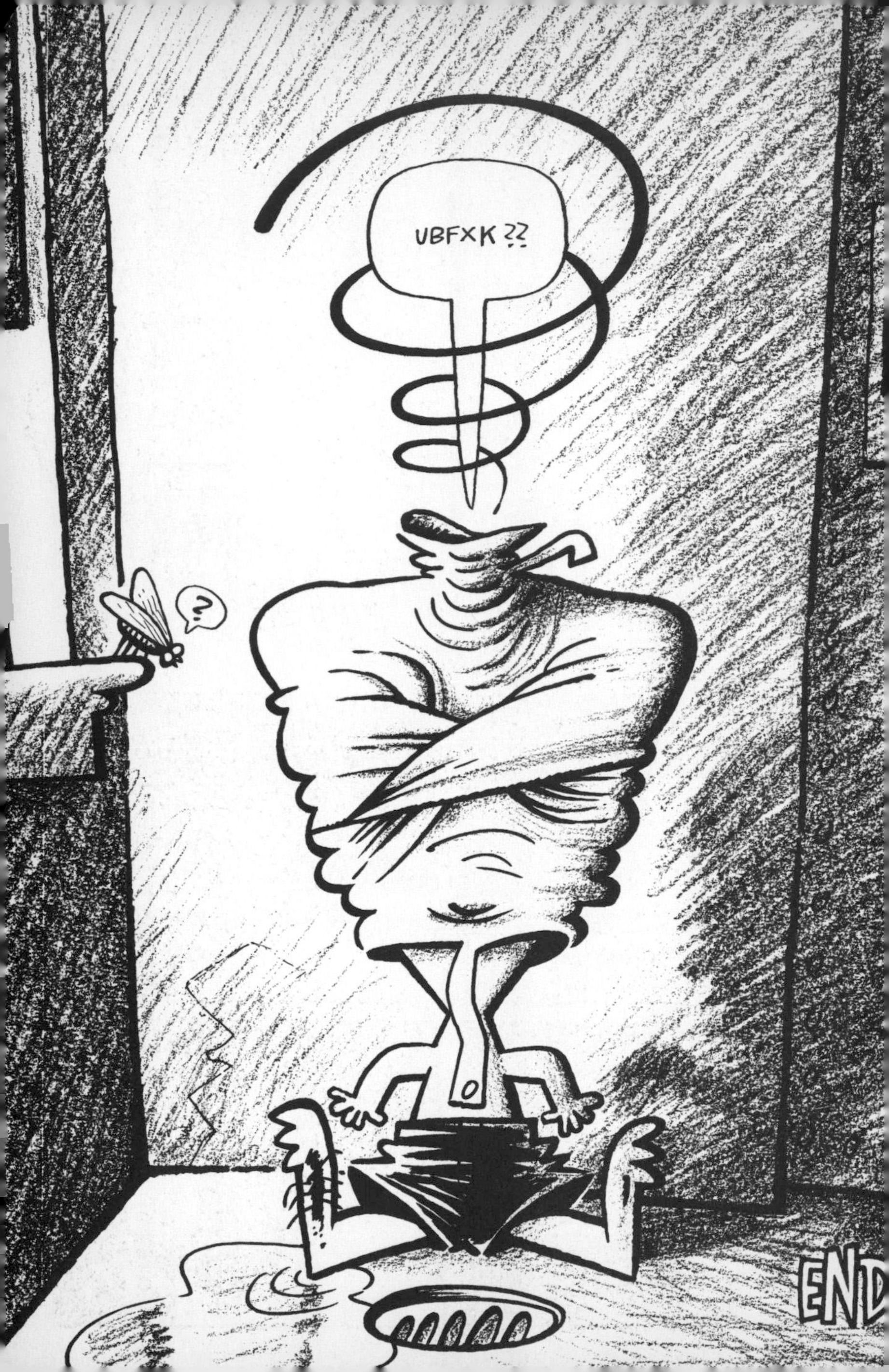

UBFXK ??
?
END

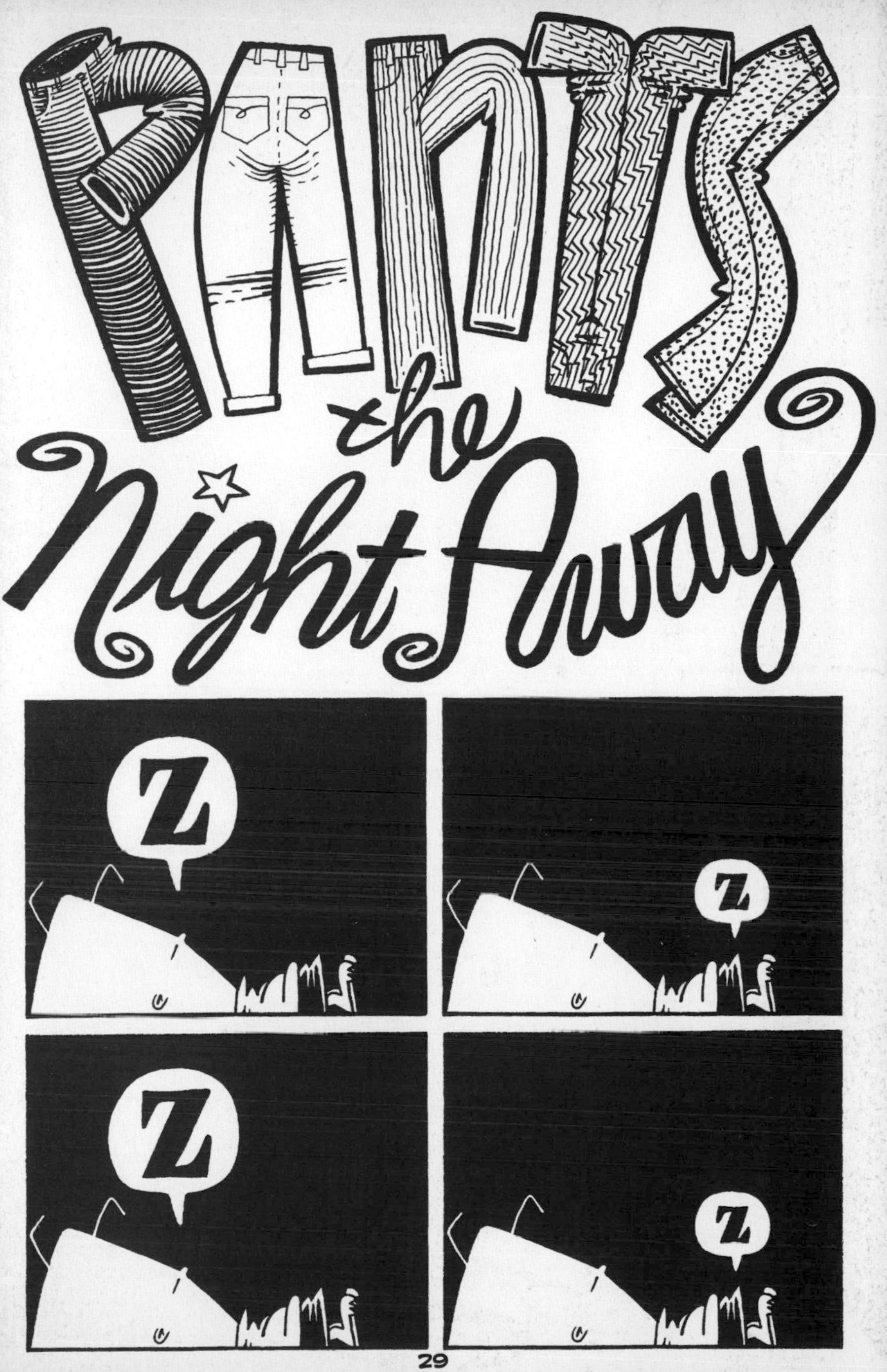
PANTS the Night Away
Z
Z
Z
Z

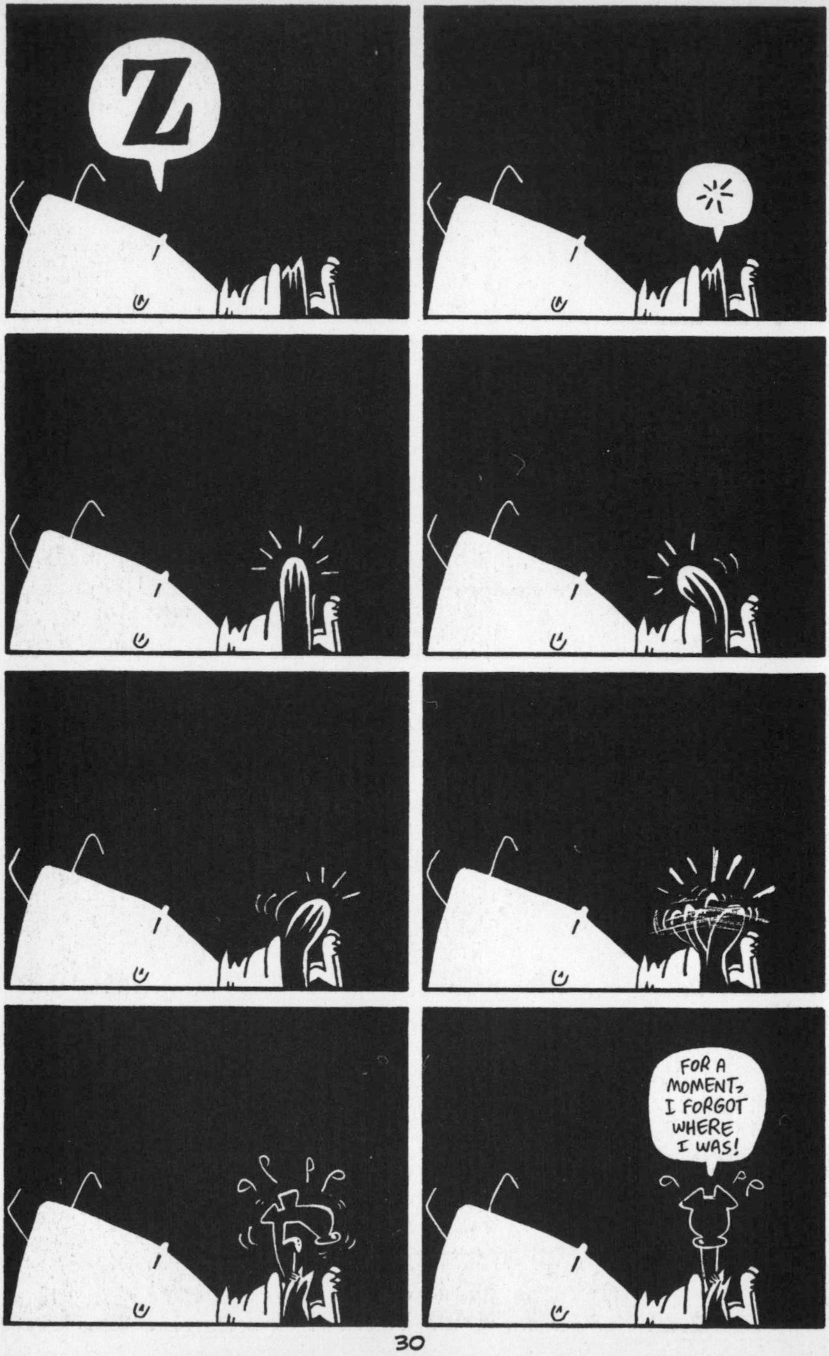
Z
FOR A MOMENT, I FORGOT WHERE I WAS!

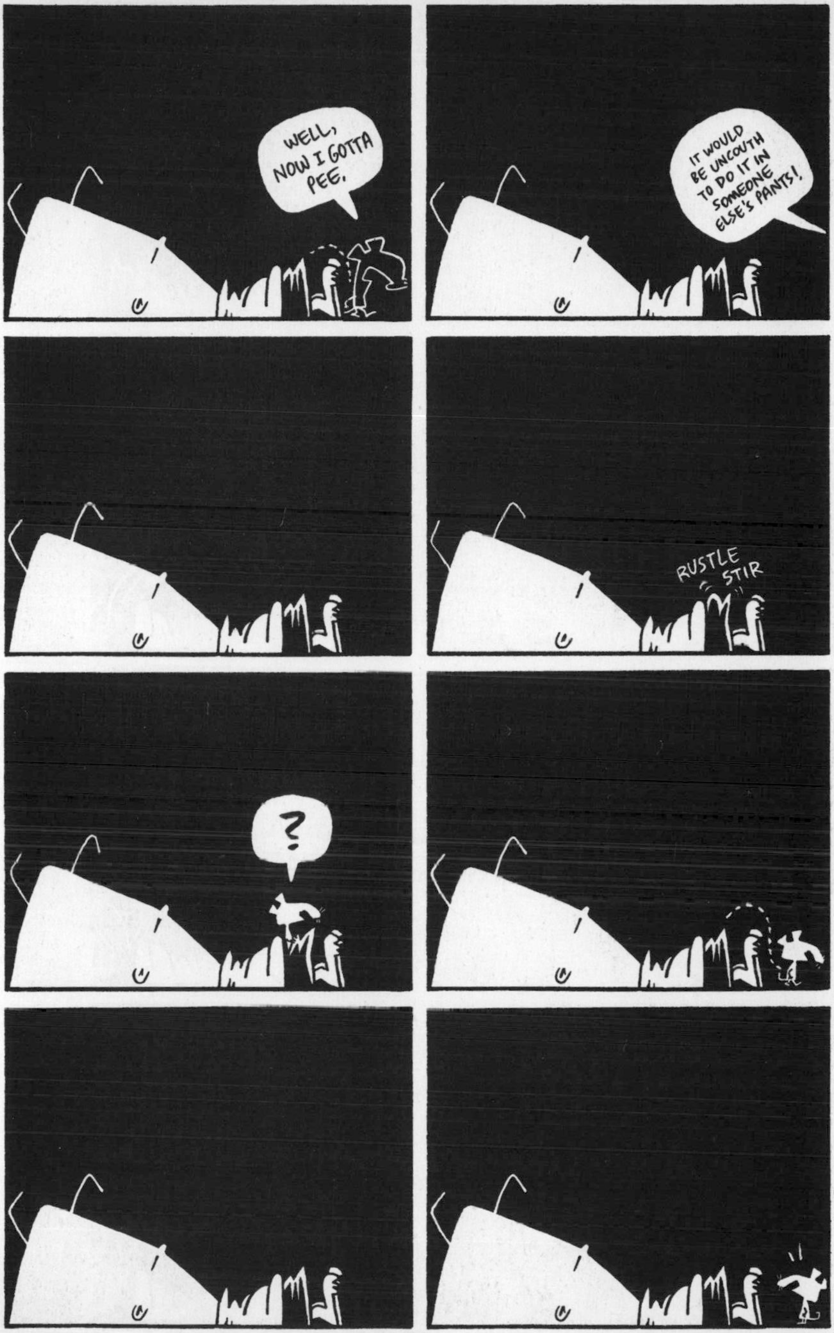
WELL, NOW I GOTTA PEE.
IT WOULD BE UNCOUTH TO DO IT IN SOMEONE ELSE'S PANTS!
RUSTLE STIR
?

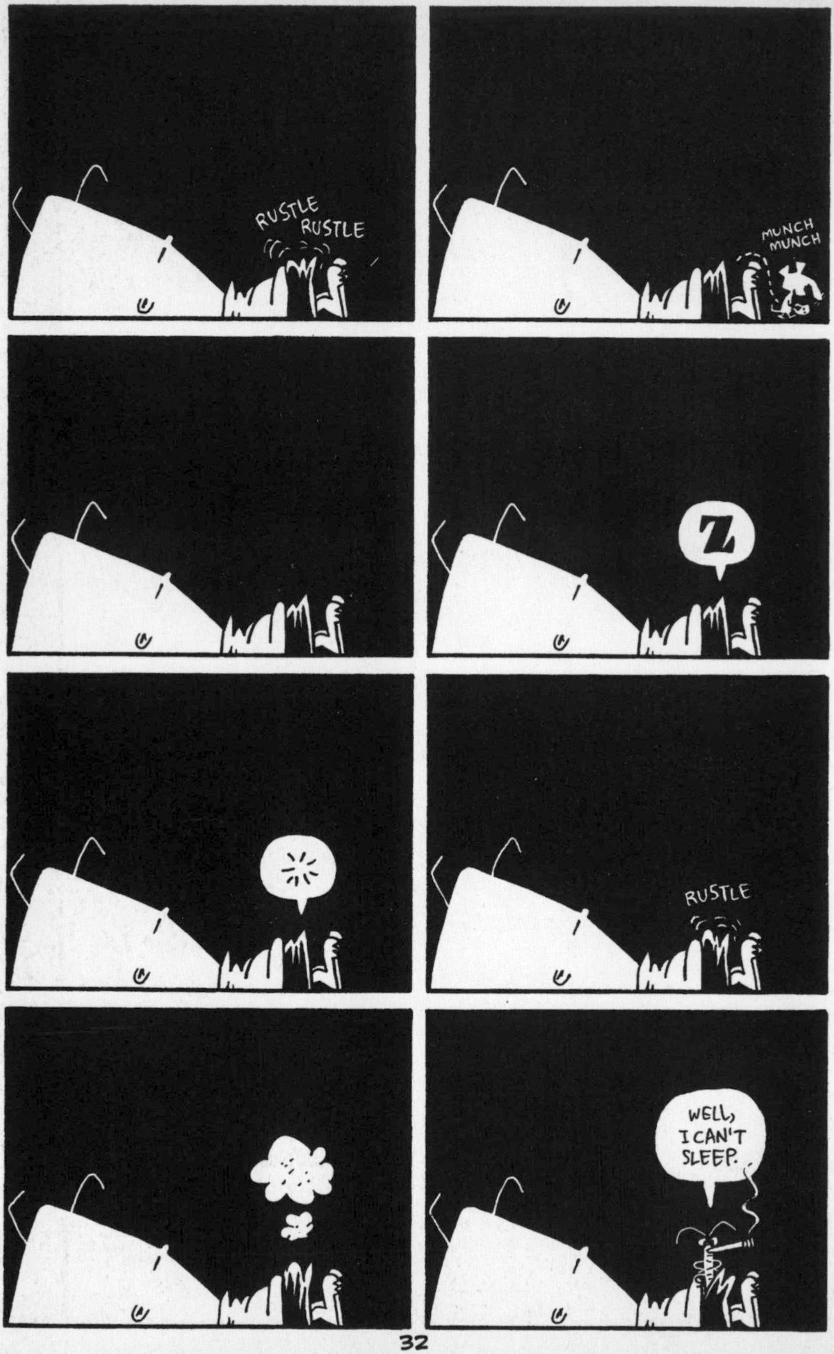
RUSTLE RUSTLE
MUNCH MUNCH
Z
RUSTLE
WELL, I CAN'T SLEEP.

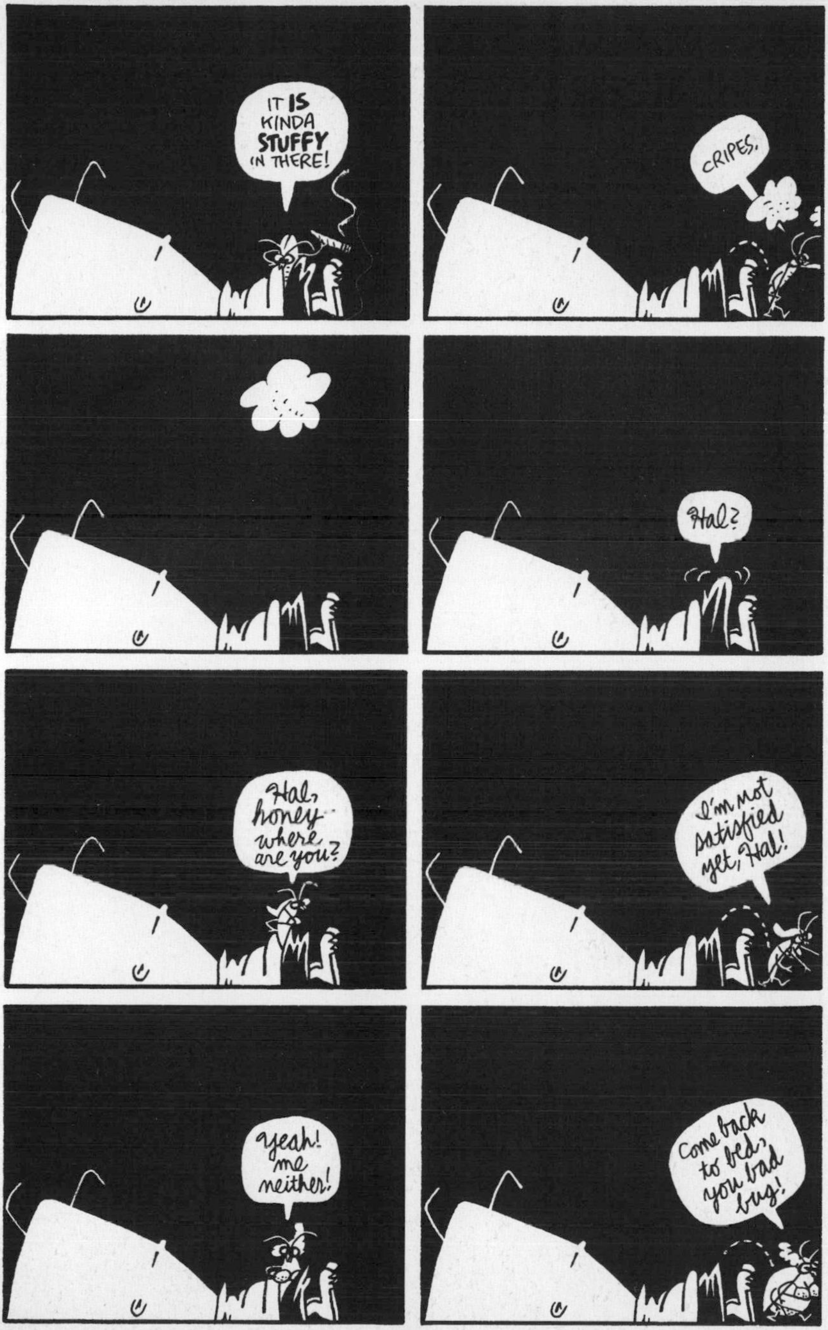
IT IS KINDA STUFFY IN THERE!
CRIPES.
Hal?
Hal, honey where are you?
I'm not satisfied yet, Hal!
yeah! me neither!
Come back to bed, you bad bug!

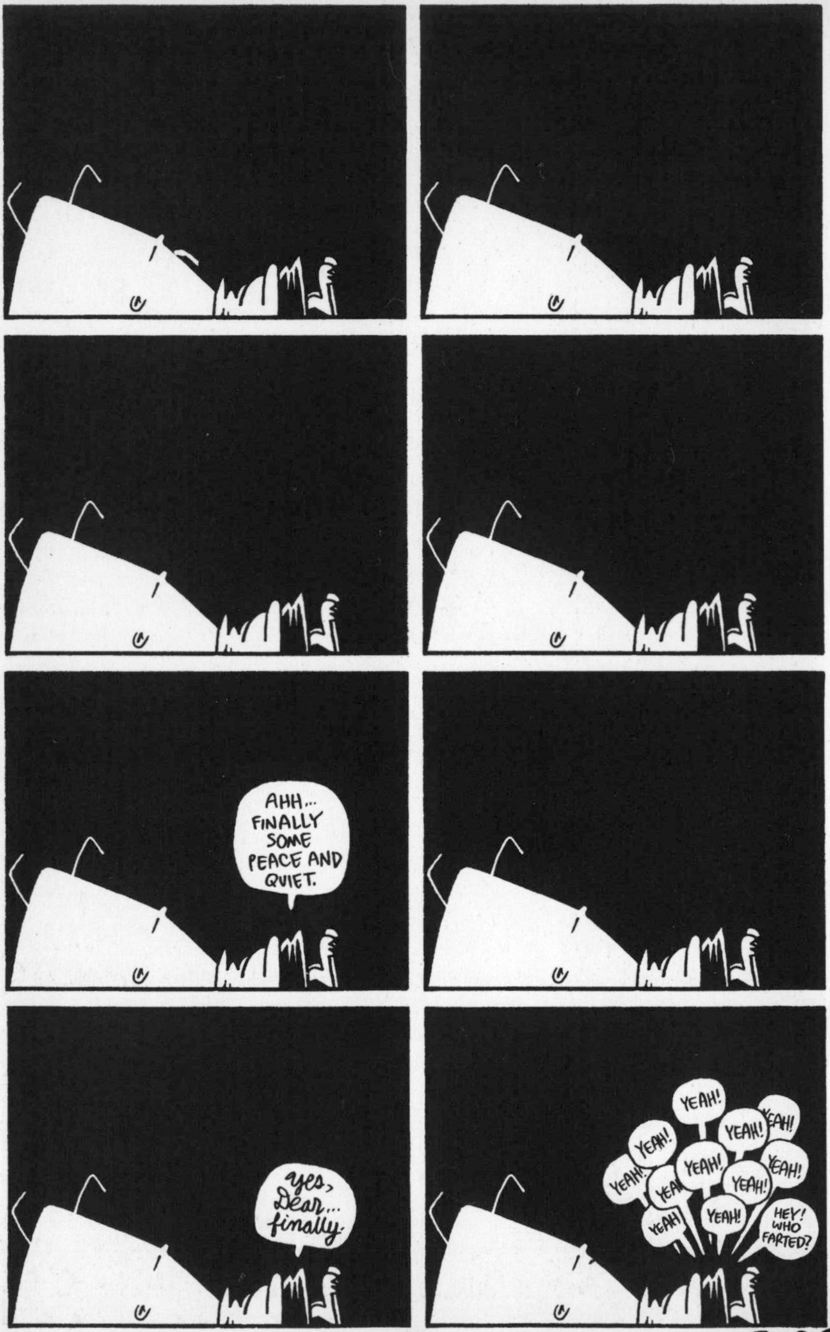
AHH... FINALLY SOME PEACE AND QUIET.
yes, Dear... finally.
YEAH!
YEAH!
YEAH!
YEAH!
YEAH!
YEAH!
YEAH!
YEAH!
YEAH!
HEY! WHO FARTED?

end

POP
SNURF
SLAM!
SNF
TO LAUNDRY ROOM

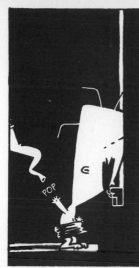

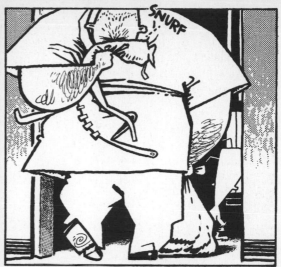

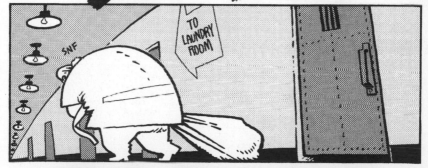

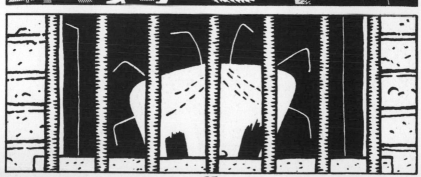

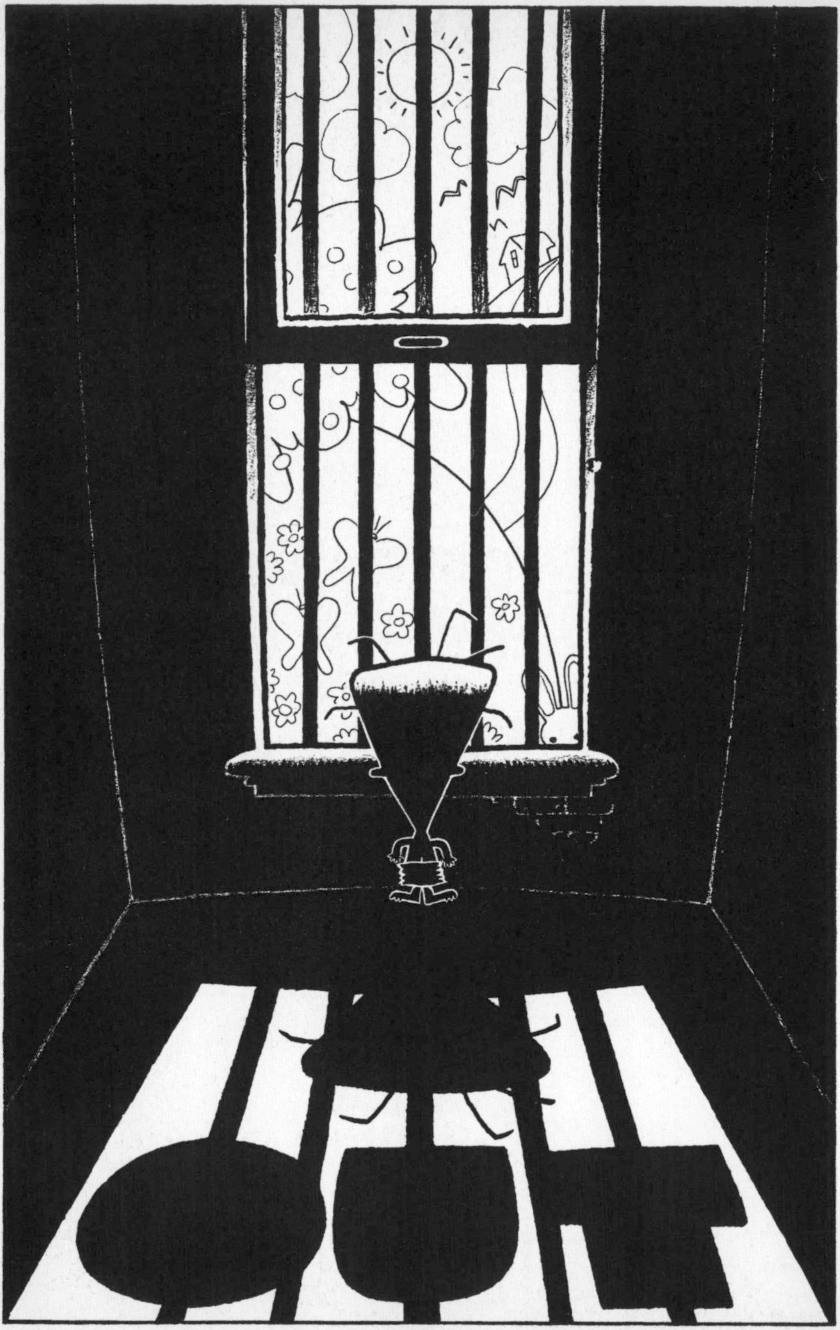

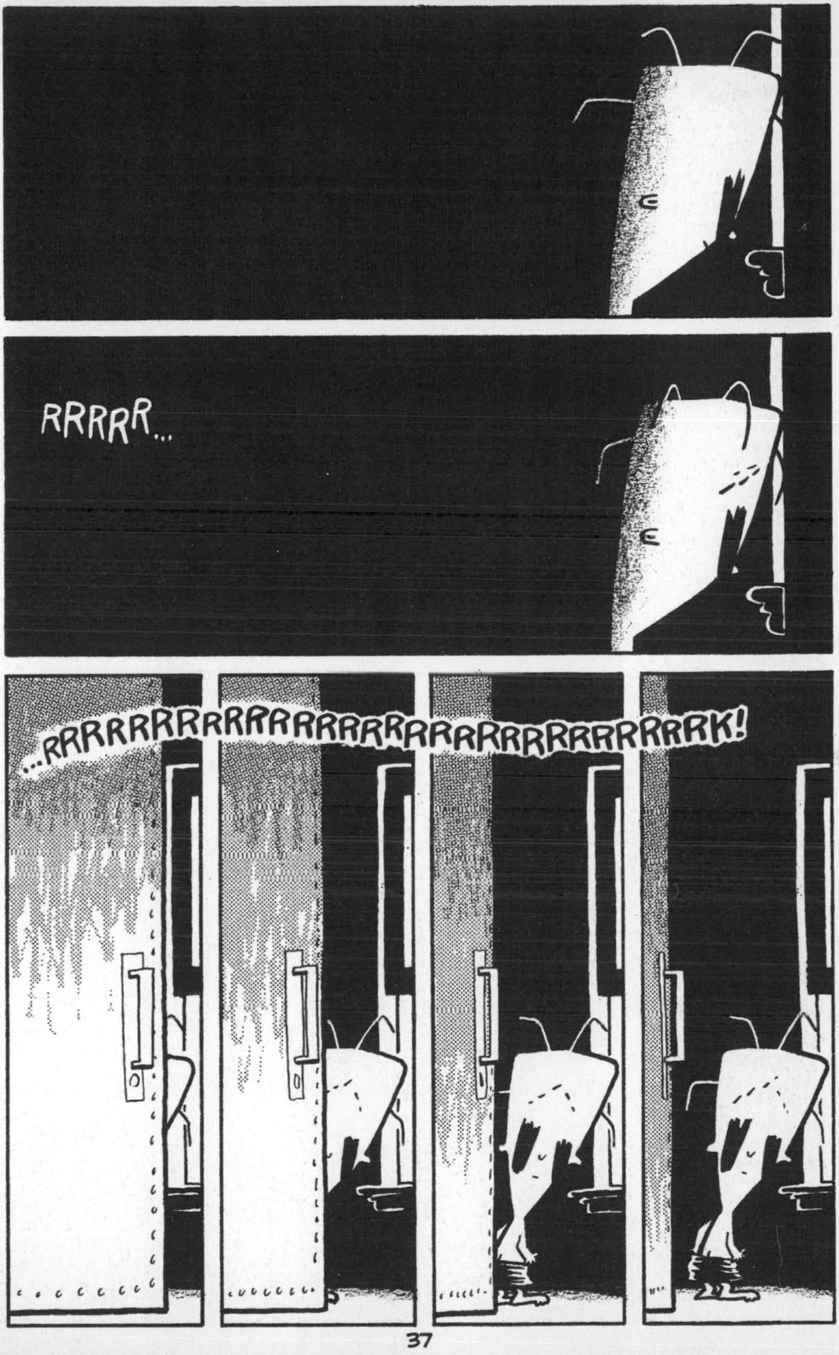
RRRRR...
...RRRRRRRRRRRRRRRRRRRRRRRRRRRRRK!

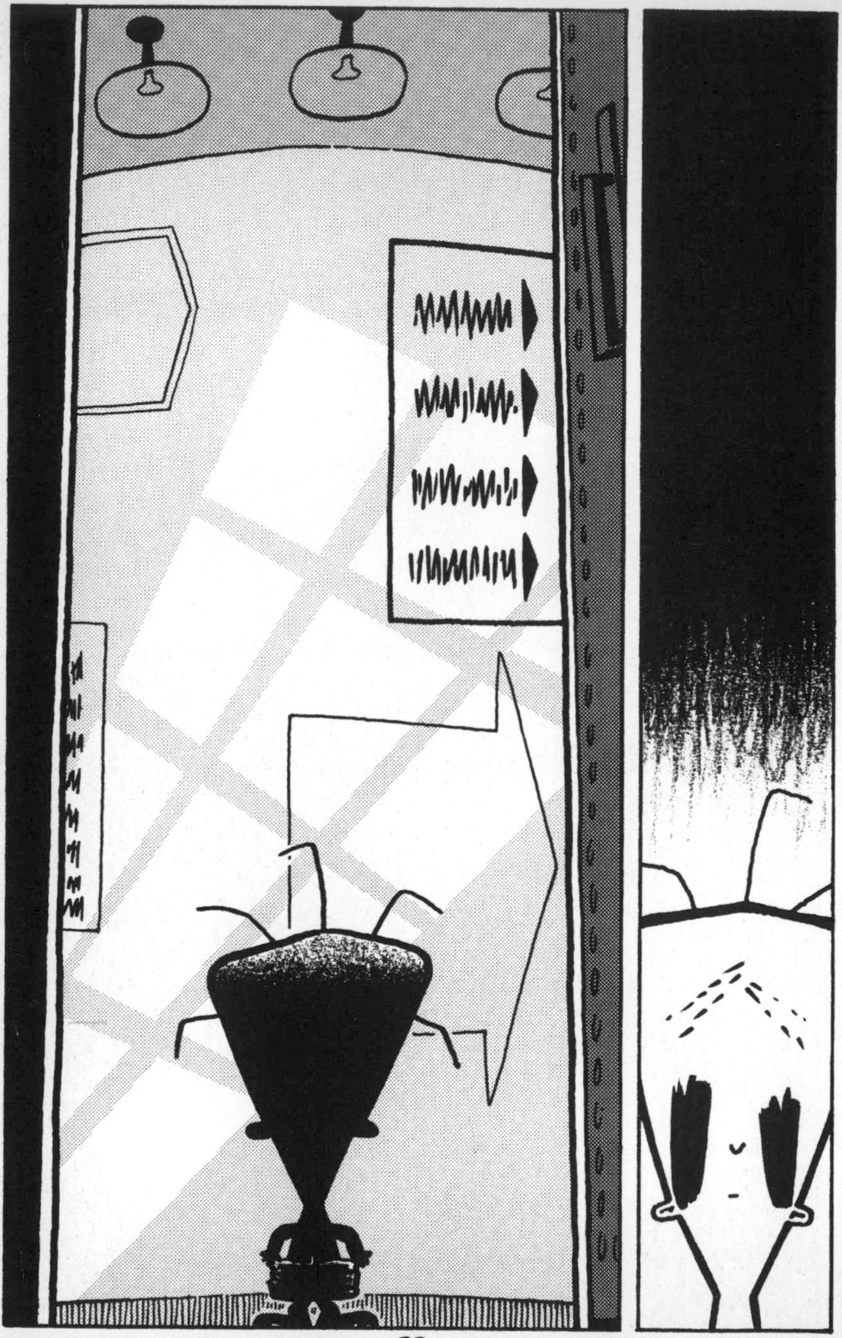

 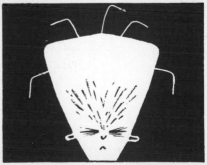

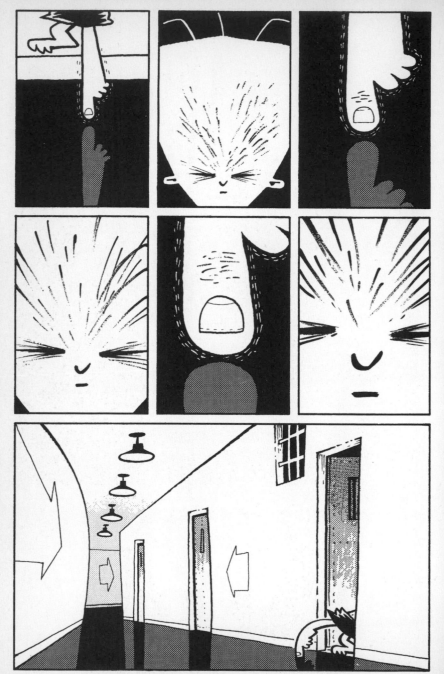

40

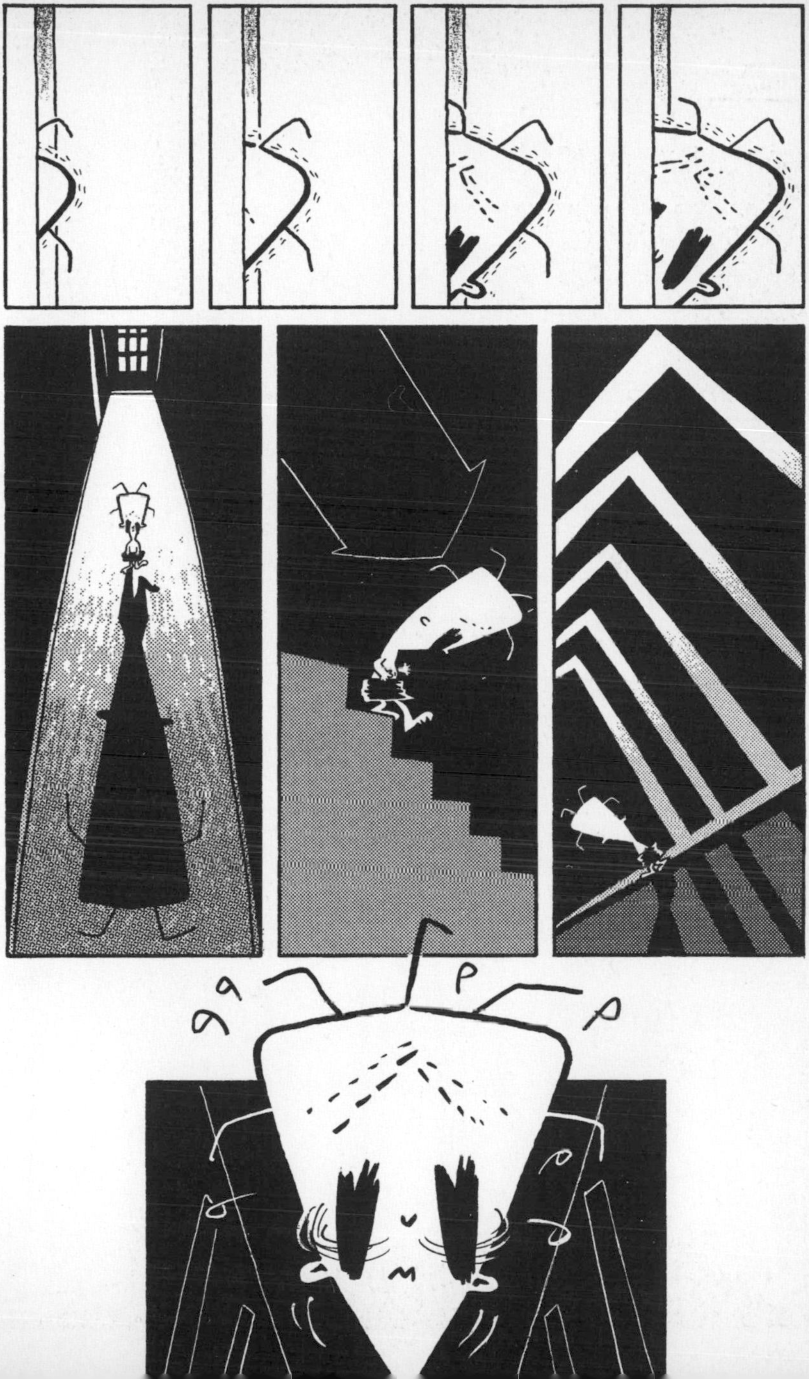

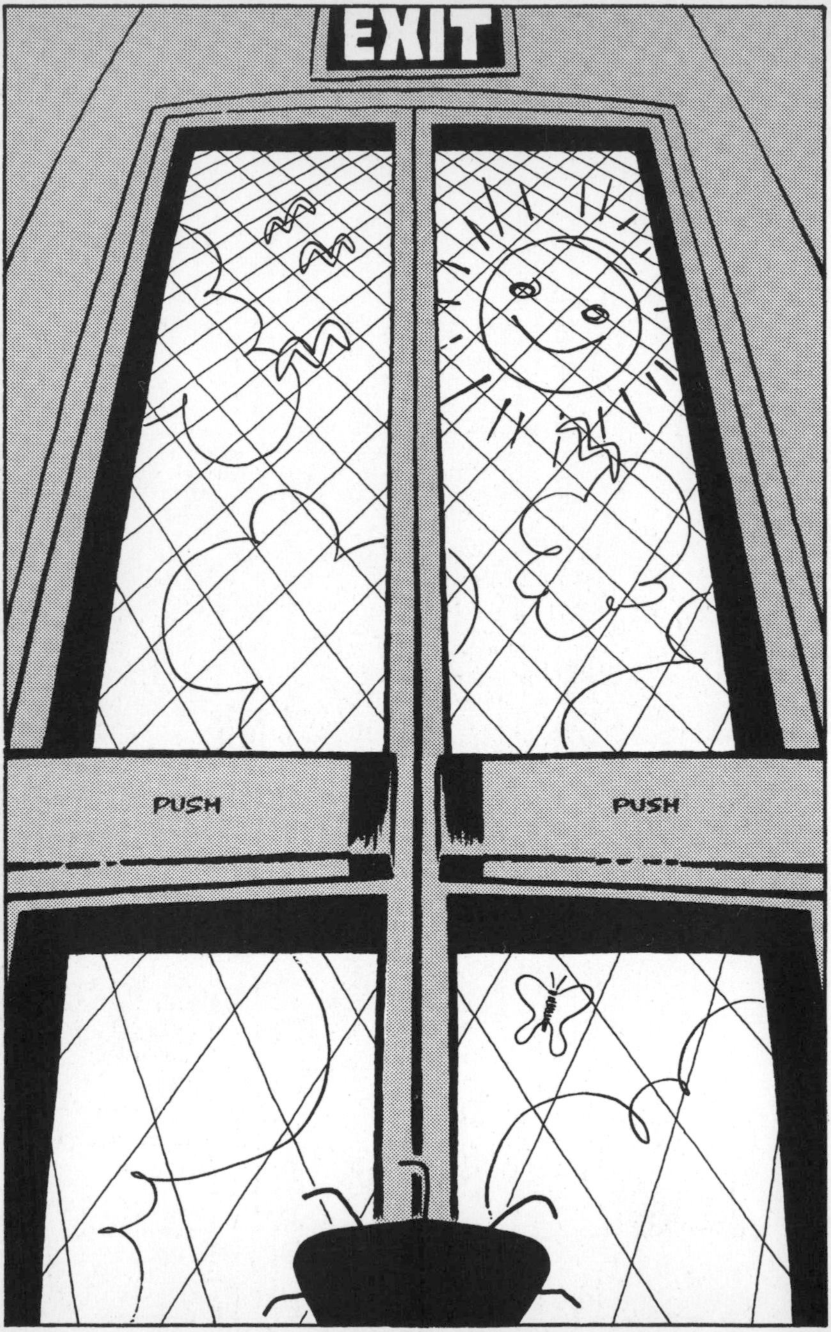
EXIT
PUSH
PUSH

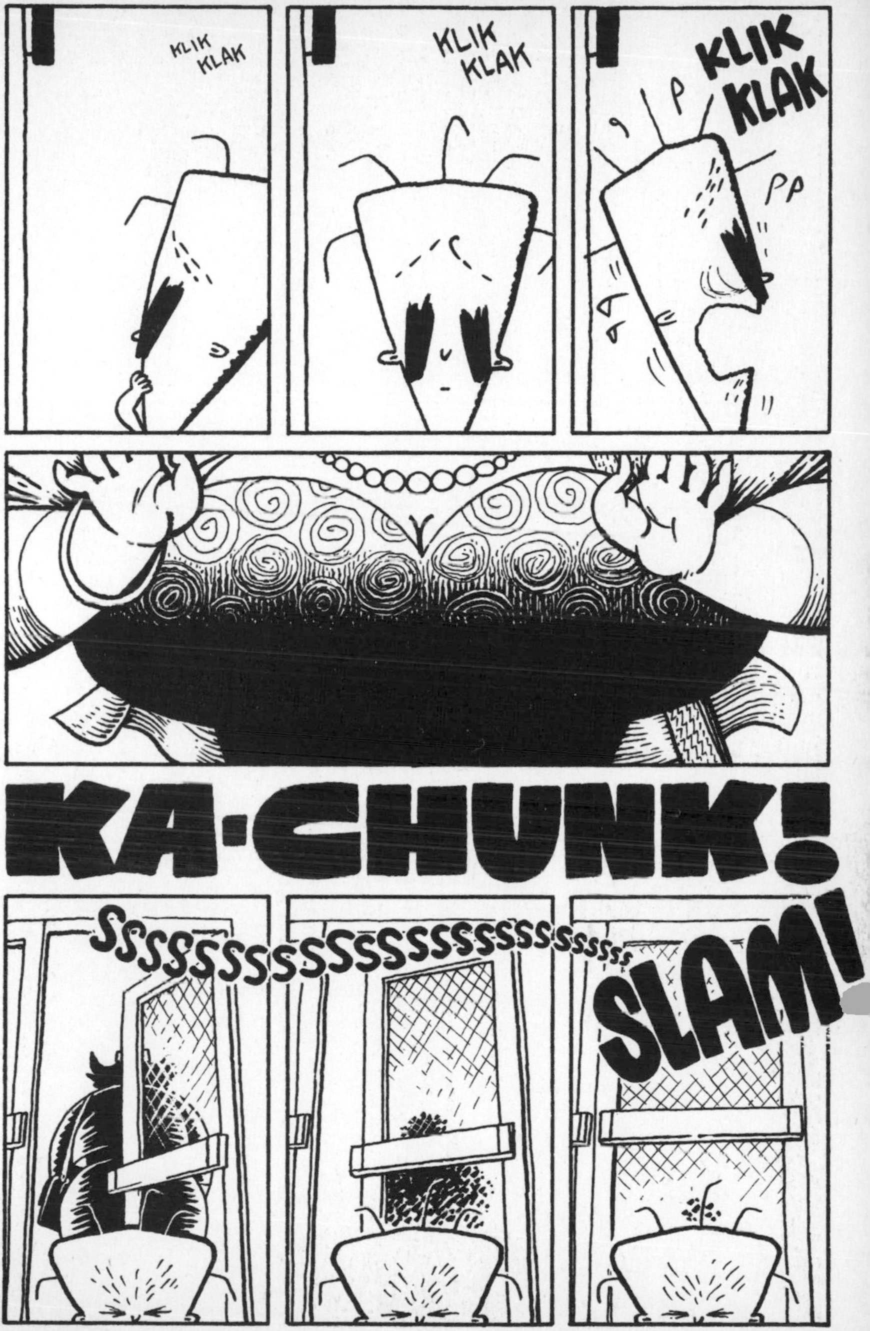
KLIK KLAK
KLIK KLAK
KLIK KLAK
KA-CHUNK!
SSSSSSSSSSSSSSSSSSSSSSSSSS
SLAM!

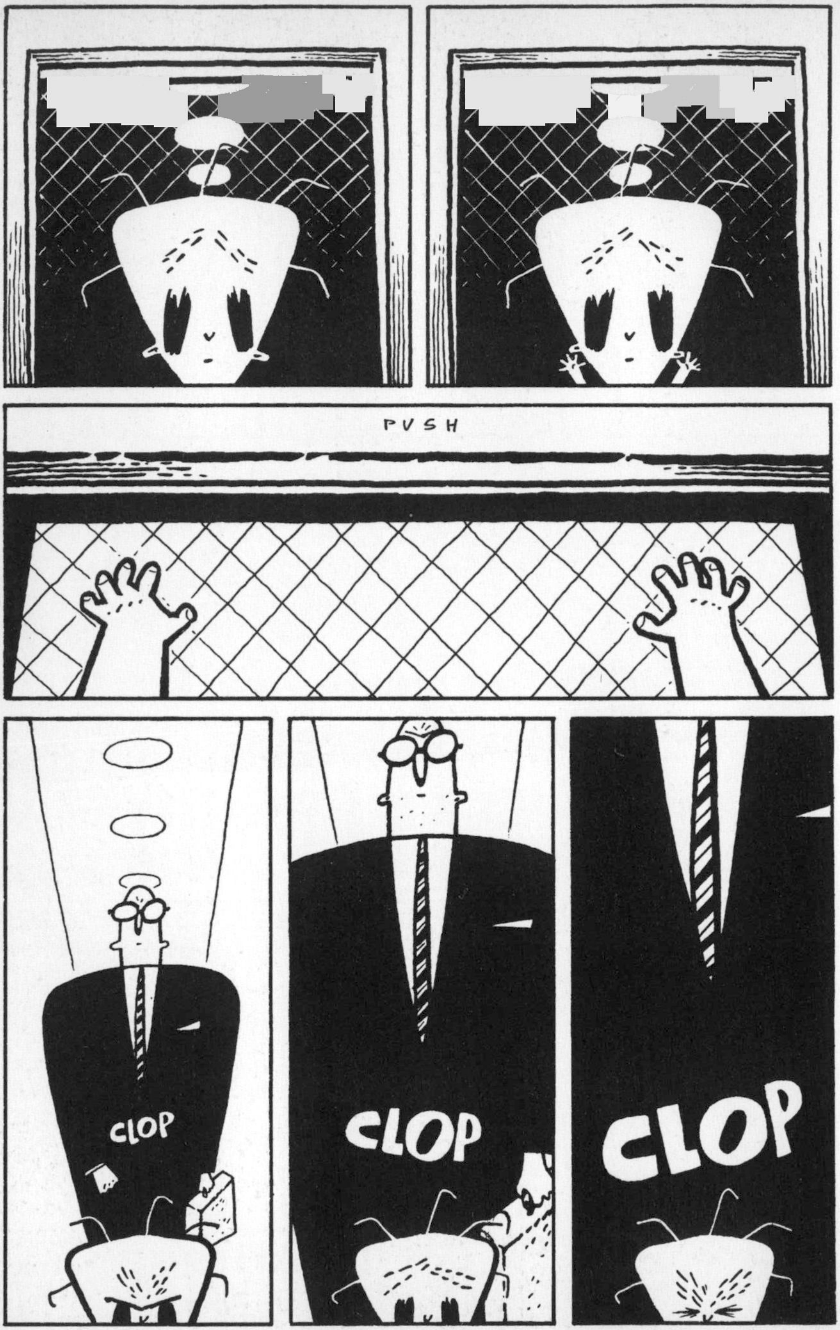
PUSH
CLOP
CLOP
CLOP

# KA·CHUNK!

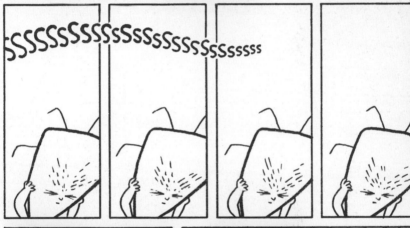

SSSSSSSSSSSSSSSSSSSSSSSSSSSSSssssssss

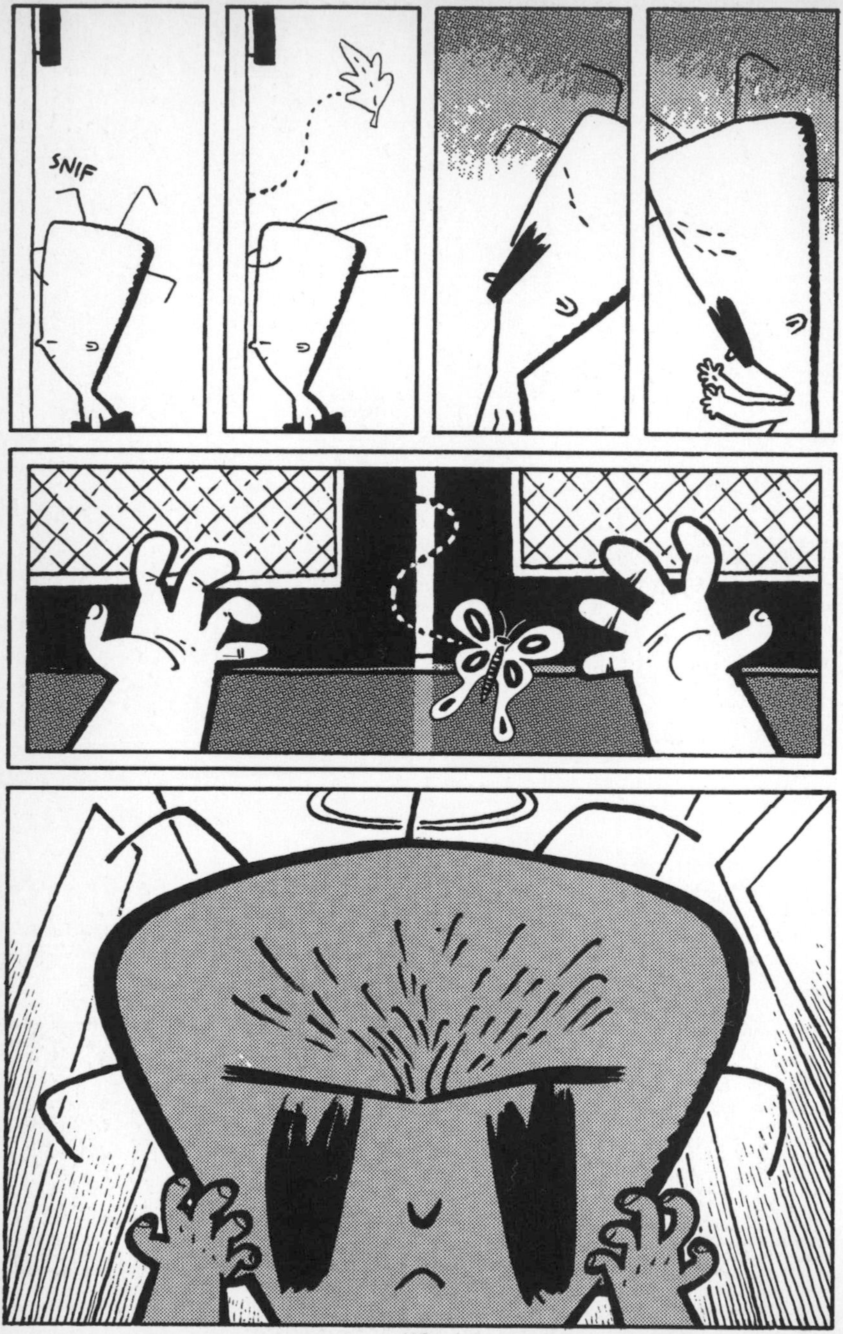
SNIF

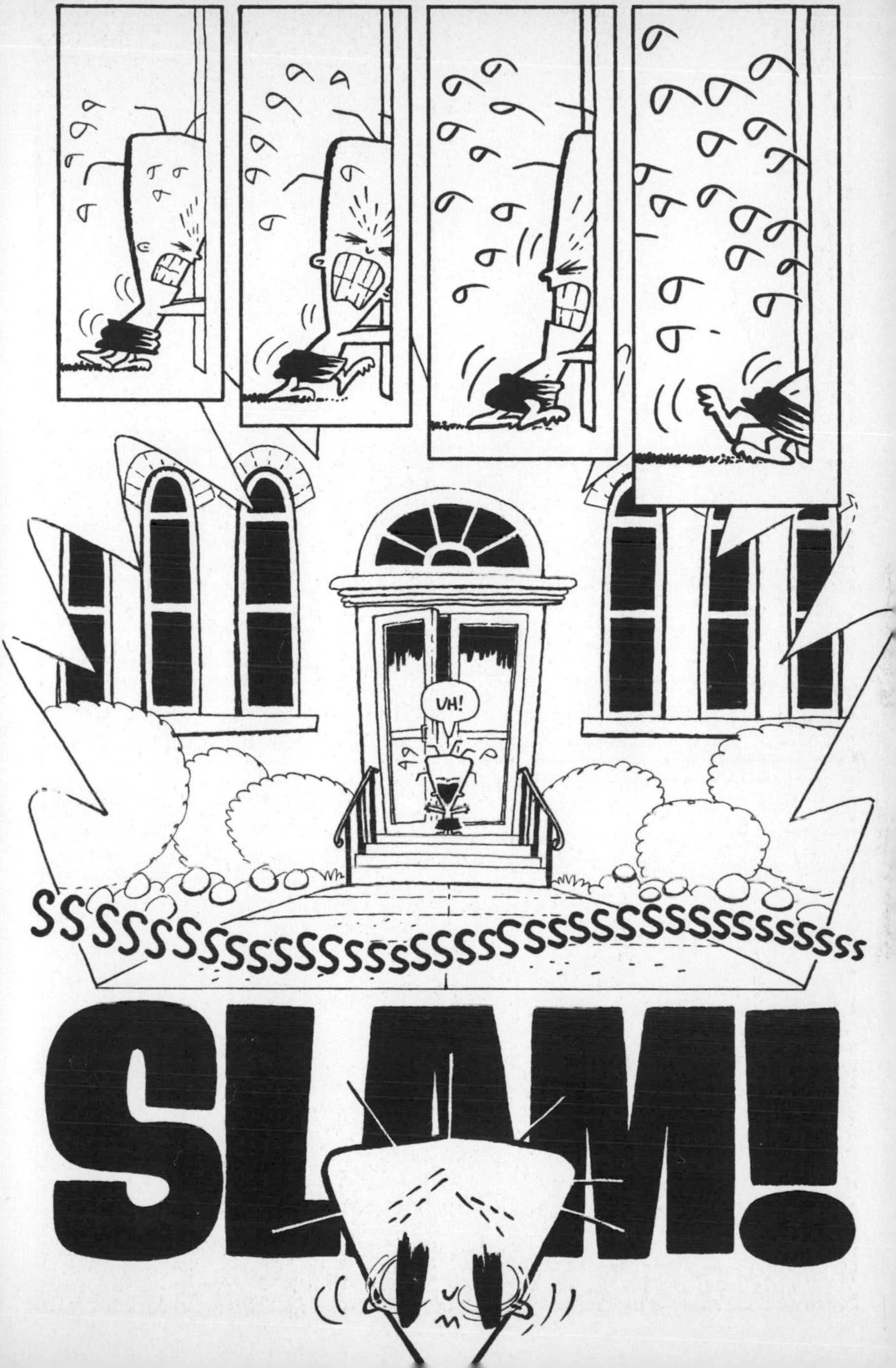
UH!
SSSSSSSSSSSSSSSSSSSSSSSSSSSSSSSSSSSSSS
SLAM!

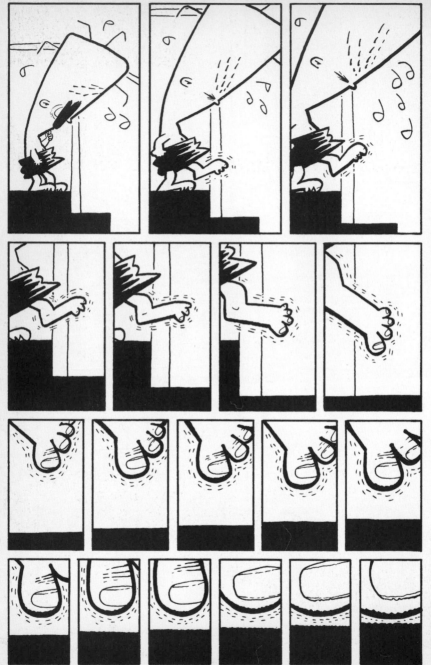

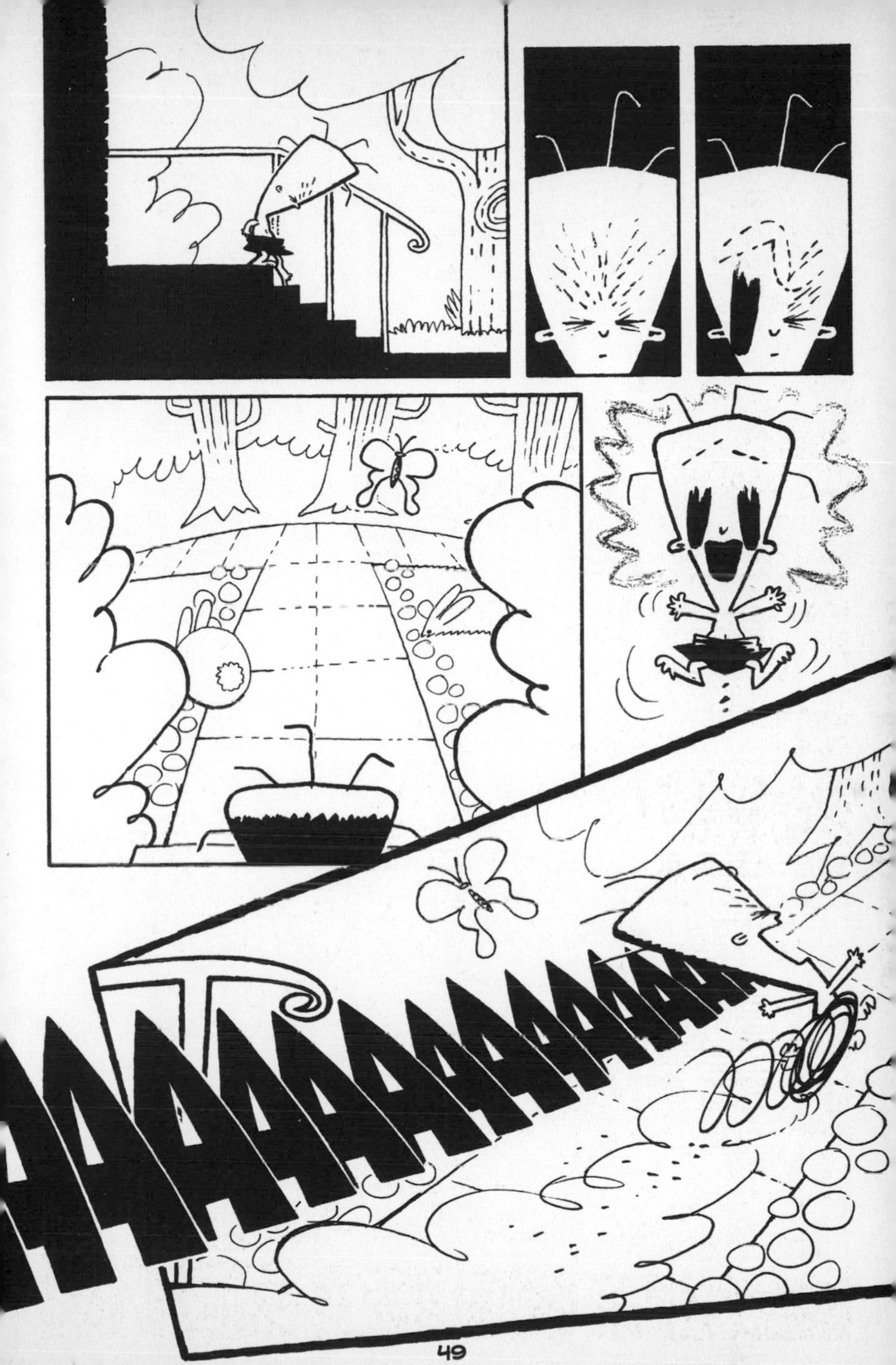
AAAAAAAAAAAAAAAAAAAAAA

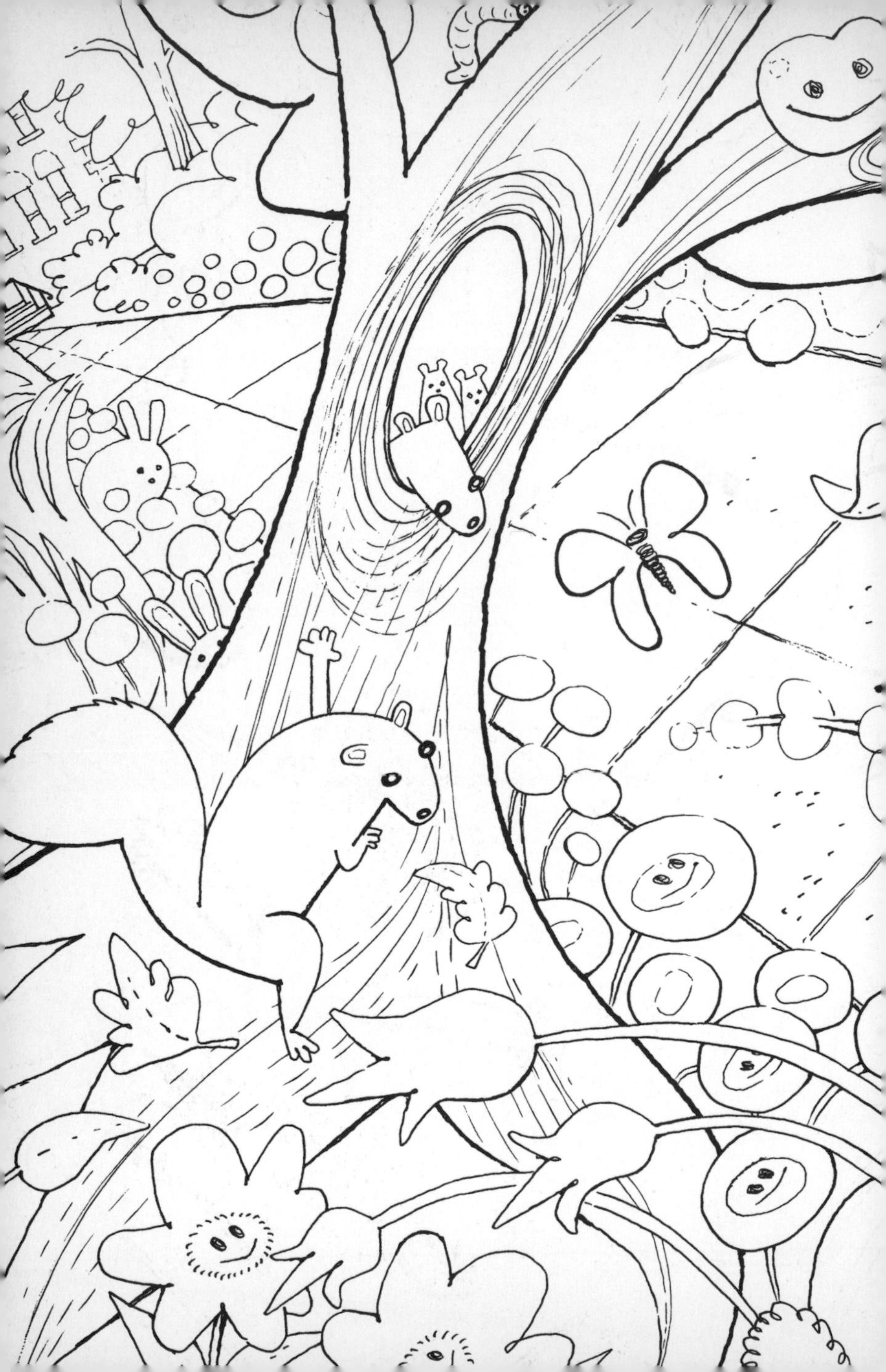

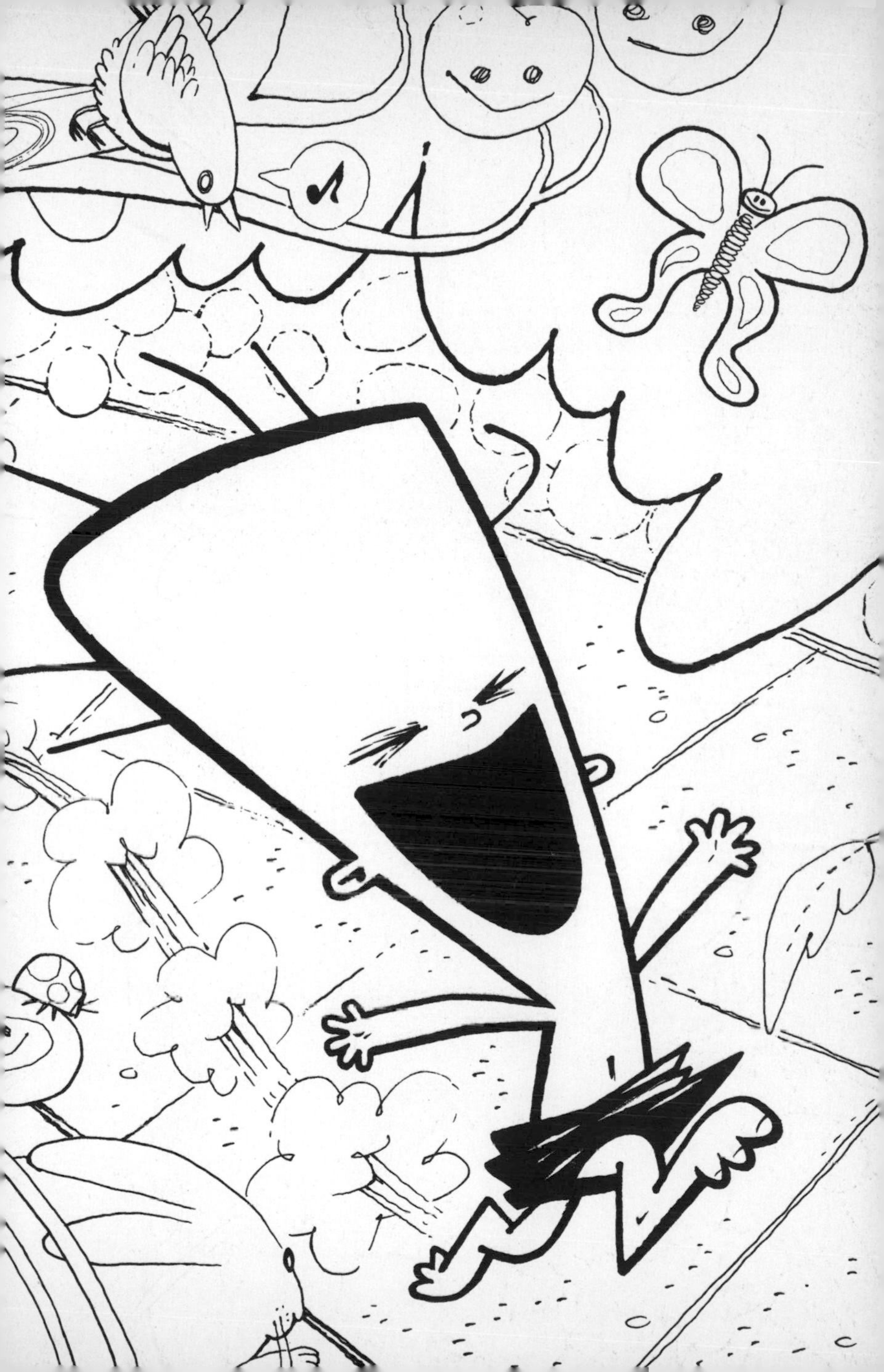

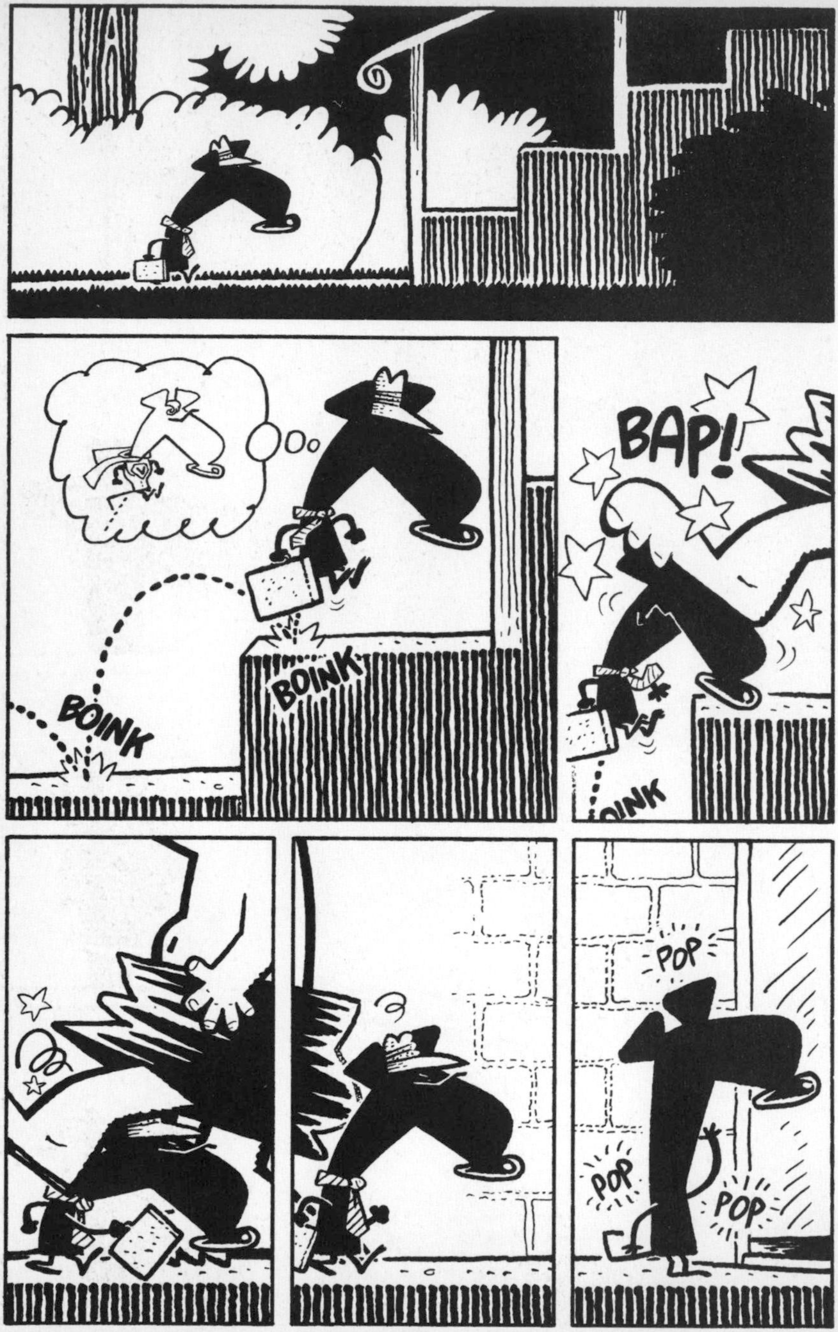
BOINK
BOINK
BAP!
OINK
POP
POP
POP

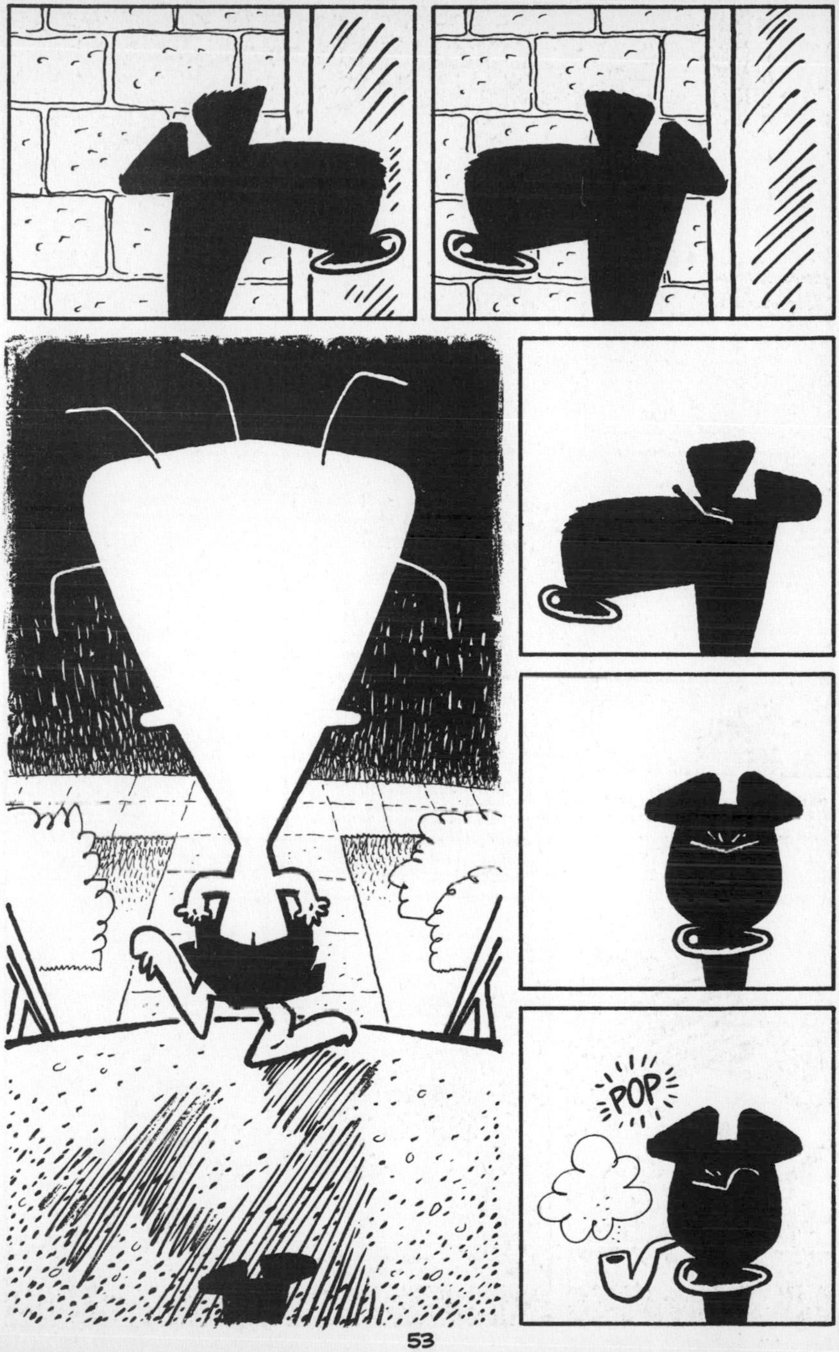
POP

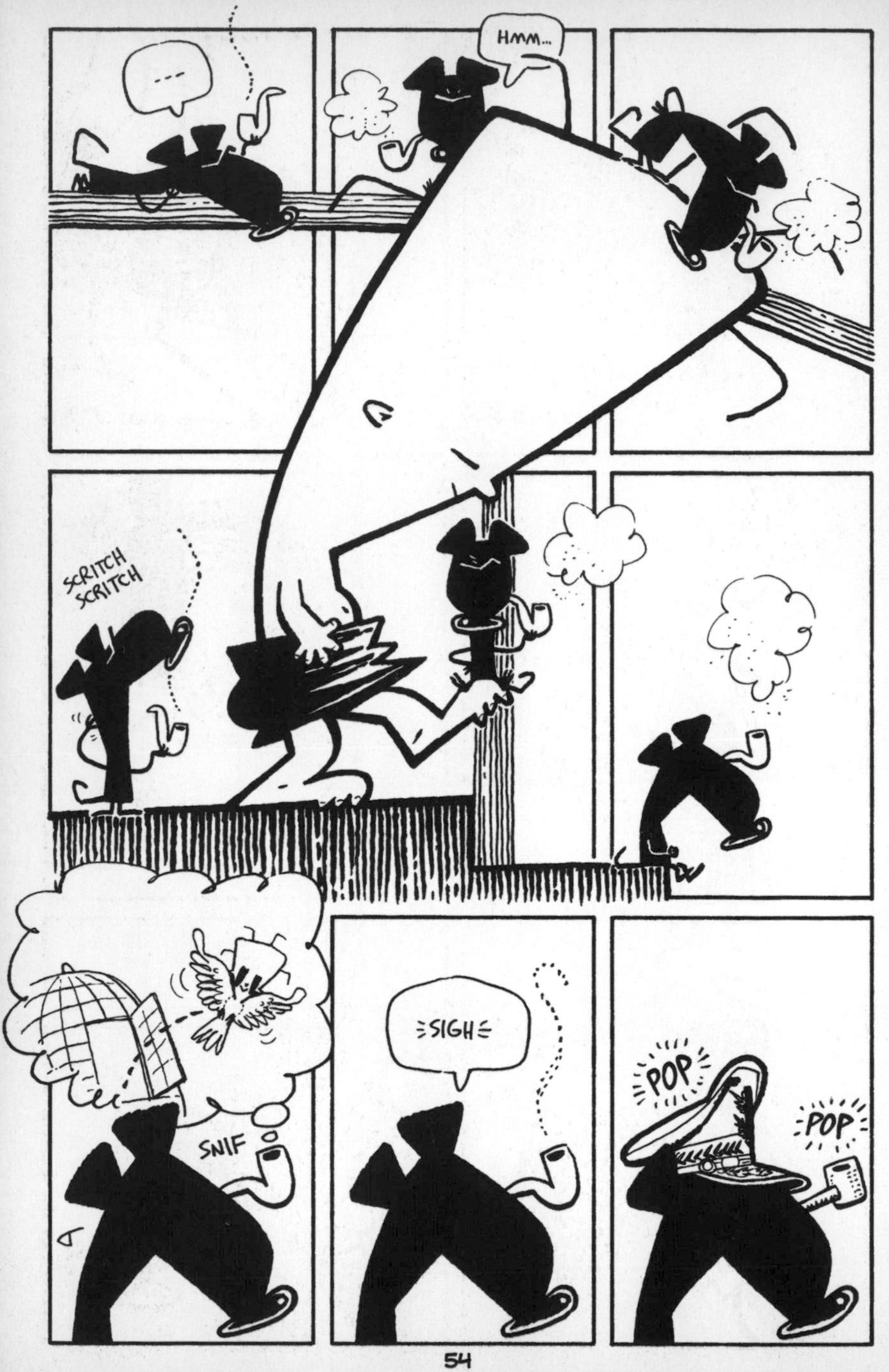

. . .
HMM...
SCRITCH
SCRITCH
SNIF
SIGH
POP
POP

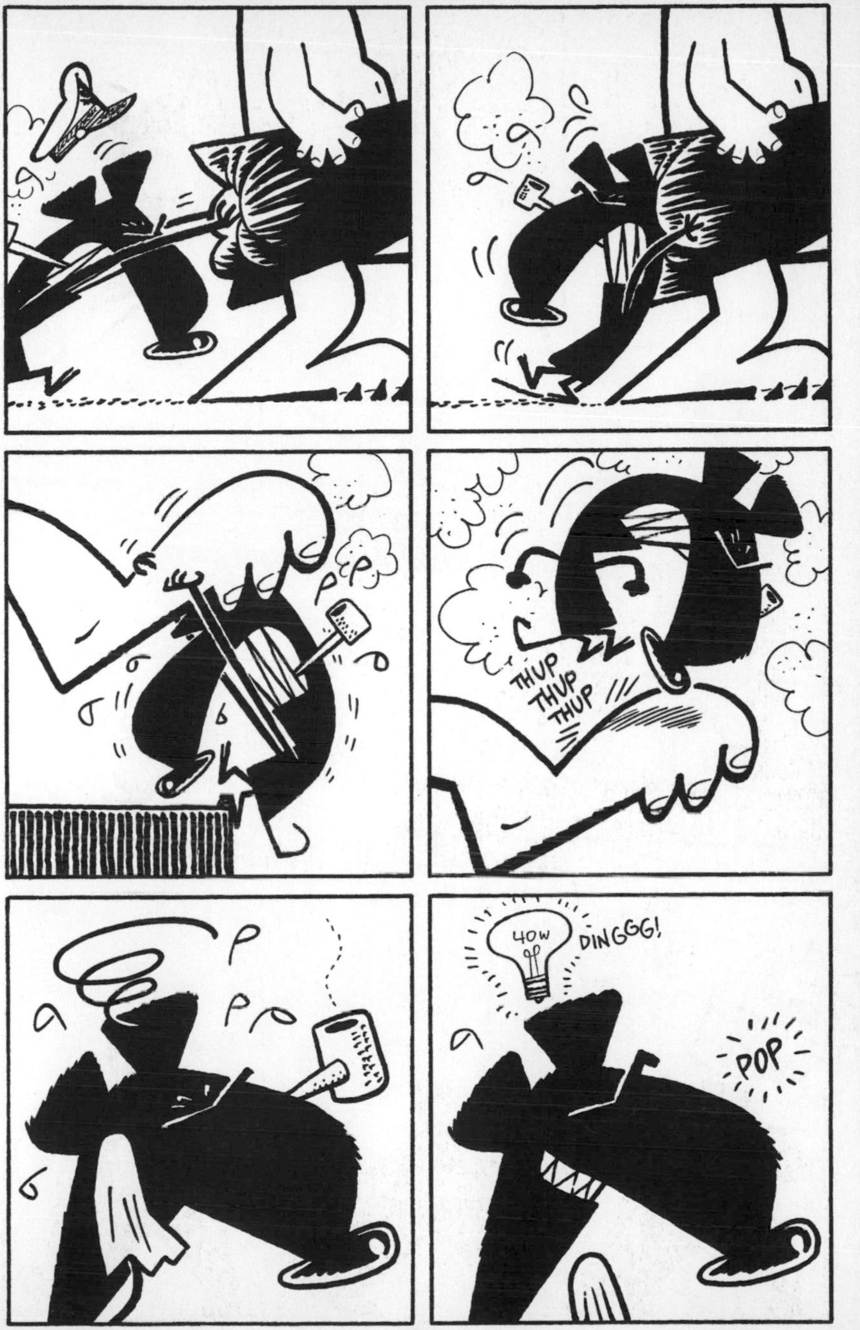
THUP
THUP
THUP
40W
DINGGG!
POP

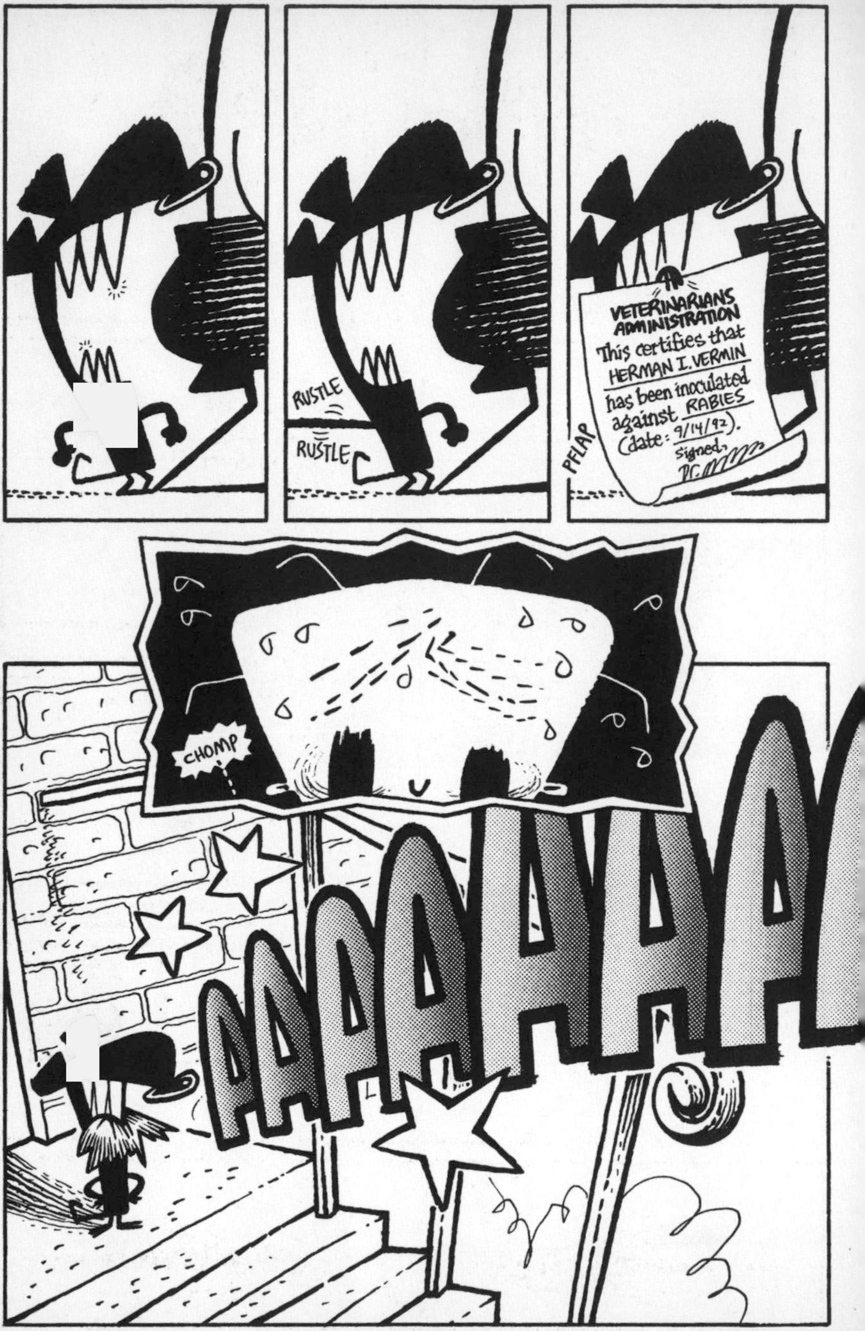
RUSTLE
RUSTLE
VETERINARIANS ADMINISTRATION
This certifies that
HERMAN I. VERMIN
has been inoculated
against RABIES
(date: 9/14/92).
Signed,
PFLAP
CHOMP
AAAAAAA

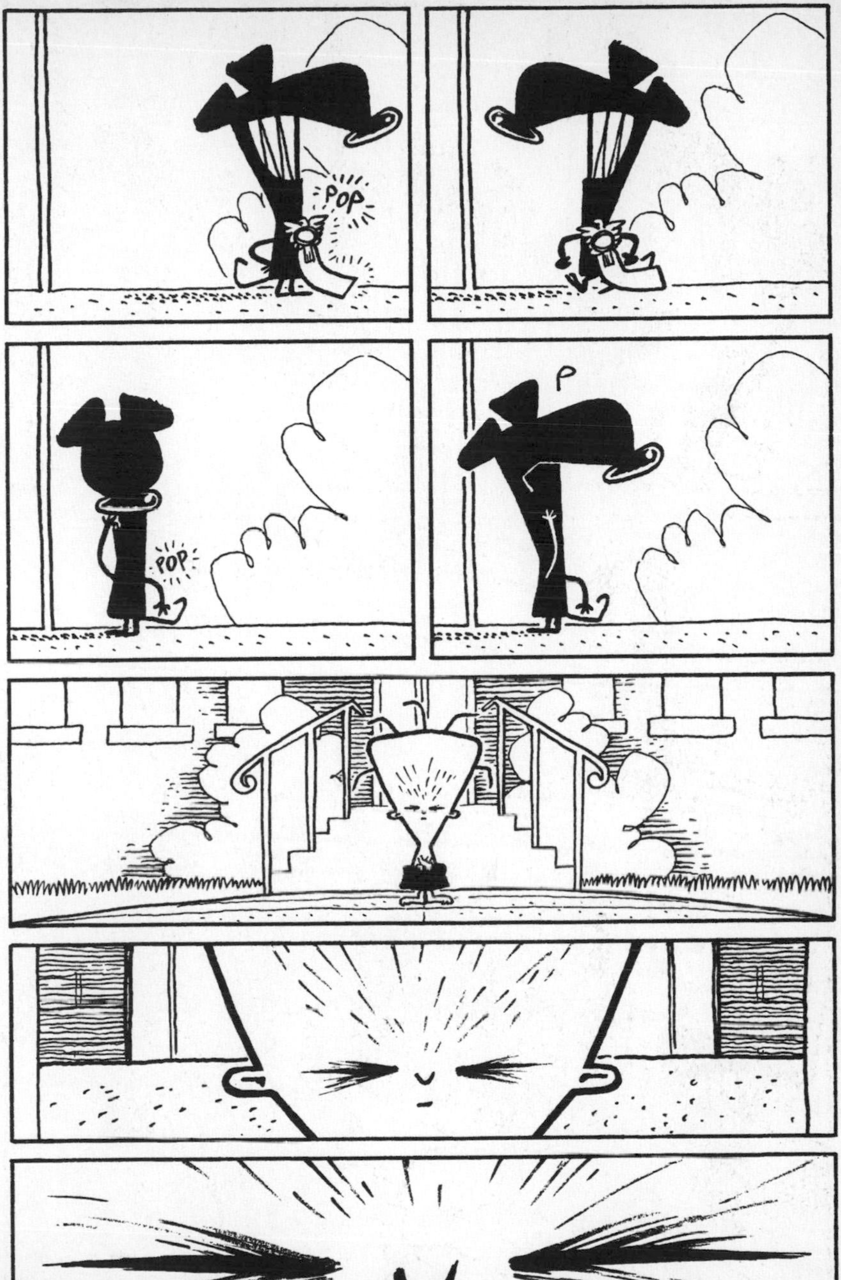
POP
POP
P

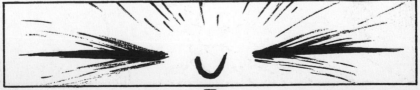

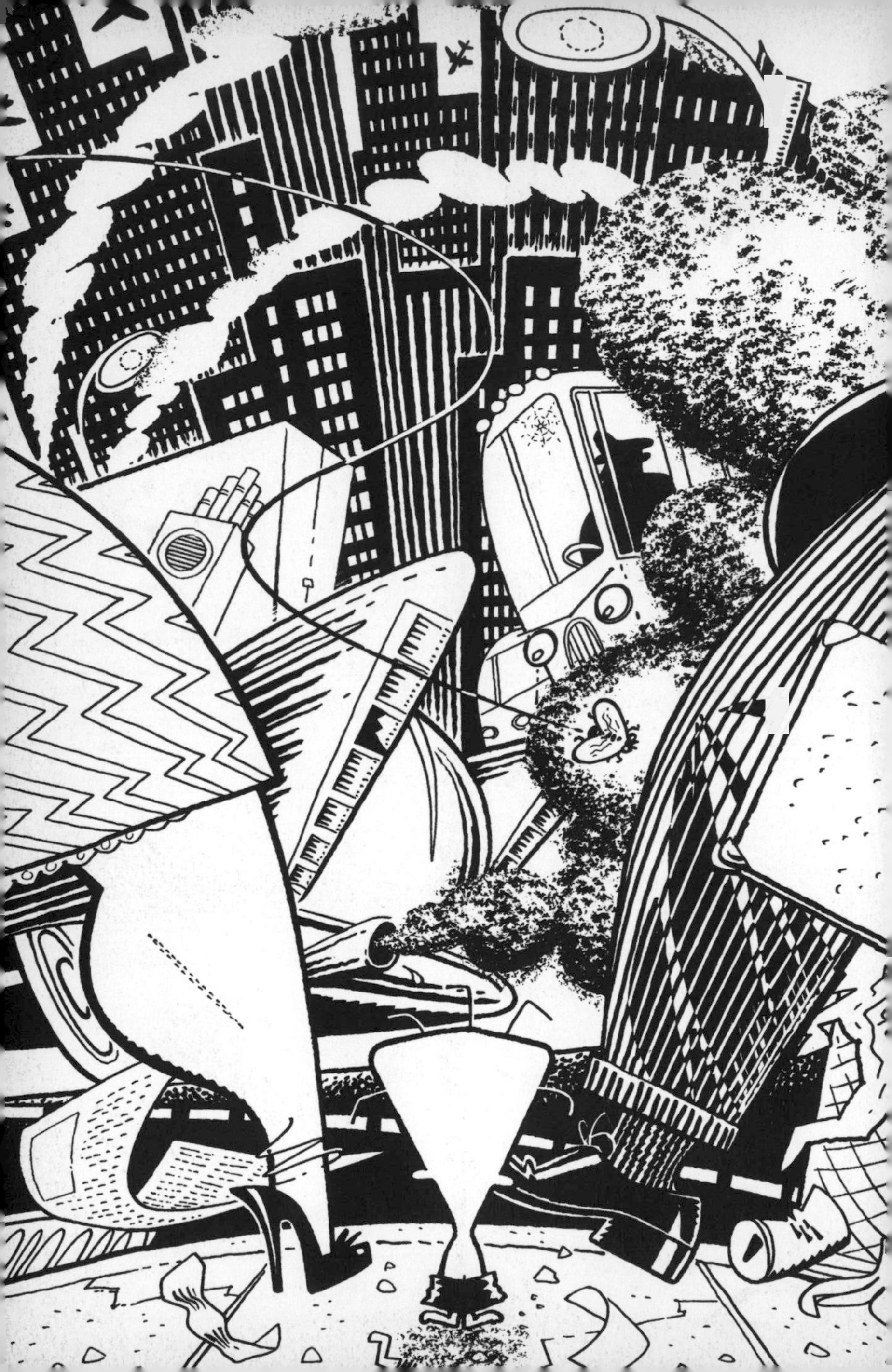

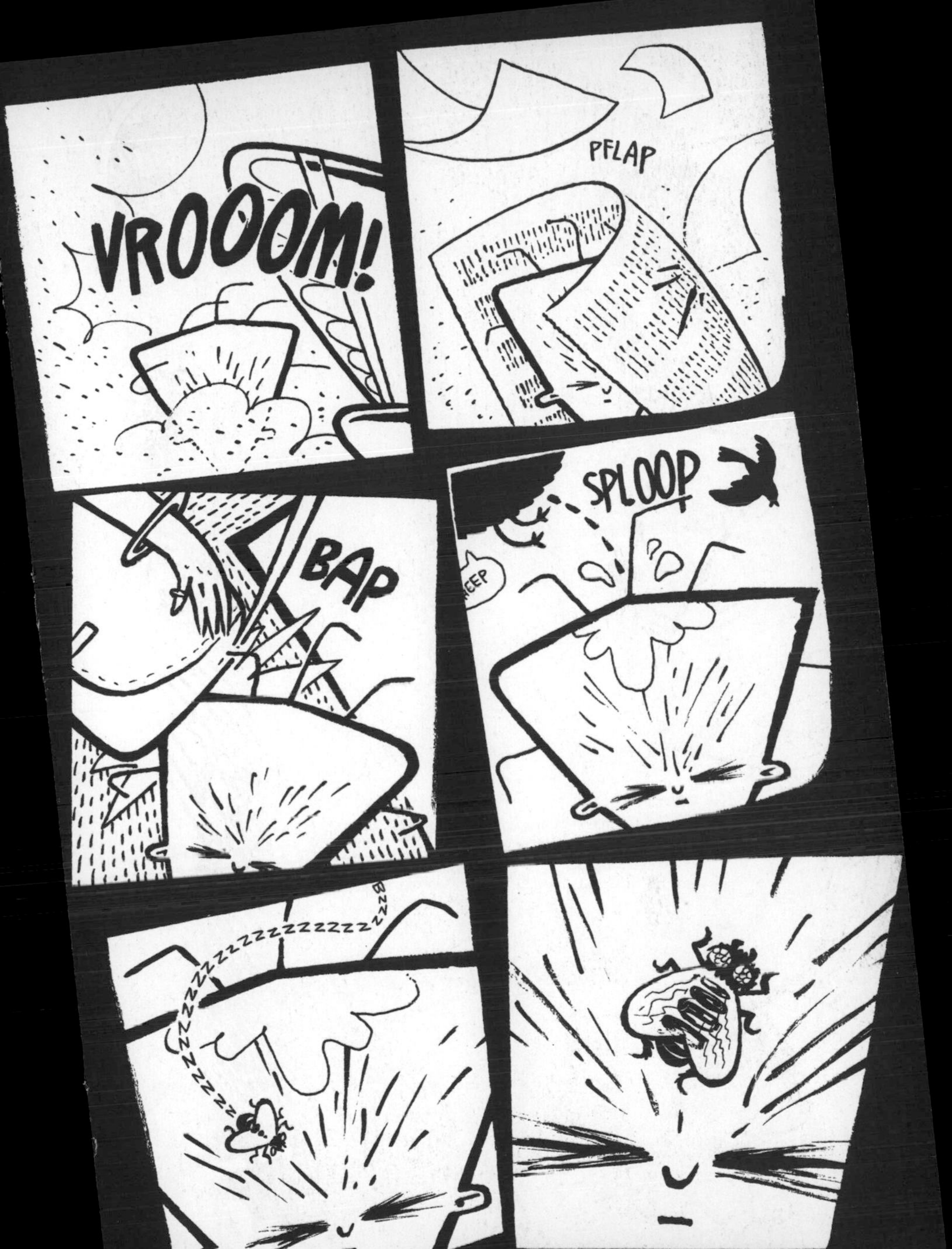
VROOOM!
PFLAP
BAP
SPLOOP

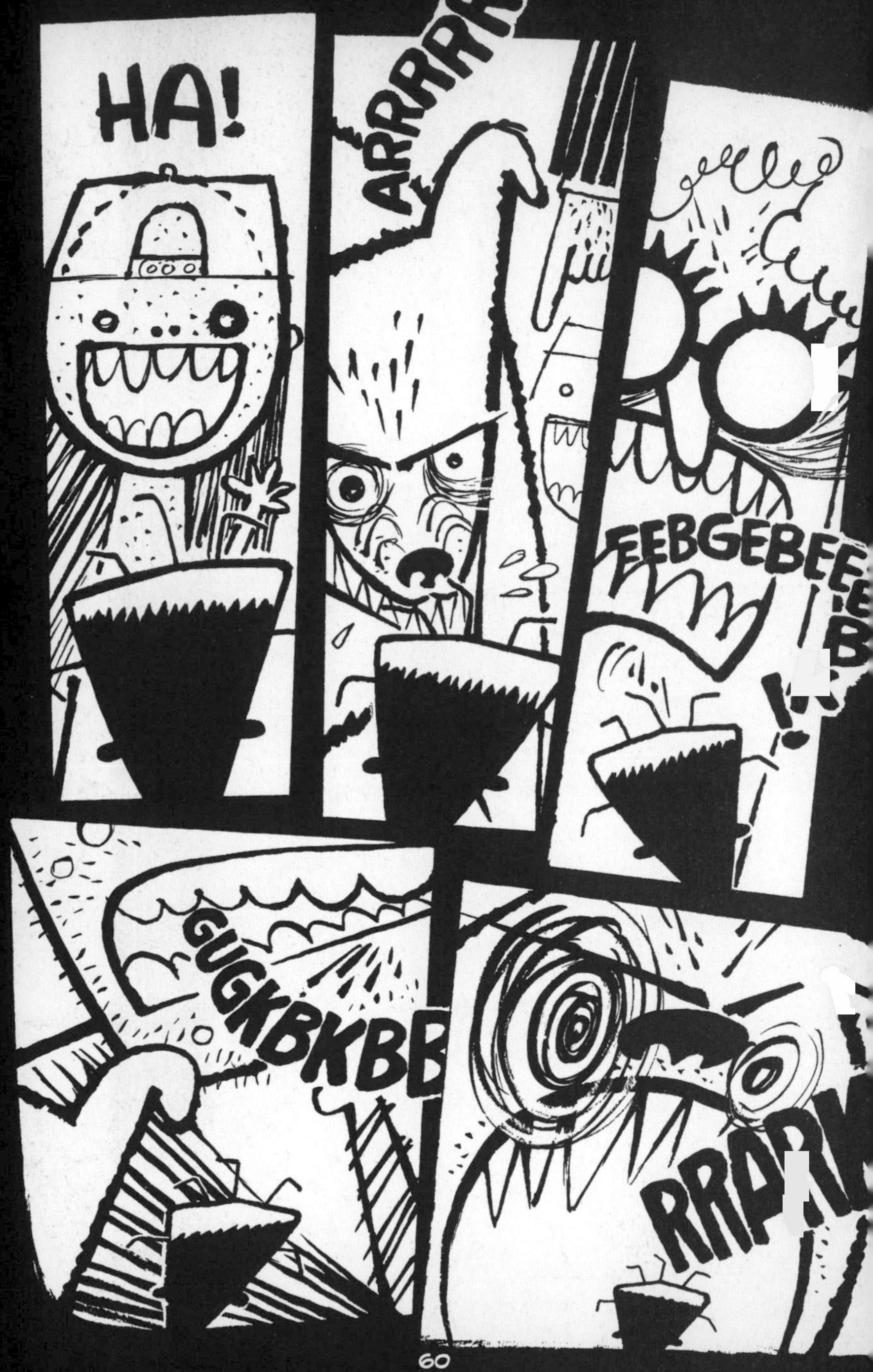
HA!
EEBGEBEEE
GUGKBKBB
RRAR

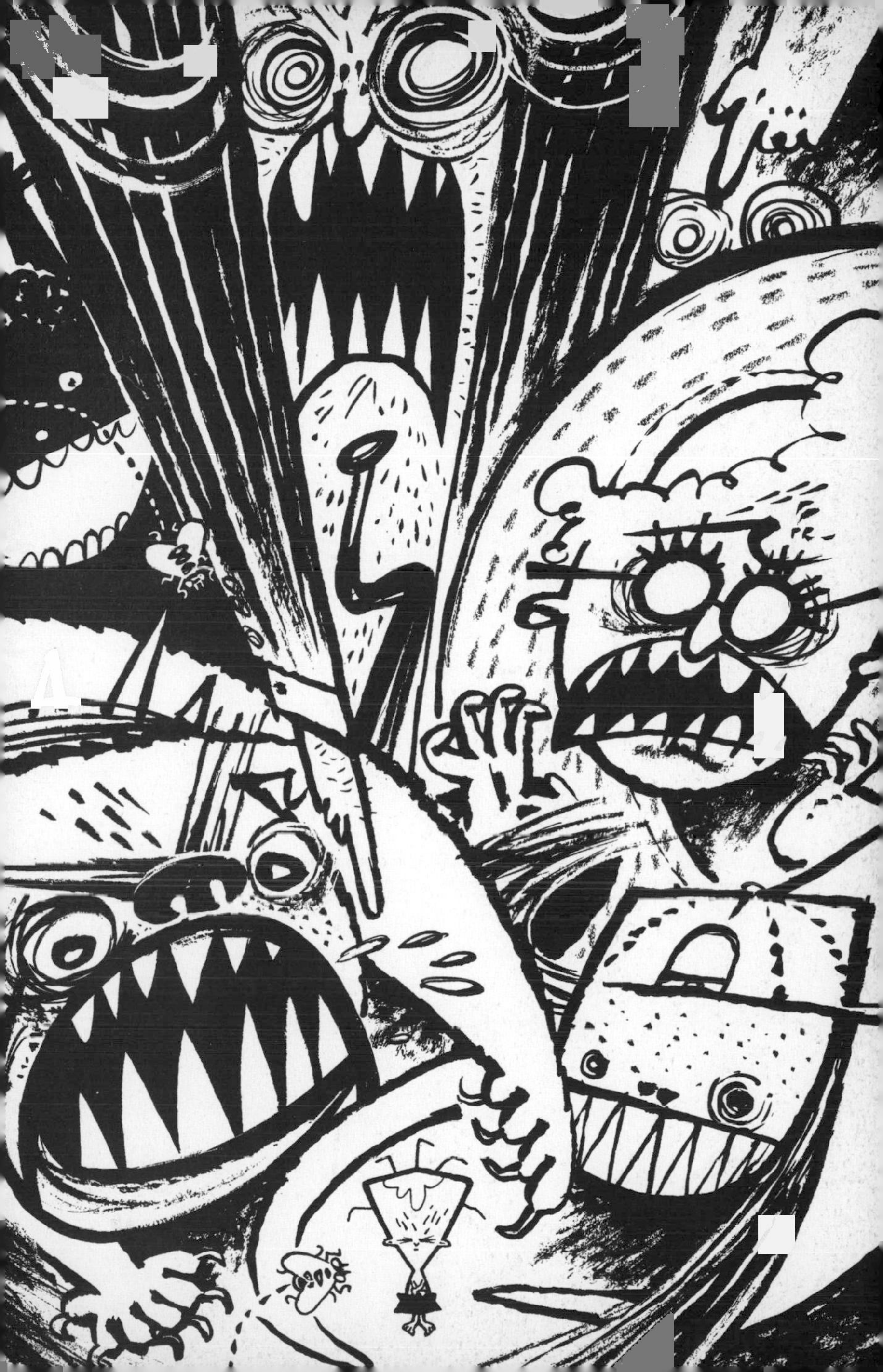

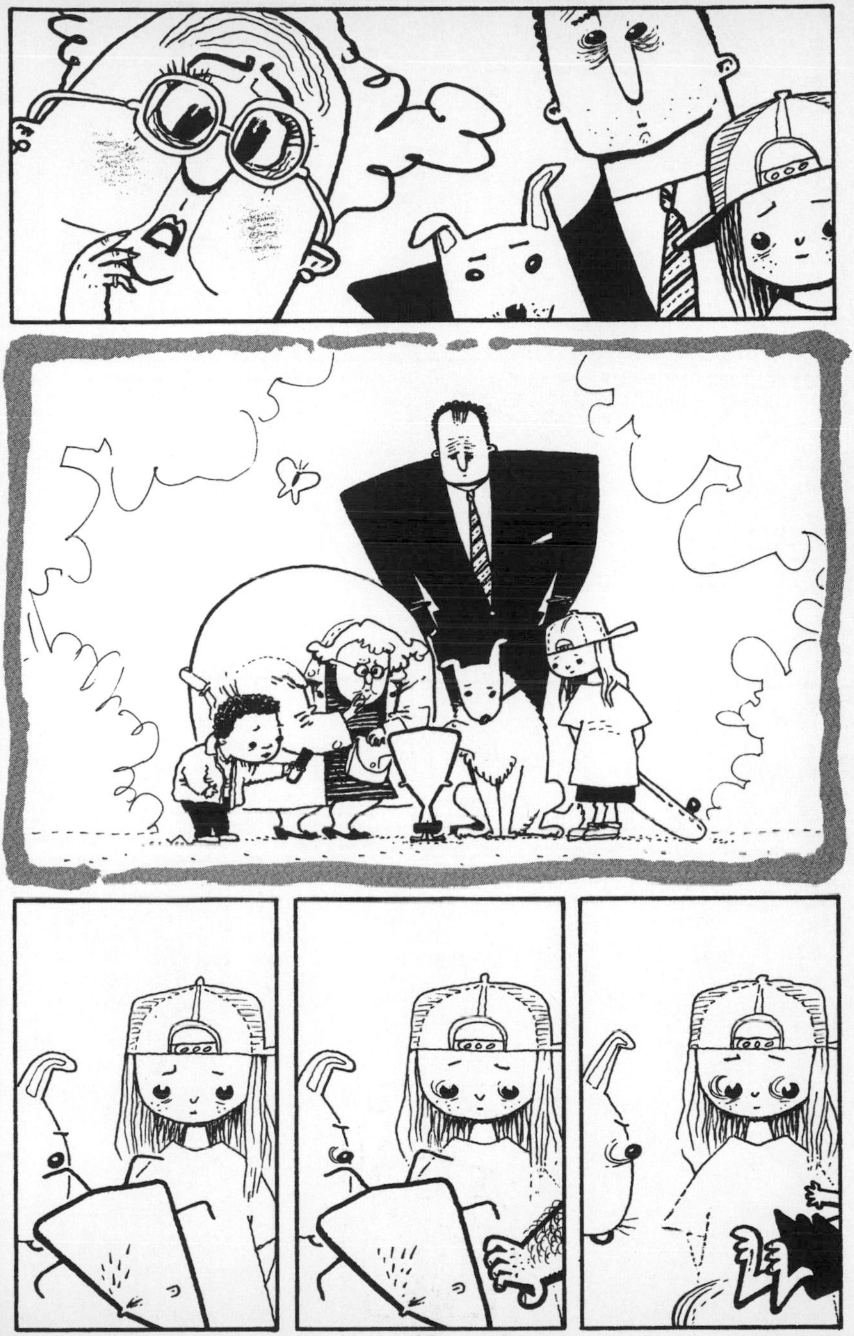

SNIF

EXIT

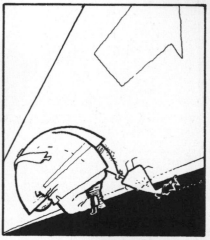

BDMP!

P!

KLATCH
KLUNK

SLAM!
Jingle Jingle
Jingle
KLUNK...
KLATCH!

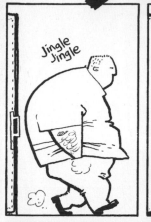

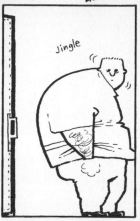

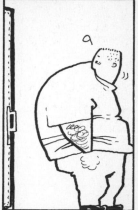

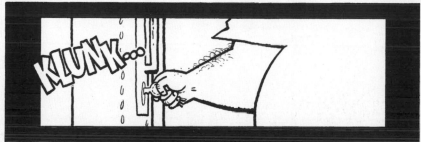

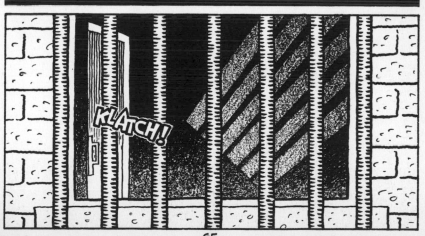

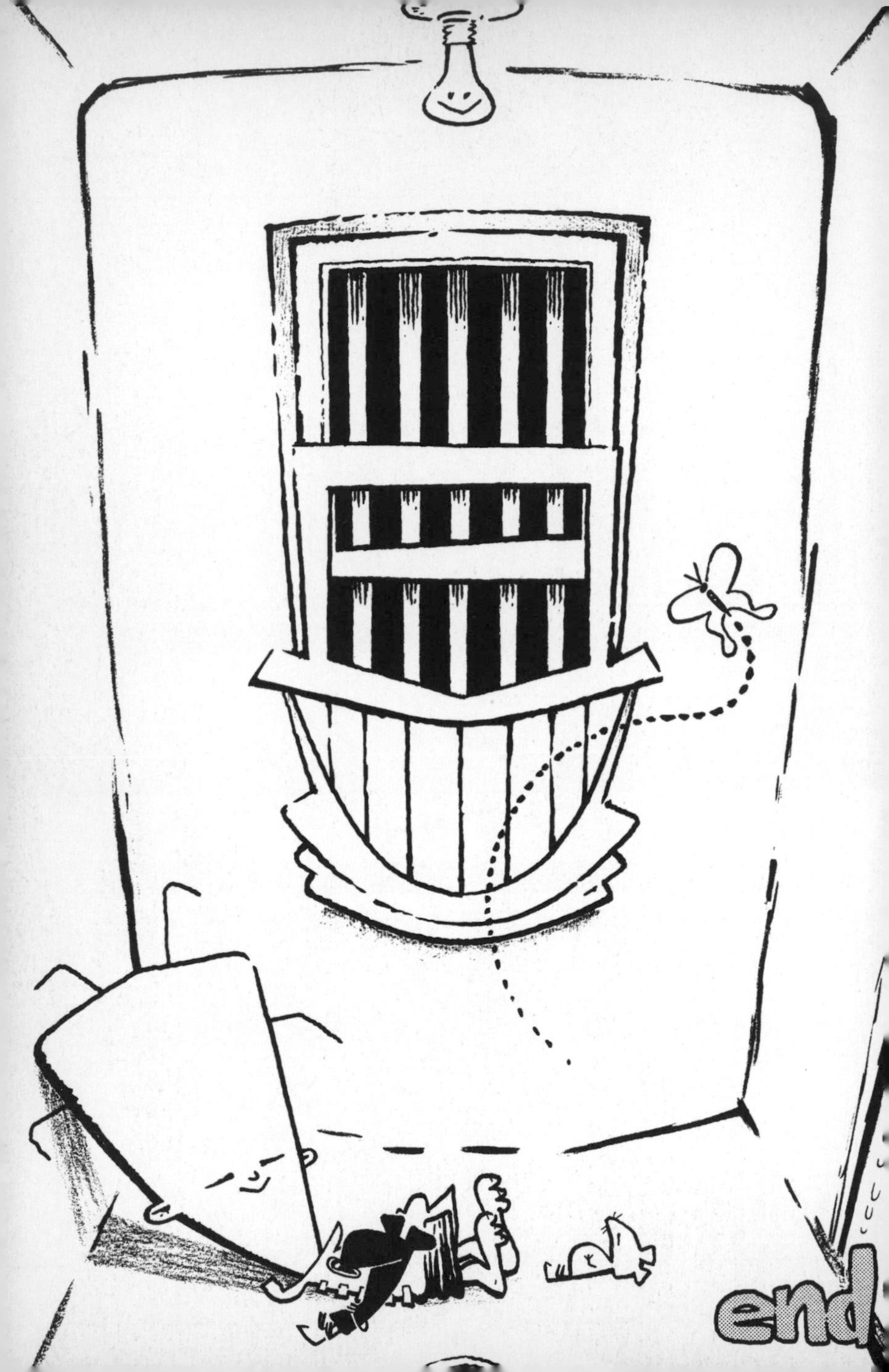
end

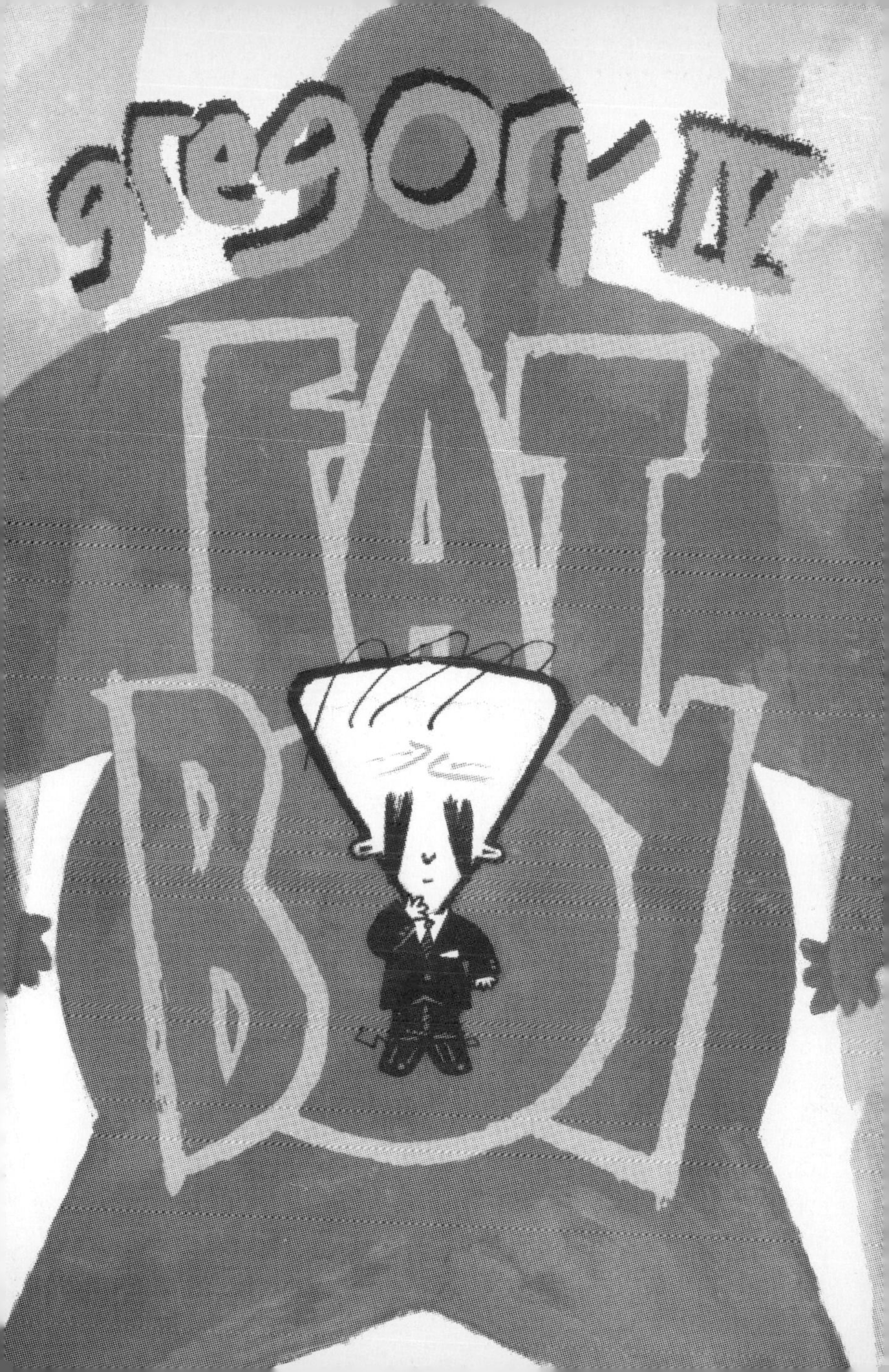
gregory IV
FAT BOY

# prologue

Hello, Gregory! You remember me, don't you? Miss Volks?

Well, guess what? Gregory's going on a trip!

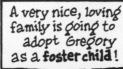

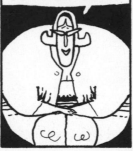

A very nice, loving family is going to adopt Gregory as a **foster child**!

Gregory will stay with them, be loved, cared for... and, hopefully, **rehabilitated**!

They're going to help Gregory overcome his **fears** and tendency to **withdraw**!

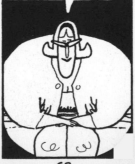

Well, now -- what does Gregory think about **that**... hmm??

Well, Miss Volks thinks **SHE** knows what's best for Gregory.

68

# gregory IV

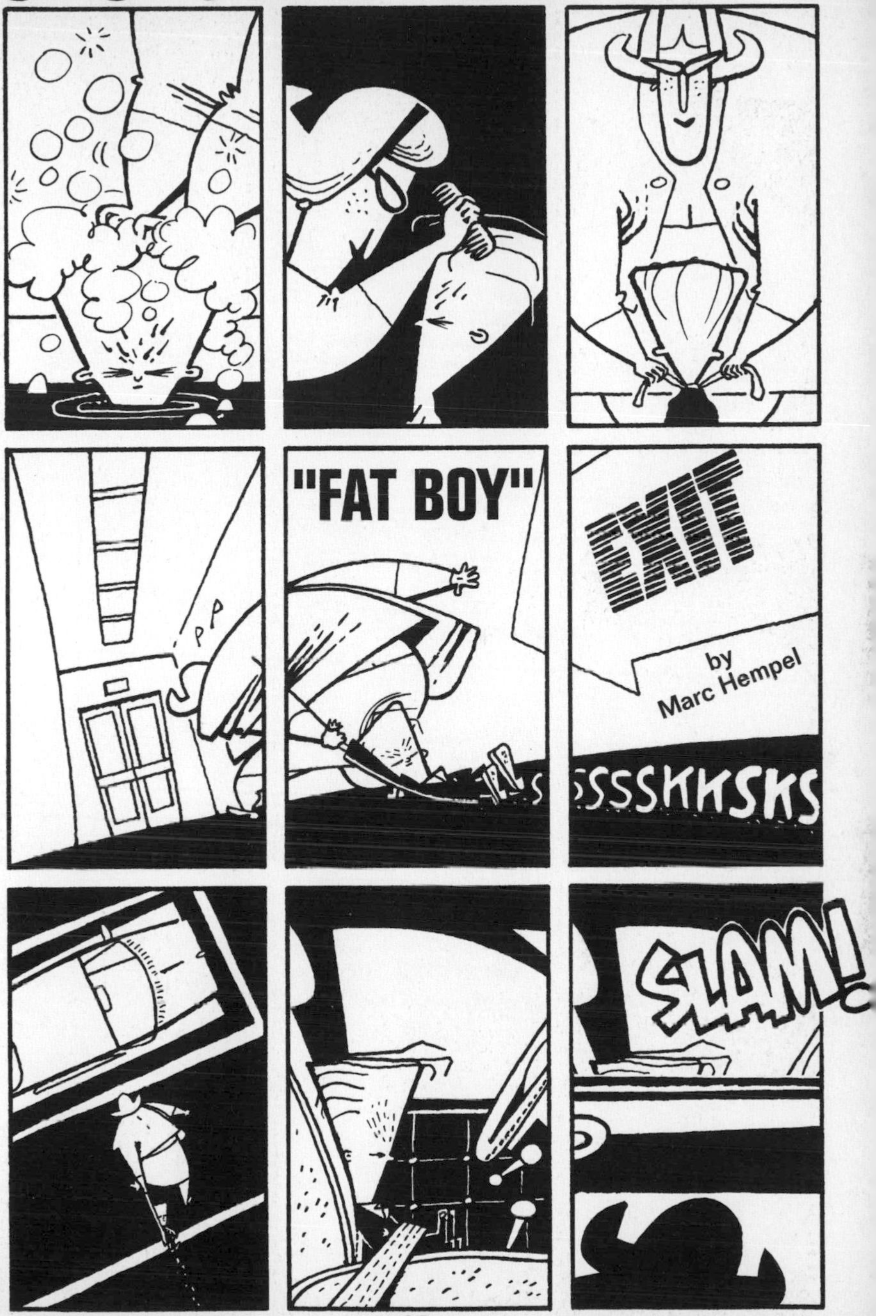
"FAT BOY"
EXIT
by
Marc Hempel
SSSSKKKSKS
SLAM!

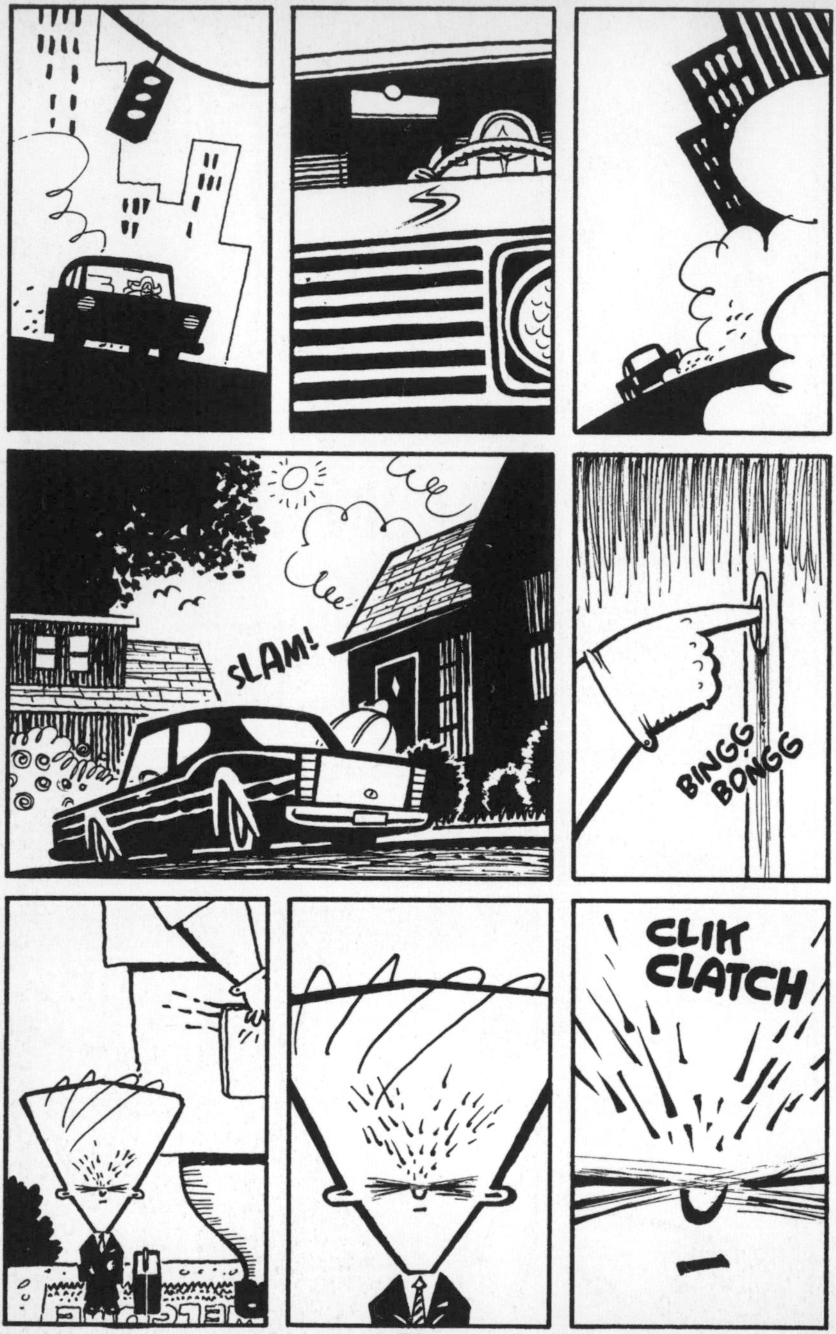
SLAM!
BINGG BONGG
CLIK
CLATCH

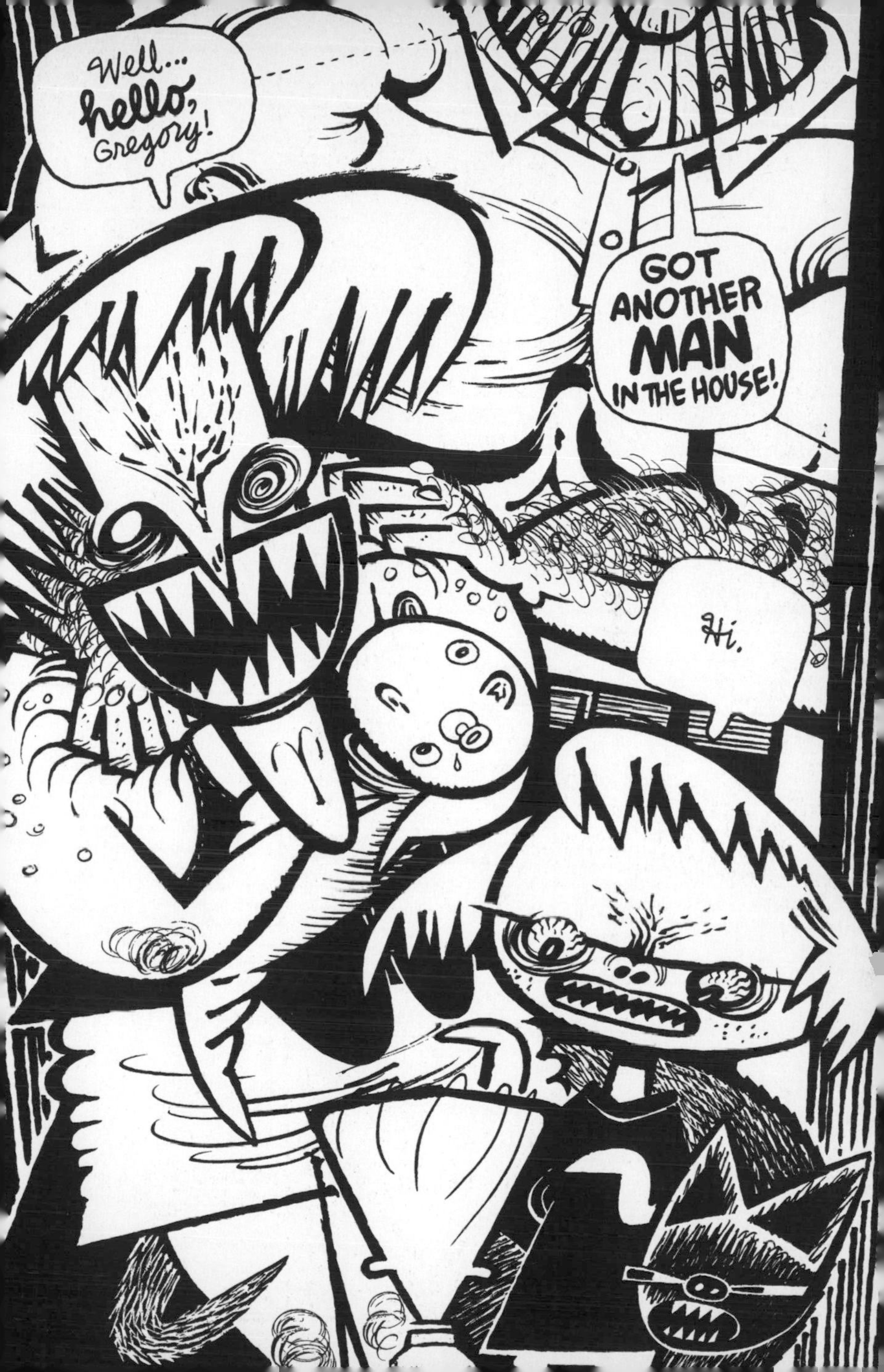
Well... hello, Gregory!
GOT ANOTHER MAN IN THE HOUSE!
Hi.

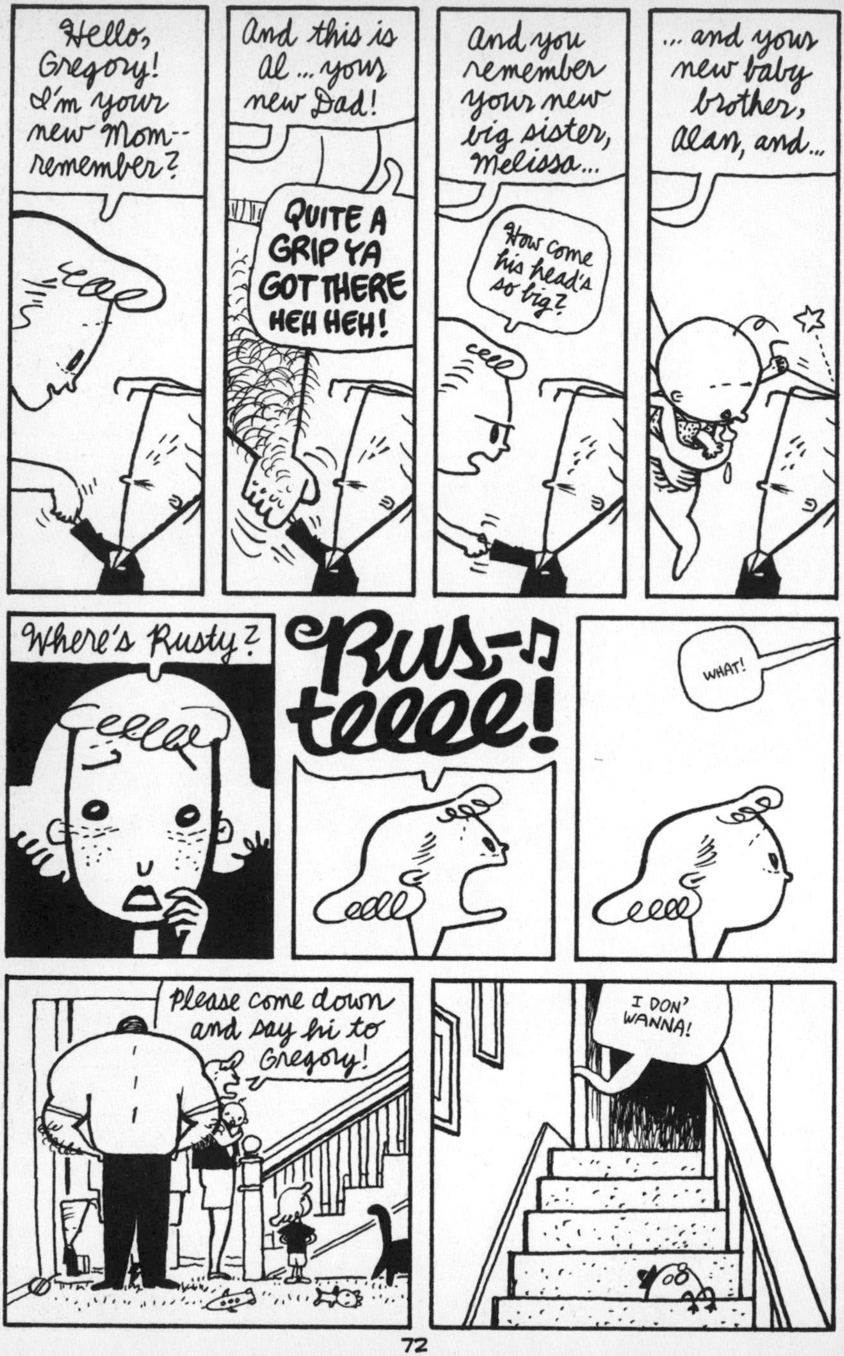
Hello, Gregory! I'm your new Mom-- remember?
And this is Al ... your new Dad!
QUITE A GRIP YA GOT THERE HEH HEH!
And you remember your new big sister, Melissa...
How come his head's so big?
... and your new baby brother, Alan, and...
Where's Rusty?
Rus-
teeee!
WHAT!
Please come down and say hi to Gregory!
I DON' WANNA!

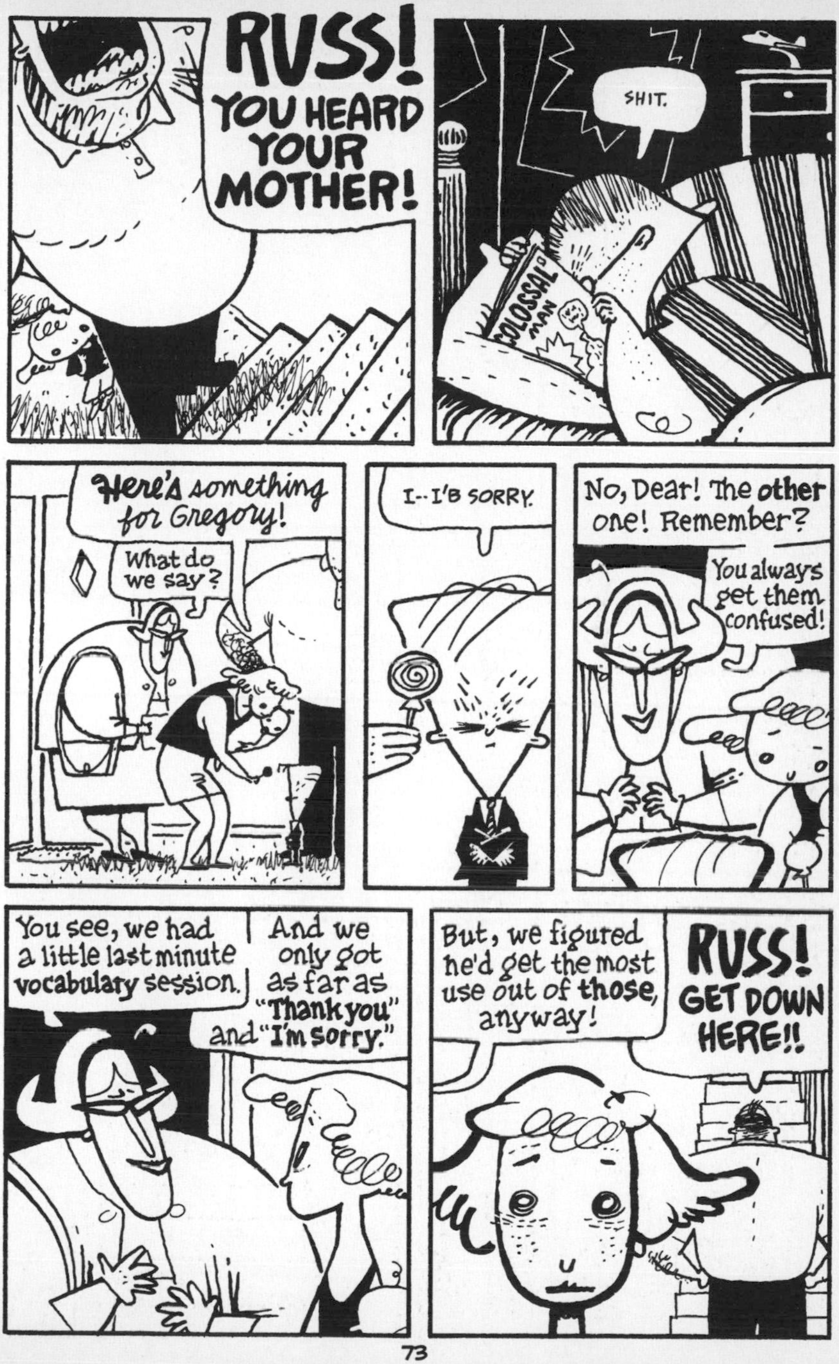
RUSS! YOU HEARD YOUR MOTHER!
SHIT.
COLOSSAL MAN
Here's something for Gregory!
What do we say?
I-- I'B SORRY.
No, Dear! The other one! Remember?
You always get them confused!
You see, we had a little last minute vocabulary session.
And we only got as far as "Thank you" and "I'm sorry."
But, we figured he'd get the most use out of those, anyway!
RUSS! GET DOWN HERE!!

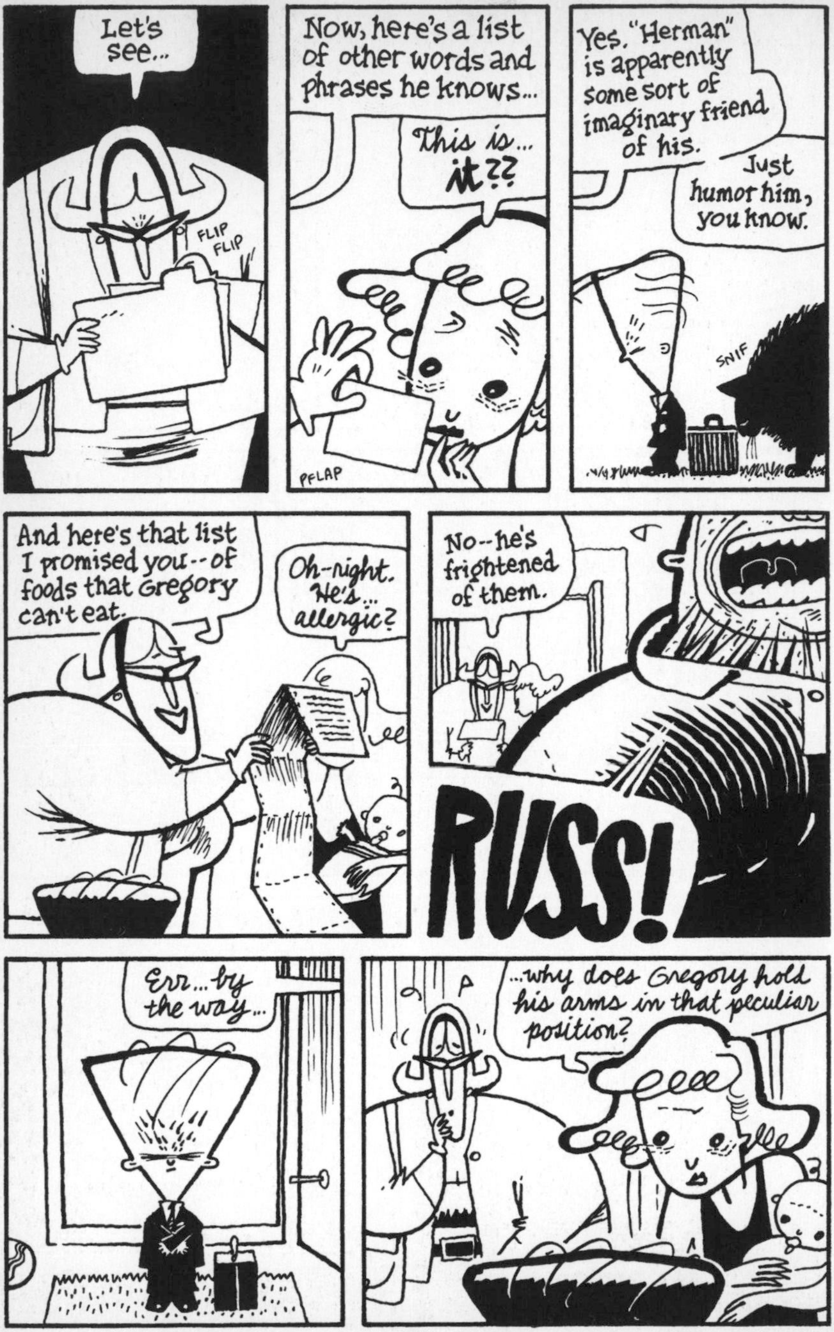
Let's see...
FLIP FLIP
Now, here's a list of other words and phrases he knows...
This is... it??
PFLAP
Yes, "Herman" is apparently some sort of imaginary friend of his.
Just humor him, you know.
SNIF
And here's that list I promised you-- of foods that Gregory can't eat.
Oh-right. He's... allergic?
No--he's frightened of them.
RUSS!
Err... by the way...
...why does Gregory hold his arms in that peculiar position?

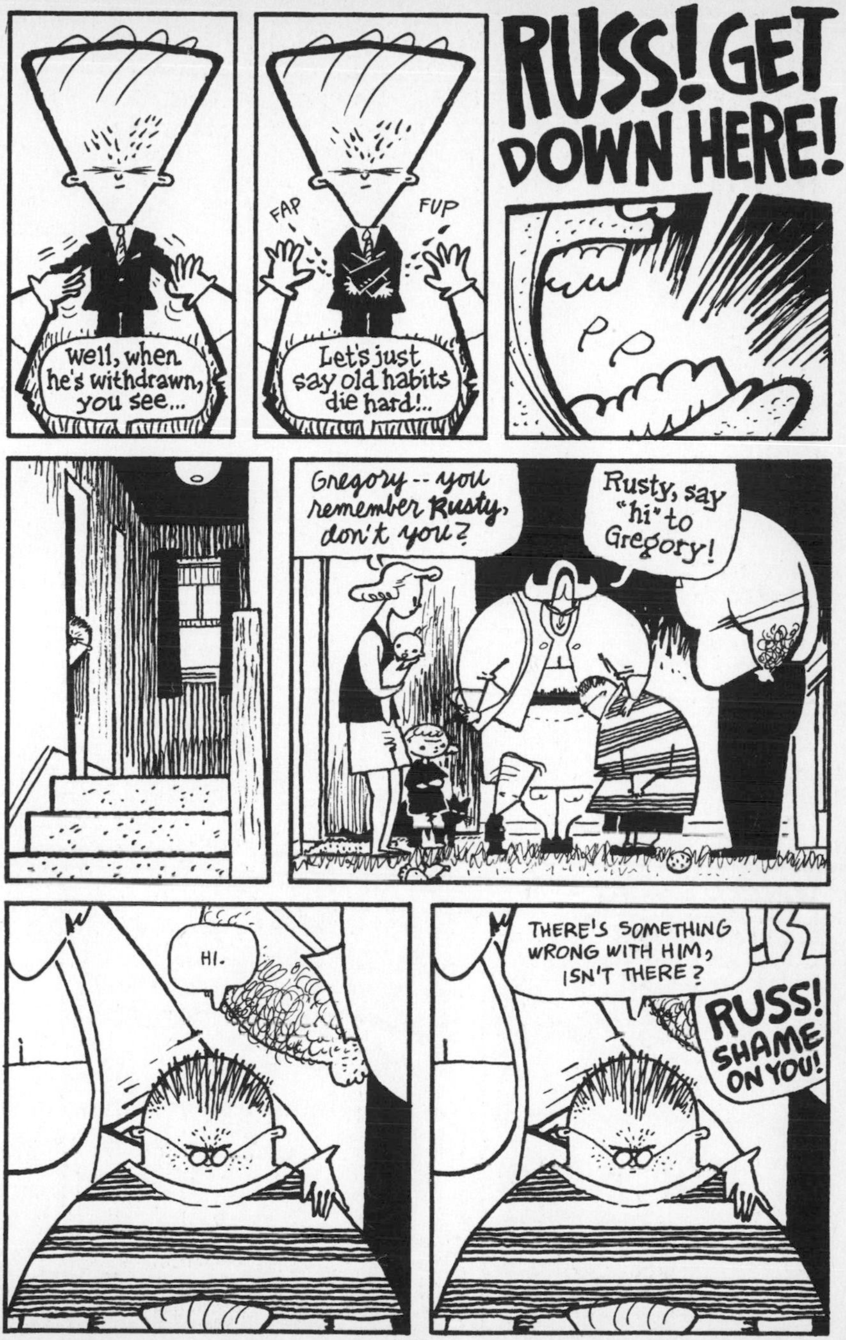

Well, when he's withdrawn, you see...
FAP
FUP
Let's just say old habits die hard!..
RUSS! GET DOWN HERE!
Gregory -- you remember Rusty, don't you?
Rusty, say "hi" to Gregory!
HI.
THERE'S SOMETHING WRONG WITH HIM, ISN'T THERE?
RUSS! SHAME ON YOU!

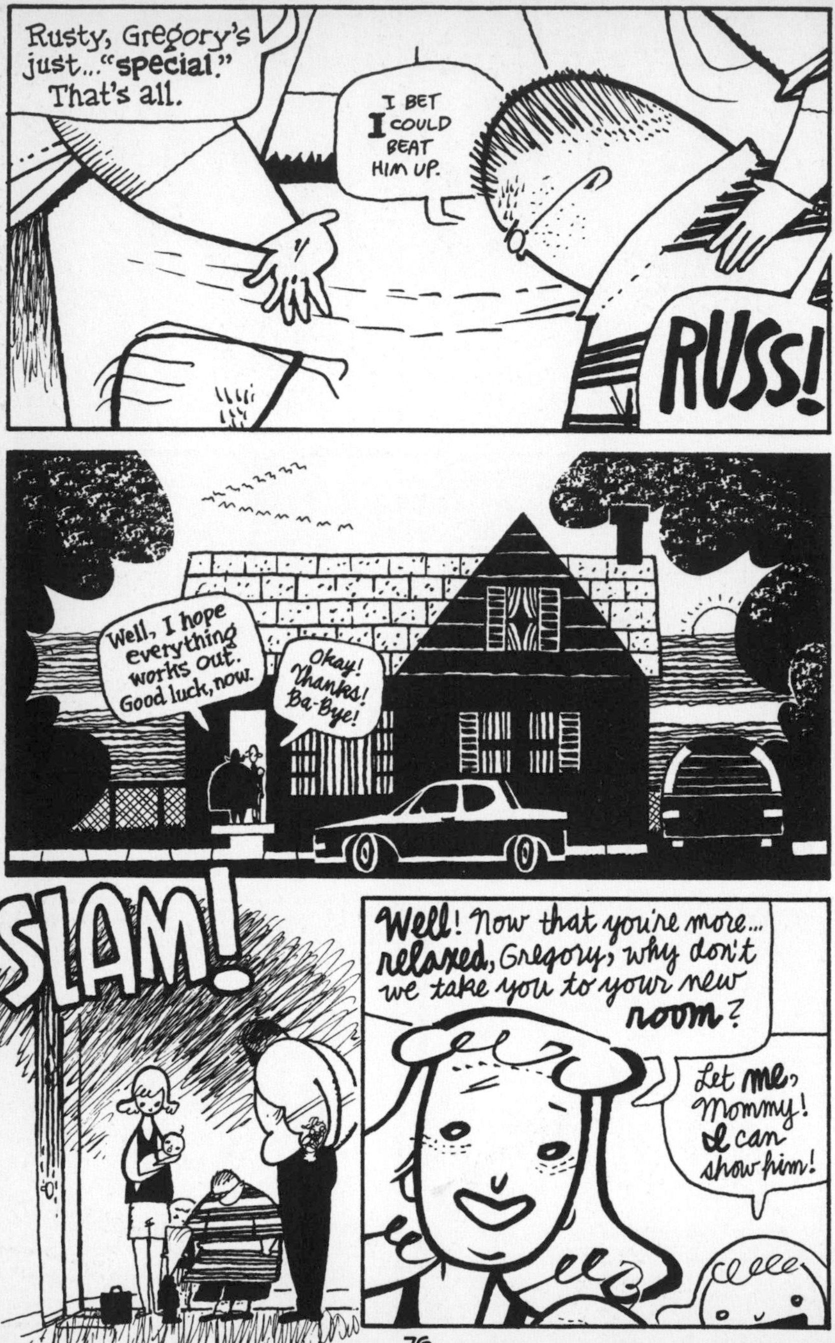
Rusty, Gregory's just... "special." That's all.
I BET I COULD BEAT HIM UP.
RUSS!
Well, I hope everything works out. Good luck, now.
Okay! Thanks! Ba-Bye!
SLAM!
Well! Now that you're more... relaxed, Gregory, why don't we take you to your new room?
Let me, Mommy! I can show him!

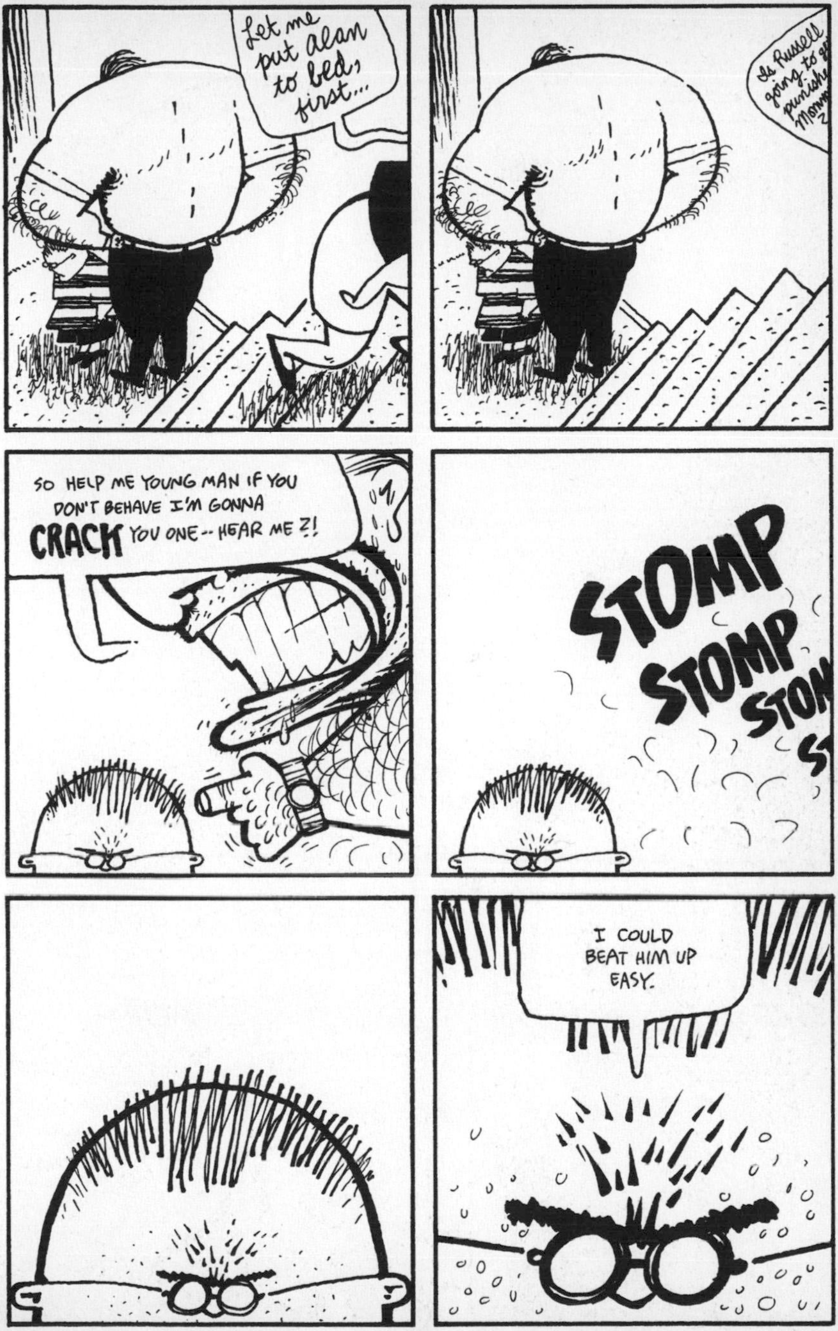
Let me put alan to bed, first...
Is Russell going to
SO HELP ME YOUNG MAN IF YOU DON'T BEHAVE I'M GONNA CRACK YOU ONE-- HEAR ME ?!
STOMP
STOMP
I COULD BEAT HIM UP EASY.

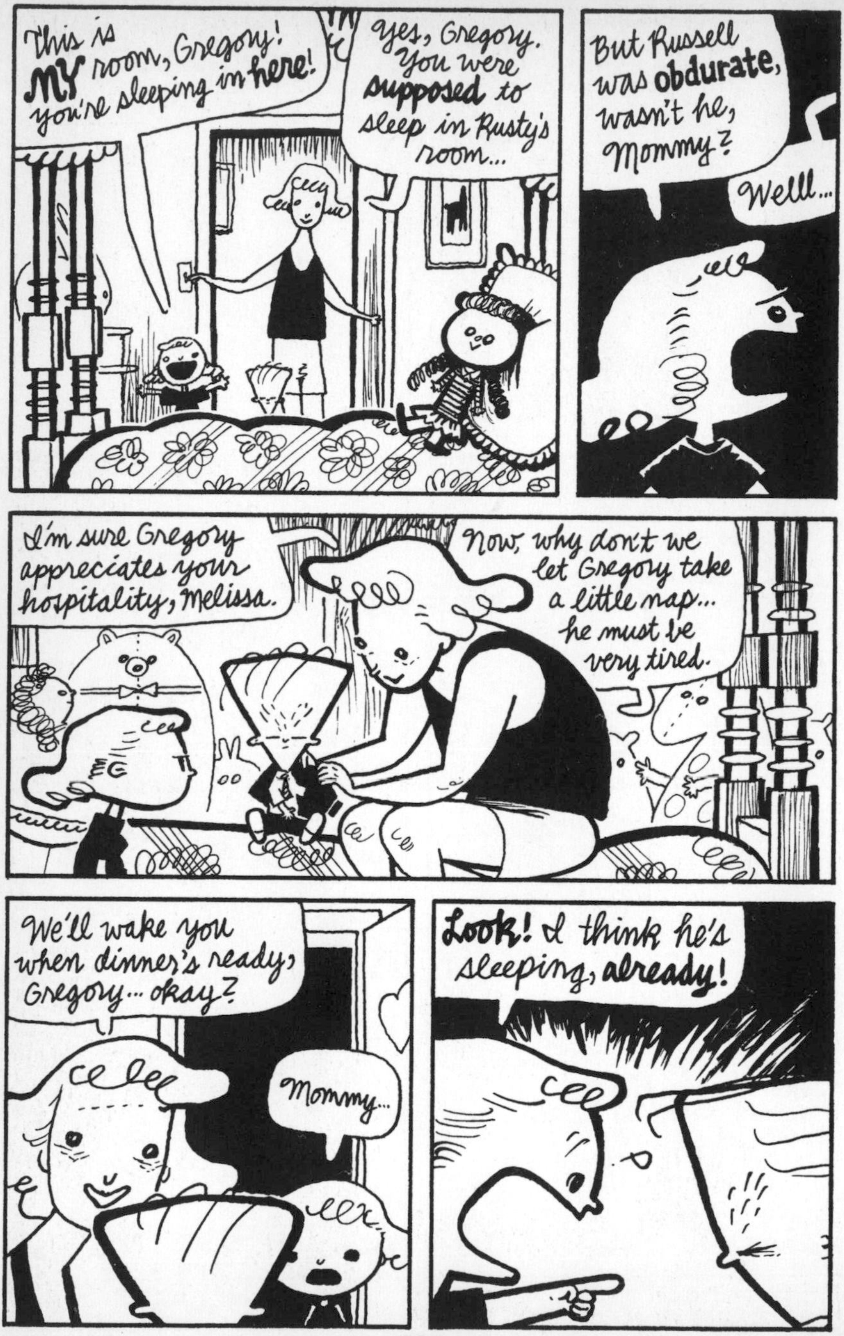
This is MY room, Gregory! you're sleeping in here!
yes, Gregory. You were supposed to sleep in Rusty's room...
But Russell was obdurate, wasn't he, Mommy?
Welll...
I'm sure Gregory appreciates your hospitality, Melissa.
Now, why don't we let Gregory take a little nap... he must be very tired.
We'll wake you when dinner's ready, Gregory... okay?
Mommy...
Look! I think he's sleeping, already!

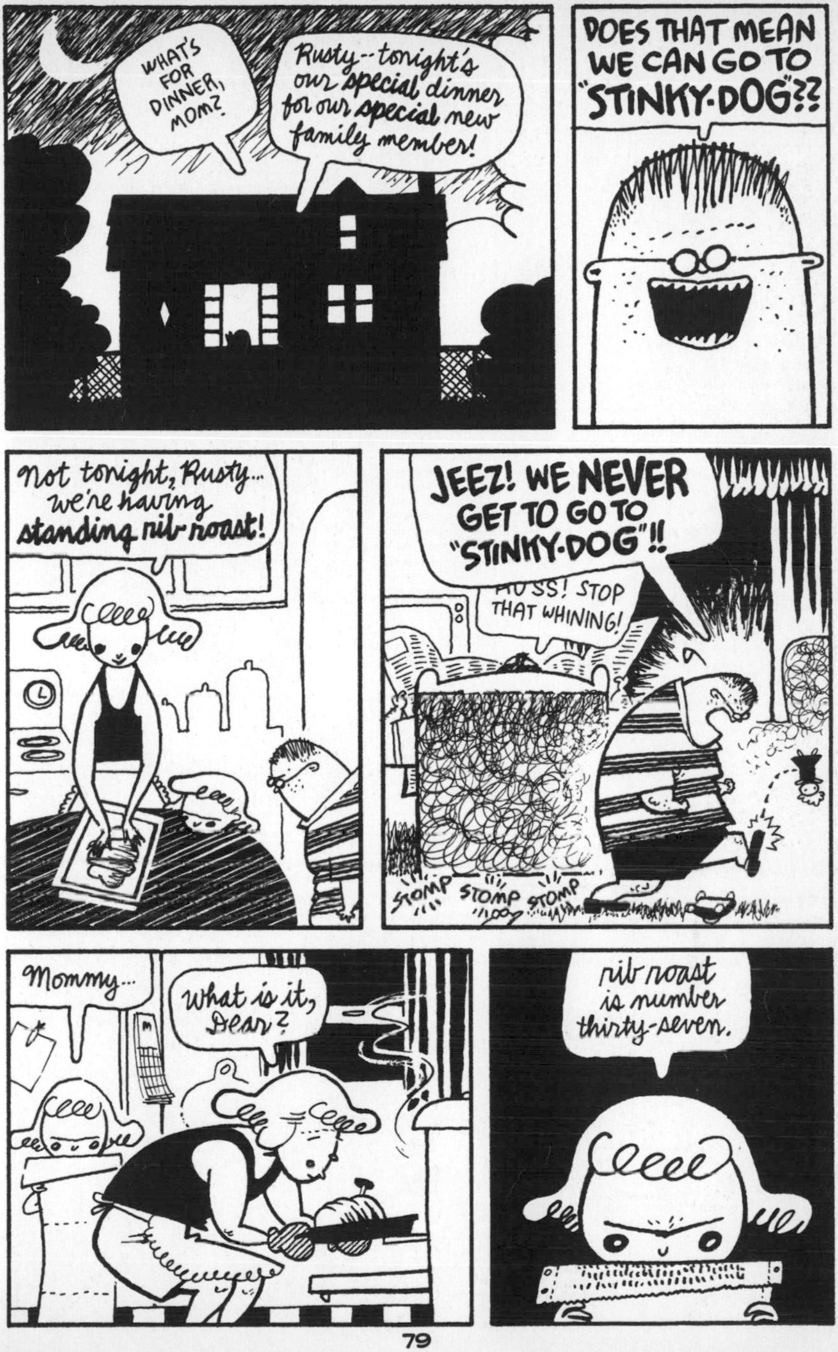
WHAT'S FOR DINNER, MOM?
Rusty--tonight's our special dinner for our special new family member!
DOES THAT MEAN WE CAN GO TO "STINKY-DOG"??
Not tonight, Rusty... we're having standing rib-roast!
JEEZ! WE NEVER GET TO GO TO "STINKY-DOG"!!
SS! STOP THAT WHINING!
STOMP STOMP STOMP
Mommy...
What is it, Dear?
rib roast is number thirty-seven.

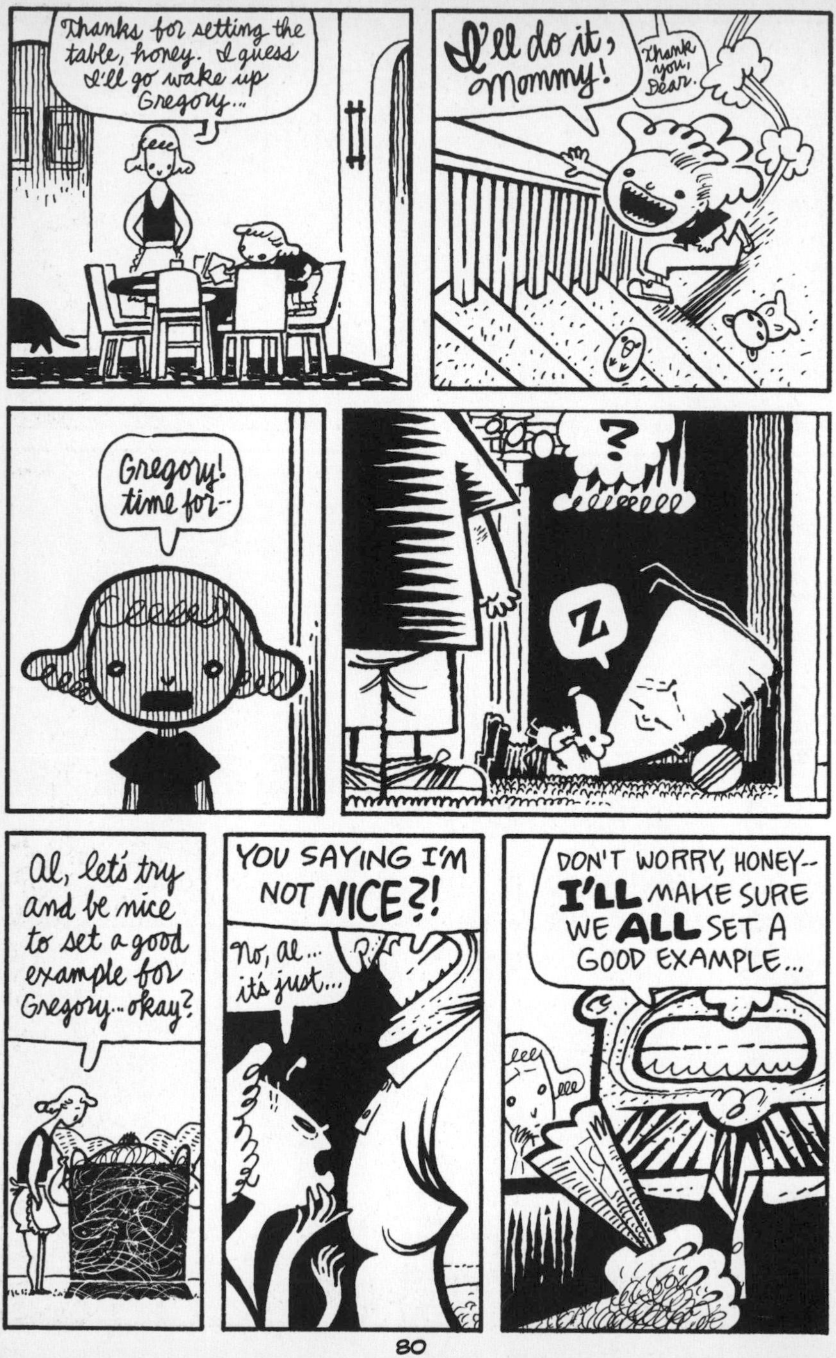
Thanks for setting the table, honey. I guess I'll go wake up Gregory...
I'll do it, Mommy!
Thank you, Dear.
Gregory! time for--
?
Z
Al, let's try and be nice to set a good example for Gregory...okay?
YOU SAYING I'M NOT NICE?!
No, Al... it's just...
DON'T WORRY, HONEY-- I'LL MAKE SURE WE ALL SET A GOOD EXAMPLE...

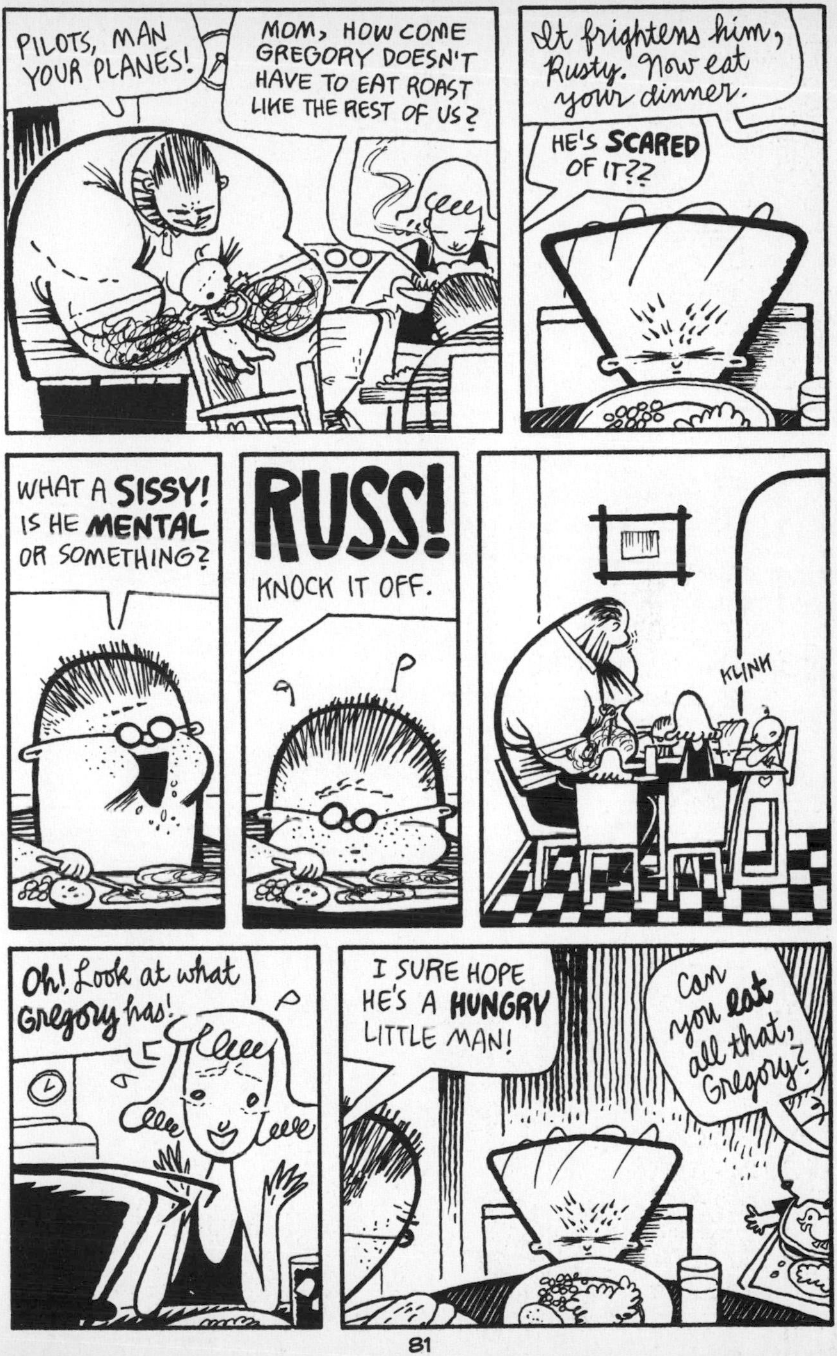
PILOTS, MAN YOUR PLANES!
MOM, HOW COME GREGORY DOESN'T HAVE TO EAT ROAST LIKE THE REST OF US?
It frightens him, Rusty. Now eat your dinner.
HE'S SCARED OF IT??
WHAT A SISSY! IS HE MENTAL OR SOMETHING?
RUSS! KNOCK IT OFF.
KLINK
Oh! Look at what Gregory has!
I SURE HOPE HE'S A HUNGRY LITTLE MAN!
Can you eat all that, Gregory?

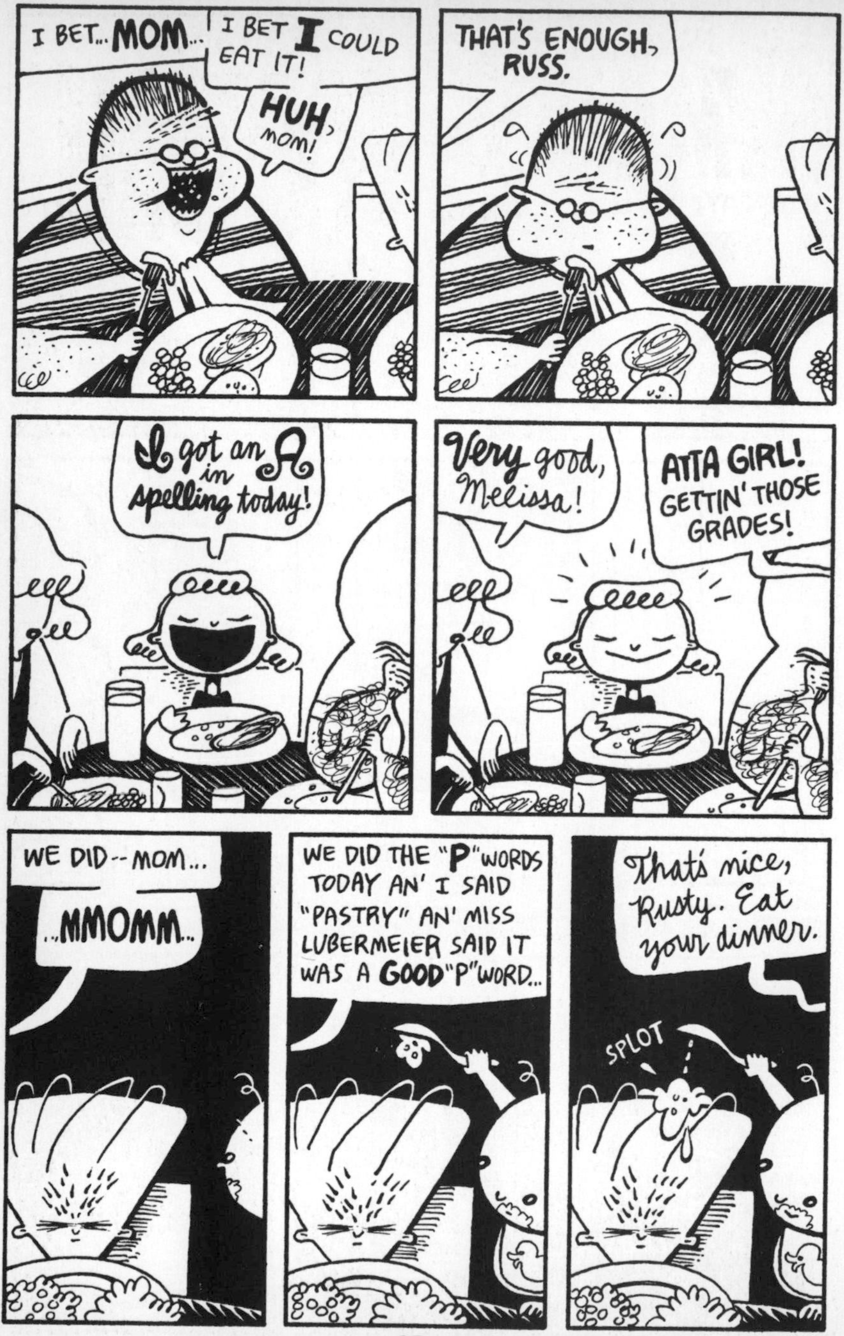

I BET... MOM...
I BET I COULD EAT IT!
HUH, MOM!
THAT'S ENOUGH, RUSS.
I got an A in spelling today!
Very good, Melissa!
ATTA GIRL! GETTIN' THOSE GRADES!
WE DID -- MOM...
...MMOMM...
WE DID THE "P" WORDS TODAY AN' I SAID "PASTRY" AN' MISS LUBERMEIER SAID IT WAS A GOOD "P" WORD...
SPLOT
That's nice, Rusty. Eat your dinner.

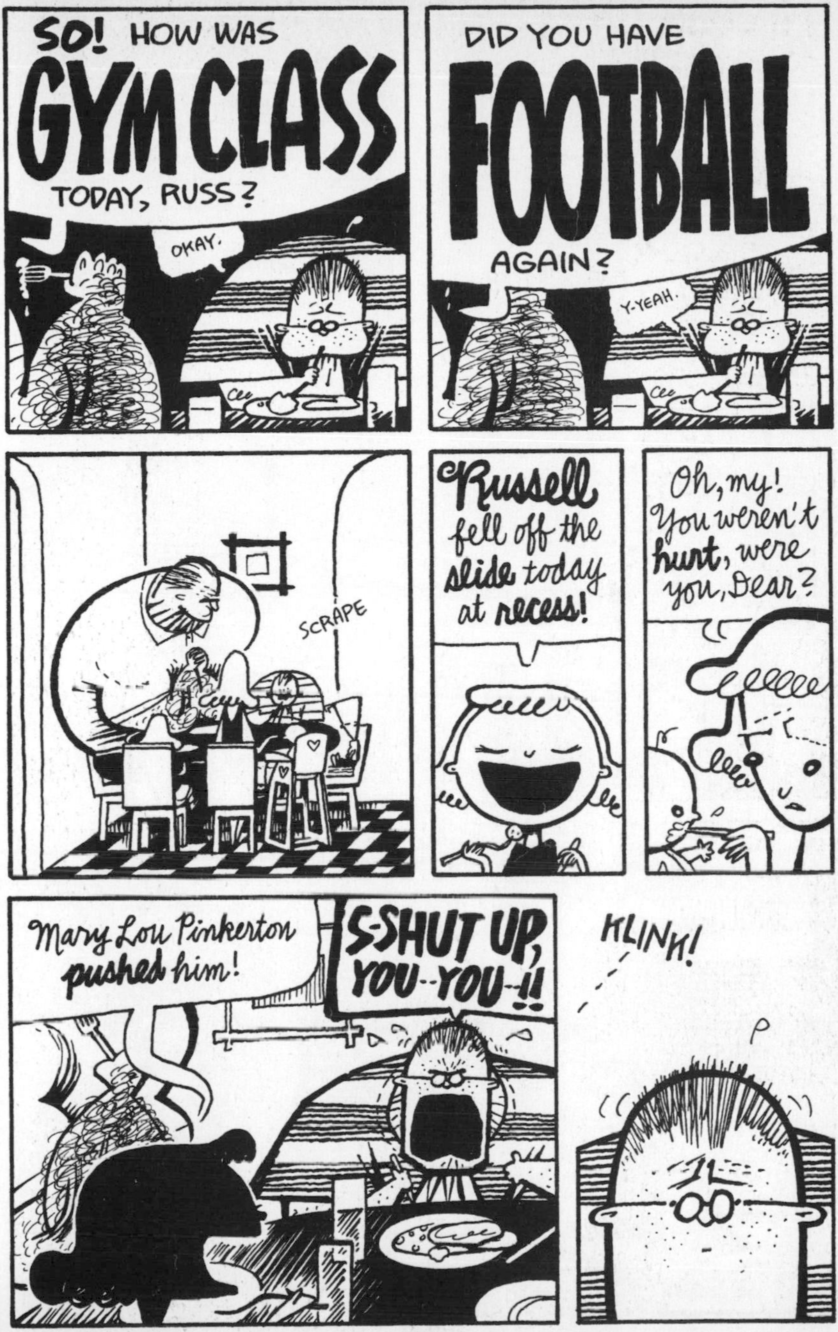
SO! HOW WAS GYM CLASS TODAY, RUSS?
OKAY.
DID YOU HAVE FOOTBALL AGAIN?
Y-YEAH.
SCRAPE
Russell fell off the slide today at recess!
Oh, my! You weren't hurt, were you, Dear?
Mary Lou Pinkerton pushed him!
S-SHUT UP, YOU--YOU--!!
KLINK!

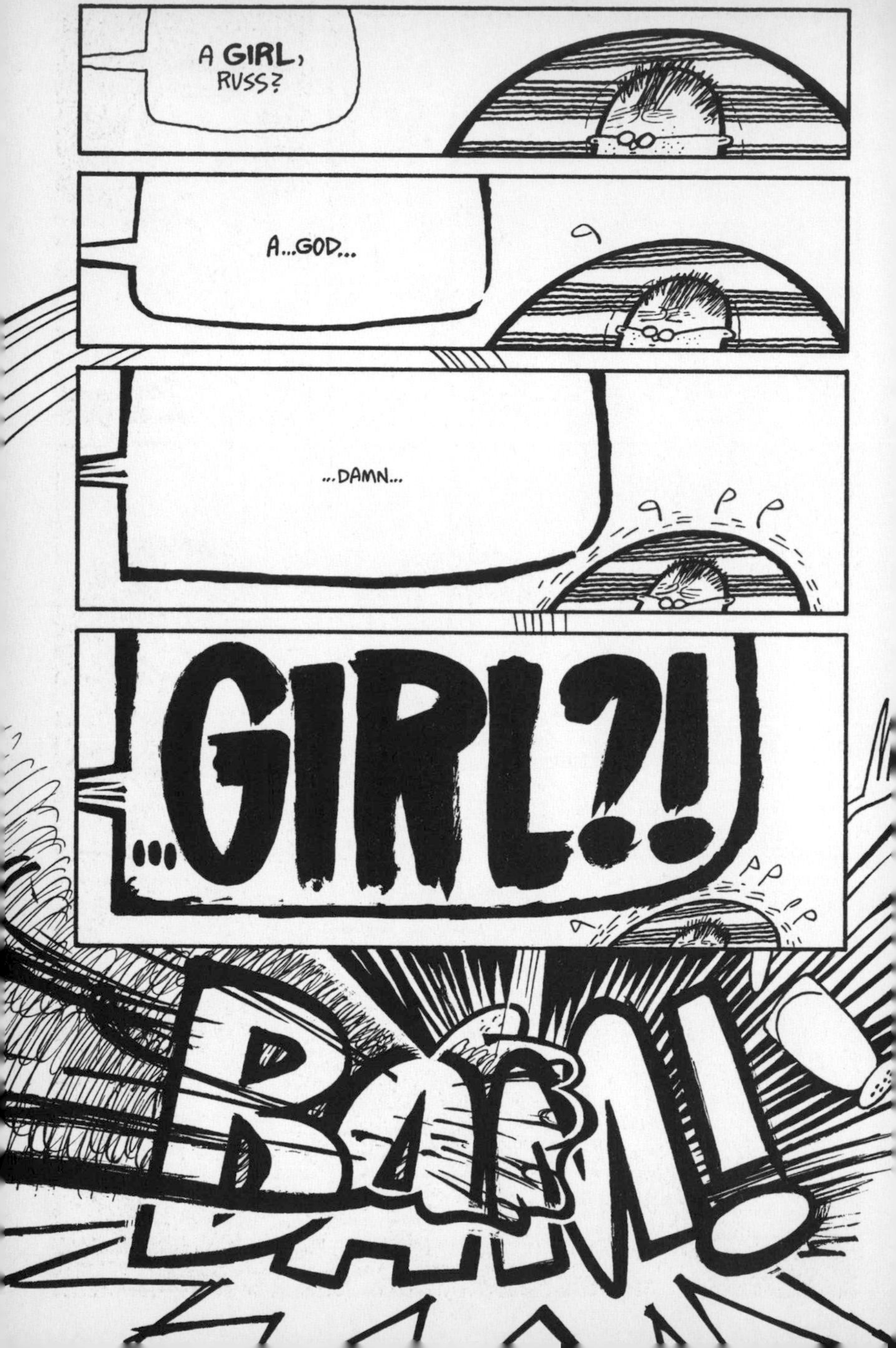
A GIRL, RUSS?
A...GOD...
...DAMN...
...GIRL?!
BAM!

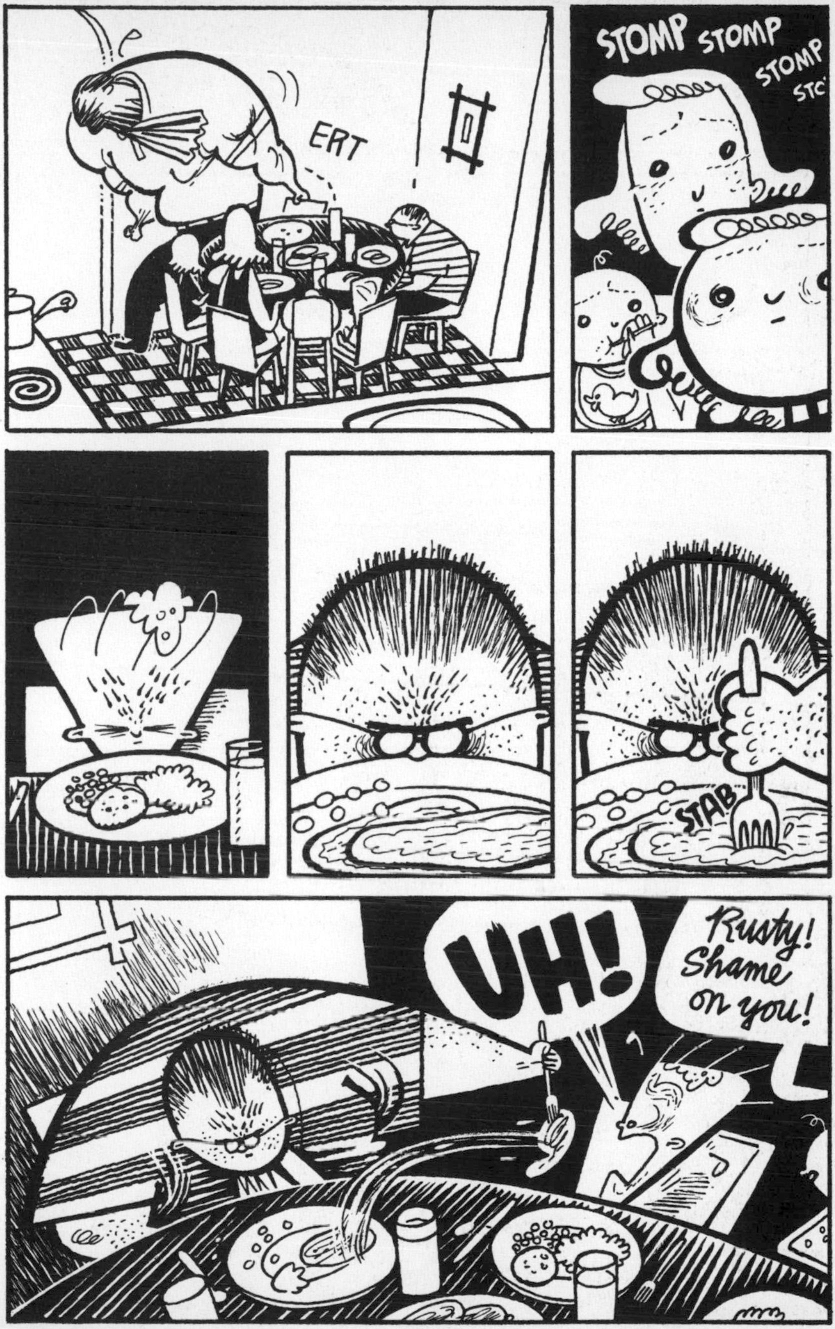
ERT
STOMP STOMP
STOMP
STO
STAB
UH!
Rusty! Shame on you!

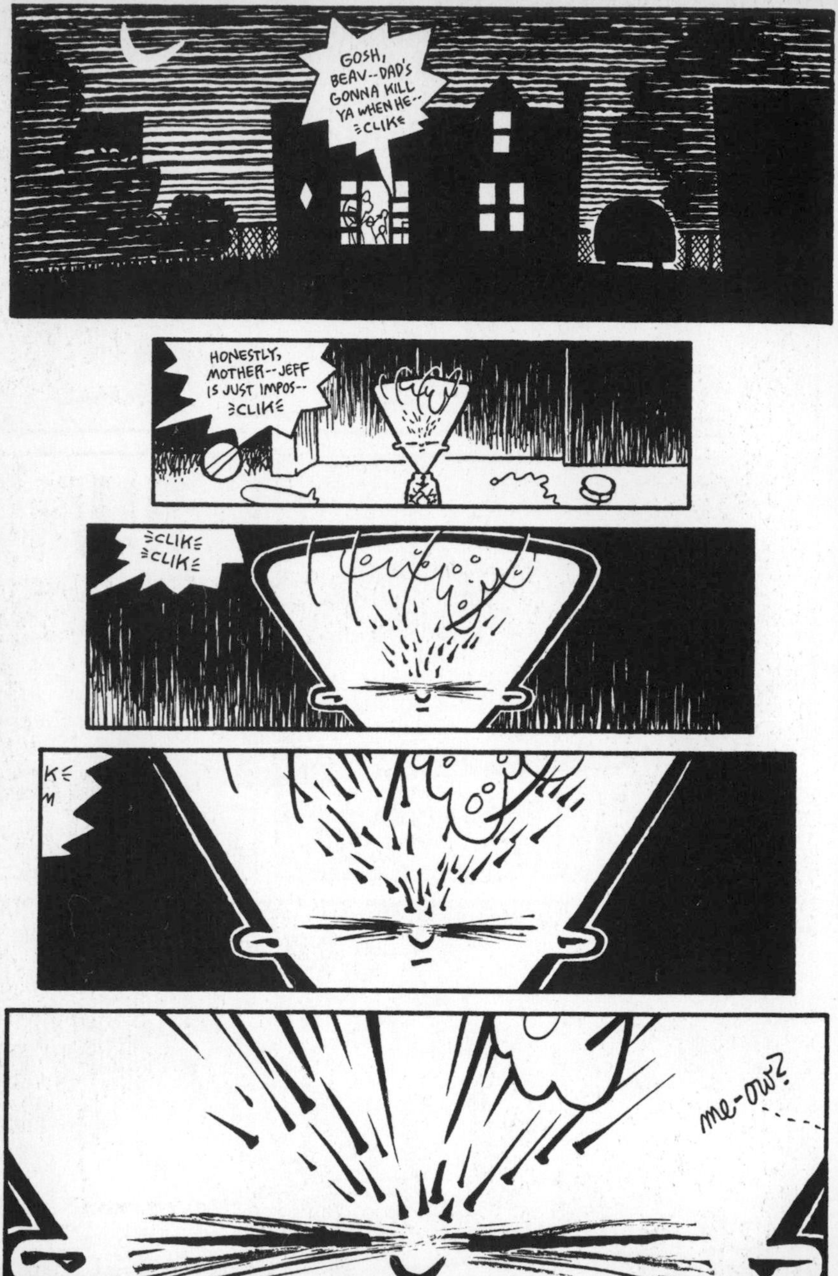
GOSH, BEAV--DAD'S GONNA KILL YA WHEN HE-- ≡CLIK≡
HONESTLY, MOTHER--JEFF IS JUST IMPOS-- ≡CLIK≡
≡CLIK≡ ≡CLIK≡
me-ow?

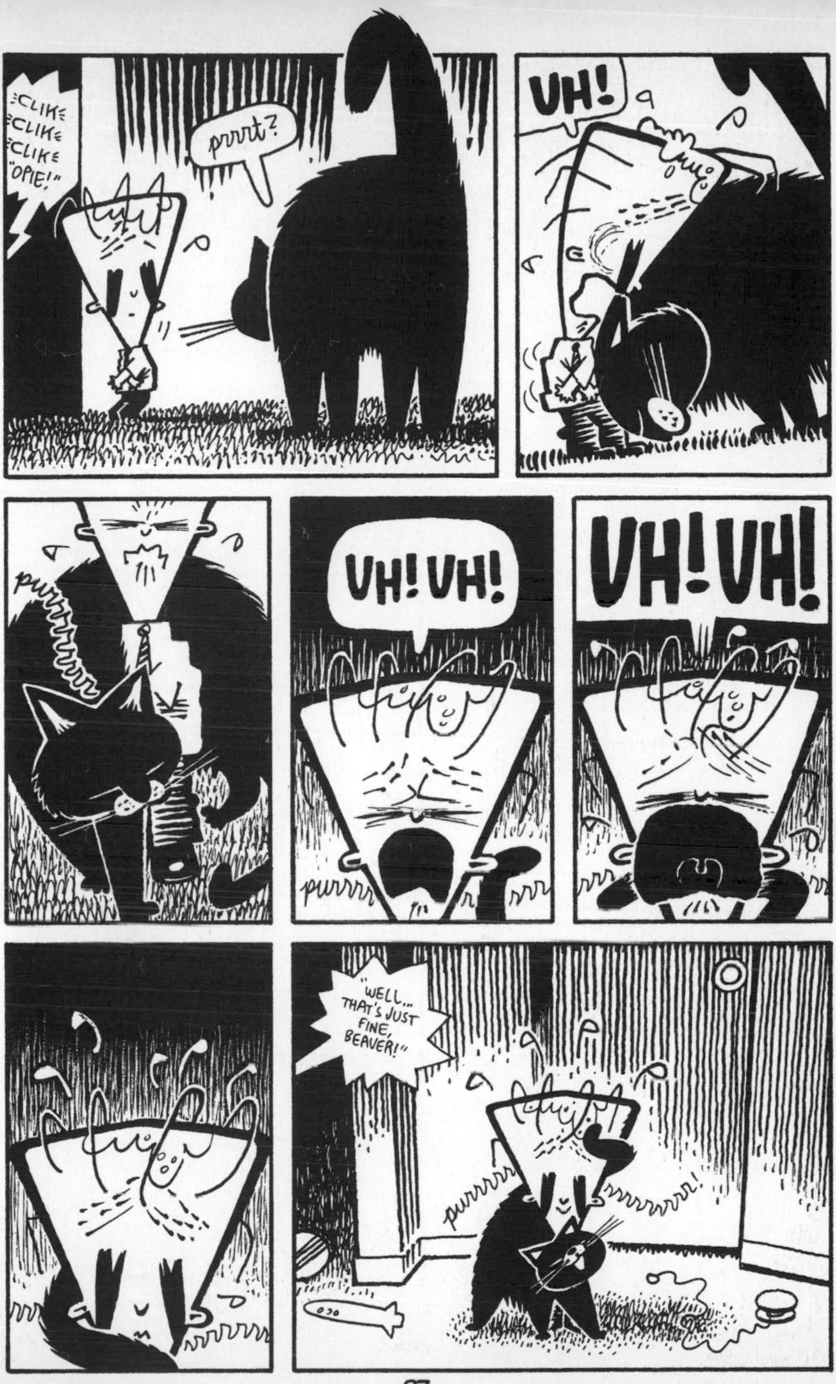
CLIK
CLIK
CLIK
"OPIE!"
prrrt?
UH!
purrrrrrrrr
UH! UH!
UH! UH!
purrrr
rrr
"WELL... THAT'S JUST FINE, BEAVER!"
purrrrr
rrrrrrrr!

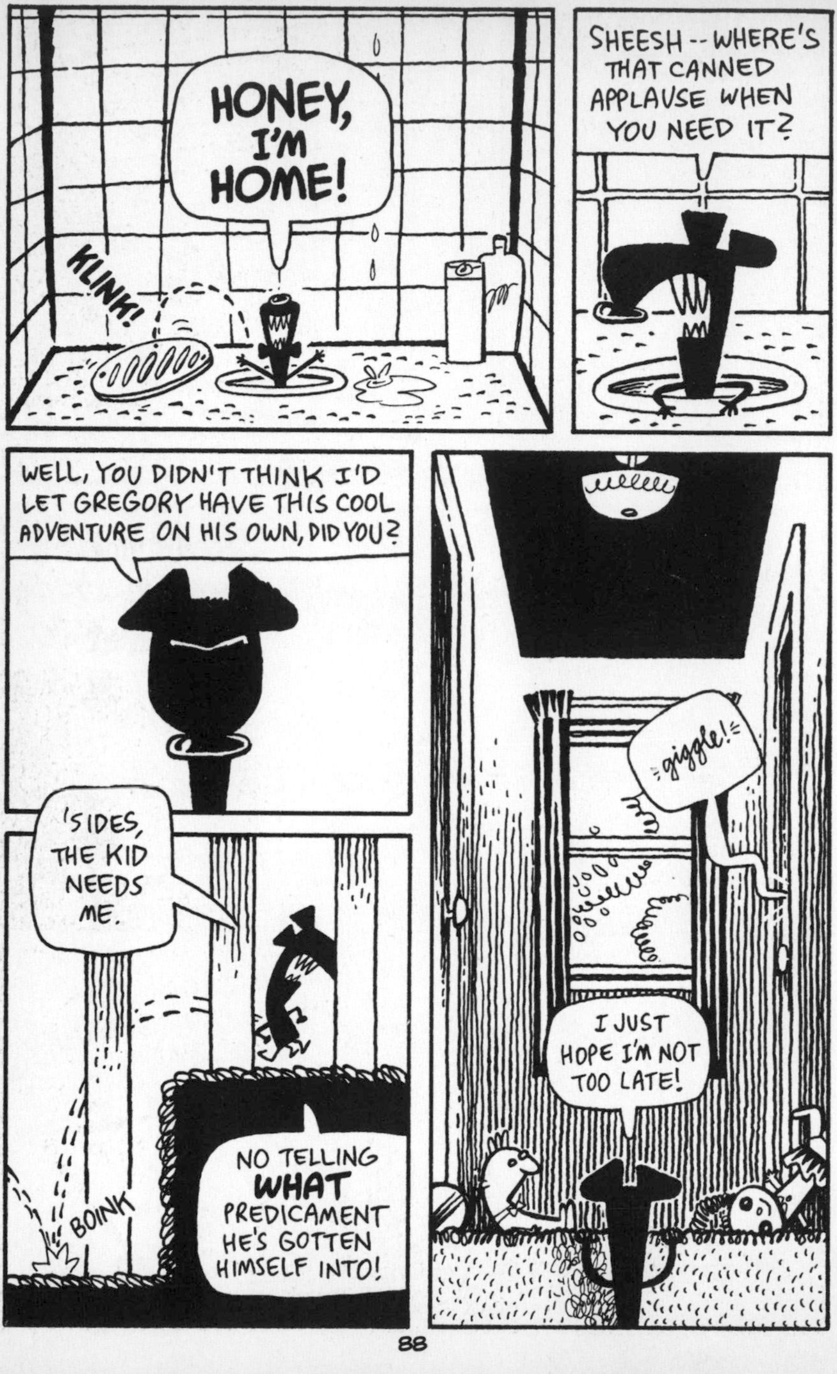
KLINK!
HONEY, I'M HOME!
SHEESH -- WHERE'S THAT CANNED APPLAUSE WHEN YOU NEED IT?
WELL, YOU DIDN'T THINK I'D LET GREGORY HAVE THIS COOL ADVENTURE ON HIS OWN, DID YOU?
'SIDES, THE KID NEEDS ME.
BOINK
NO TELLING WHAT PREDICAMENT HE'S GOTTEN HIMSELF INTO!
giggle!
I JUST HOPE I'M NOT TOO LATE!

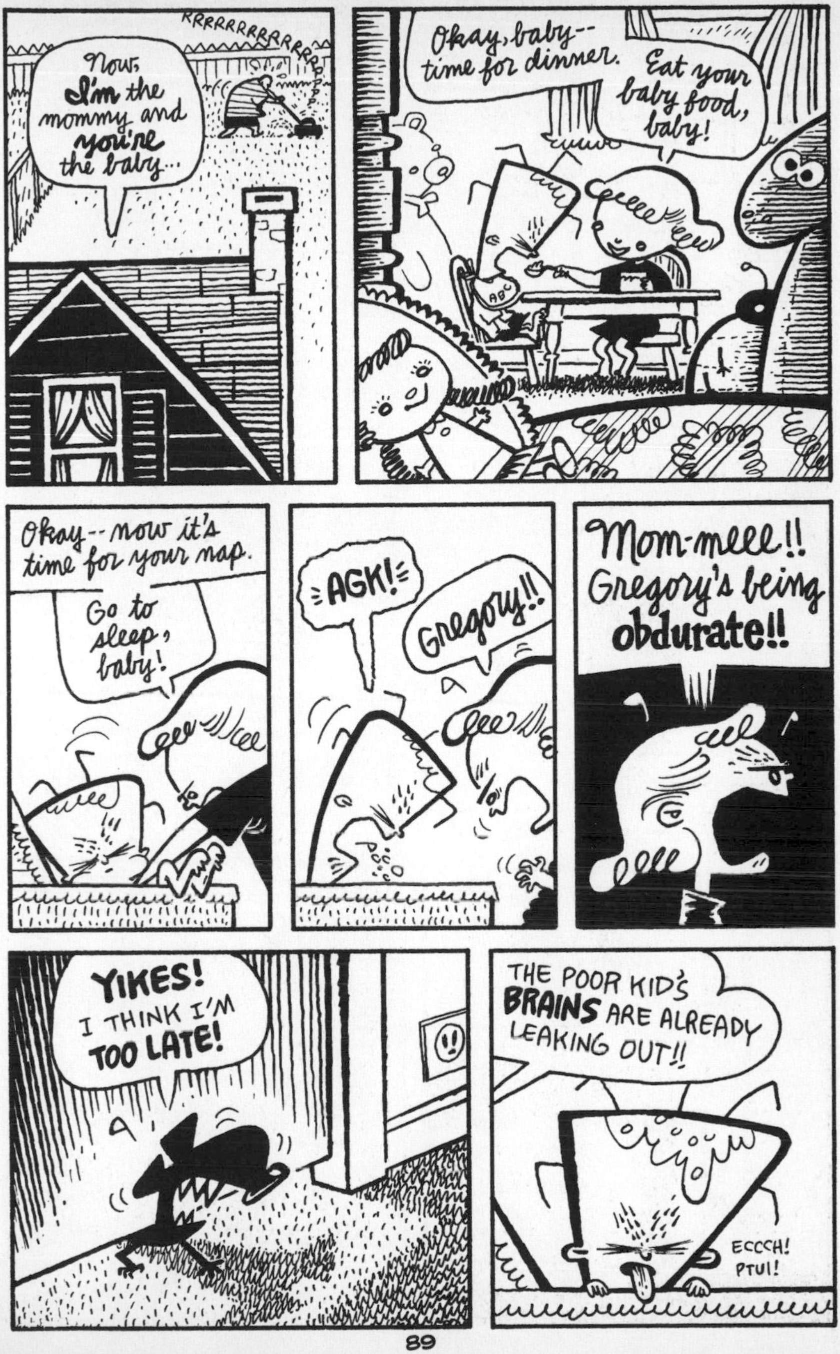
RRRRRRRRRRRRRRRRPPP
Now, I'm the mommy and you're the baby...
Okay, baby-- time for dinner.
Eat your baby food, baby!
Okay-- now it's time for your nap.
Go to sleep, baby!
AGK!
Gregory!!
Mom-meee!! Gregory's being obdurate!!
YIKES! I THINK I'M TOO LATE!
THE POOR KID'S BRAINS ARE ALREADY LEAKING OUT!!
ECCCH! PTUI!

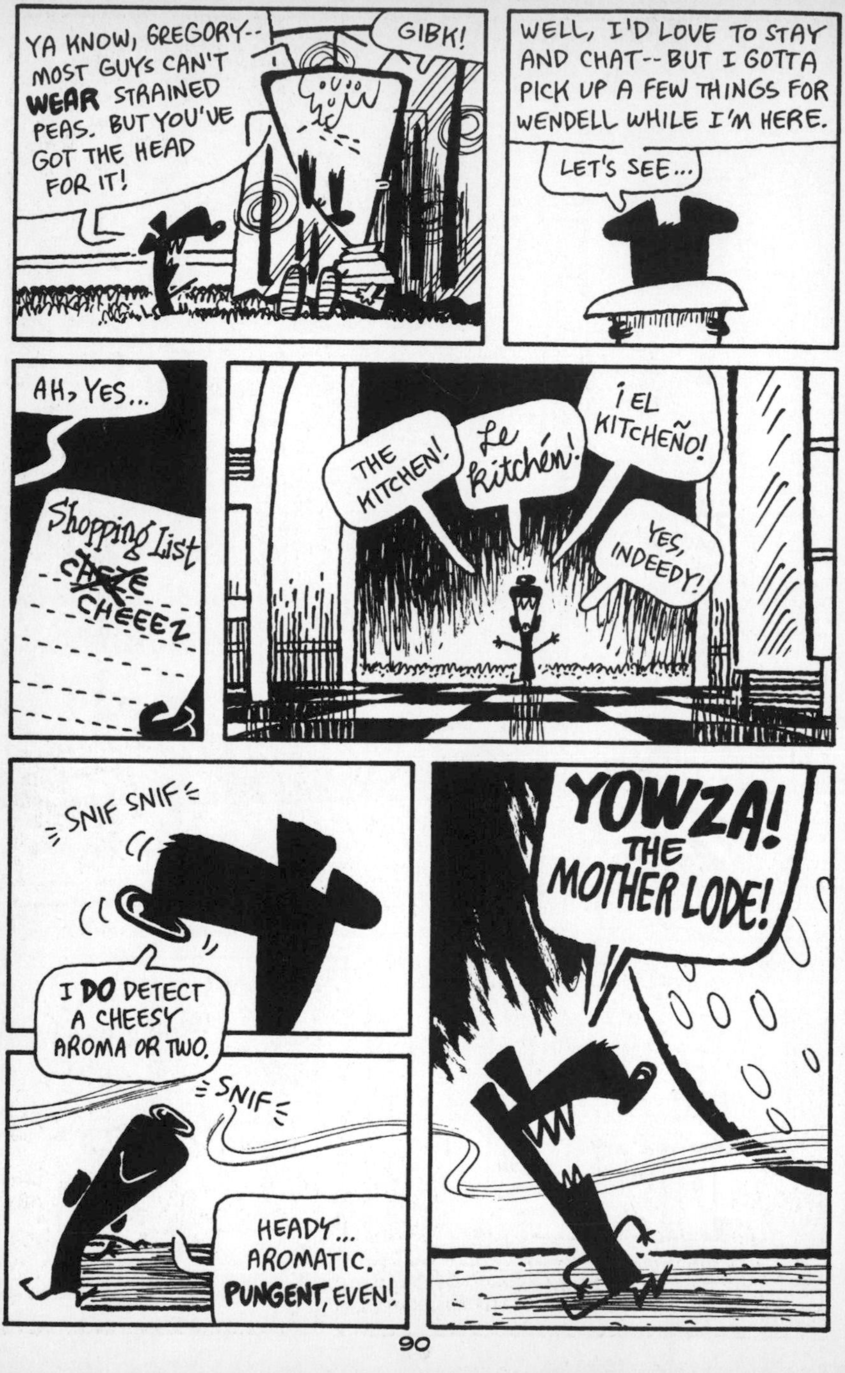
YA KNOW, GREGORY-- MOST GUYS CAN'T WEAR STRAINED PEAS. BUT YOU'VE GOT THE HEAD FOR IT!
GIBK!
WELL, I'D LOVE TO STAY AND CHAT-- BUT I GOTTA PICK UP A FEW THINGS FOR WENDELL WHILE I'M HERE.
LET'S SEE...
AH, YES...
Shopping List
CHEEZE
CHEEEZ
THE KITCHEN!
Le Kitchén!
¡EL KITCHEÑO!
YES, INDEEDY!
SNIF SNIF
I DO DETECT A CHEESY AROMA OR TWO.
SNIF
HEADY... AROMATIC. PUNGENT, EVEN!
YOWZA! THE MOTHER LODE!

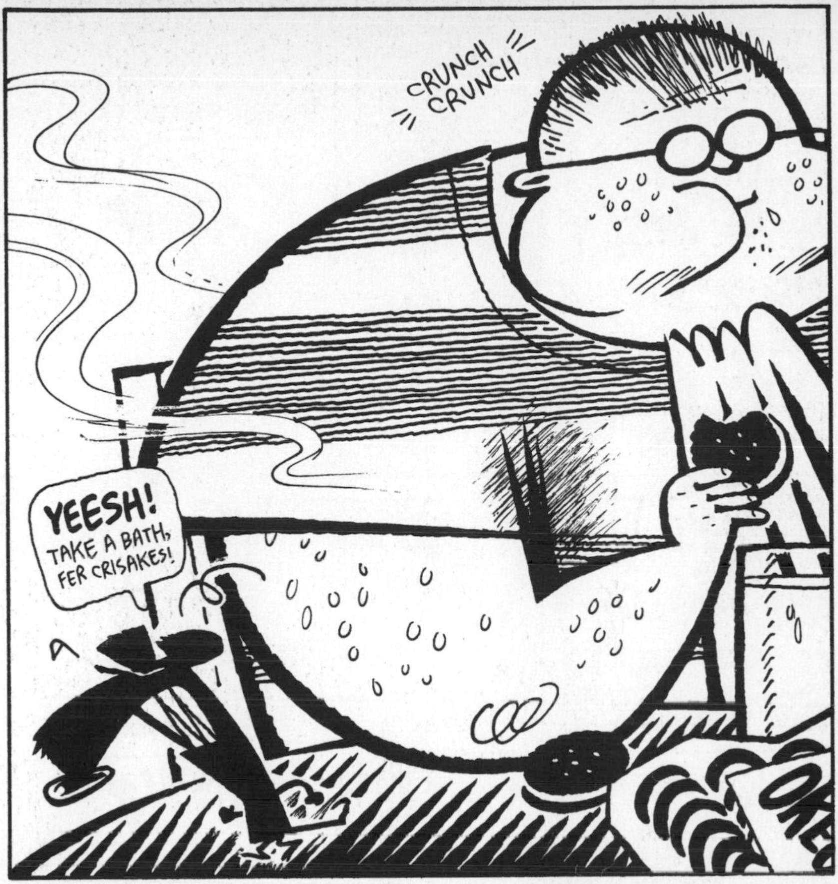
CRUNCH CRUNCH
YEESH! TAKE A BATH, FER CRISAKES!

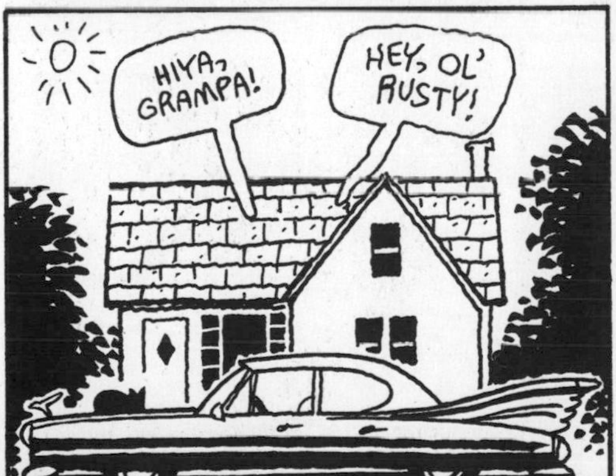
HIYA, GRAMPA!
HEY, OL' RUSTY!

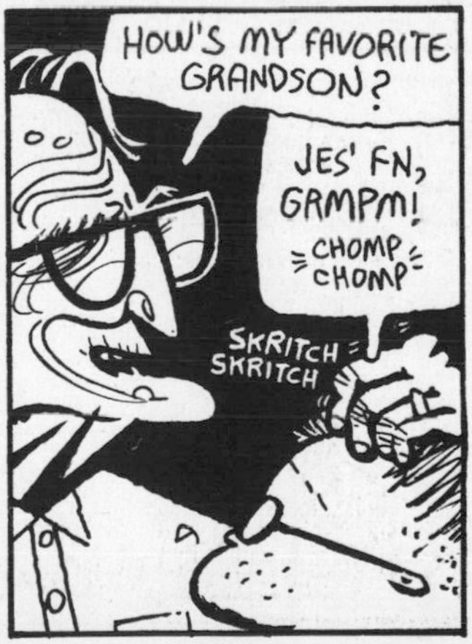
HOW'S MY FAVORITE GRANDSON?
JES' FN, GRMPM!
CHOMP CHOMP
SKRITCH SKRITCH

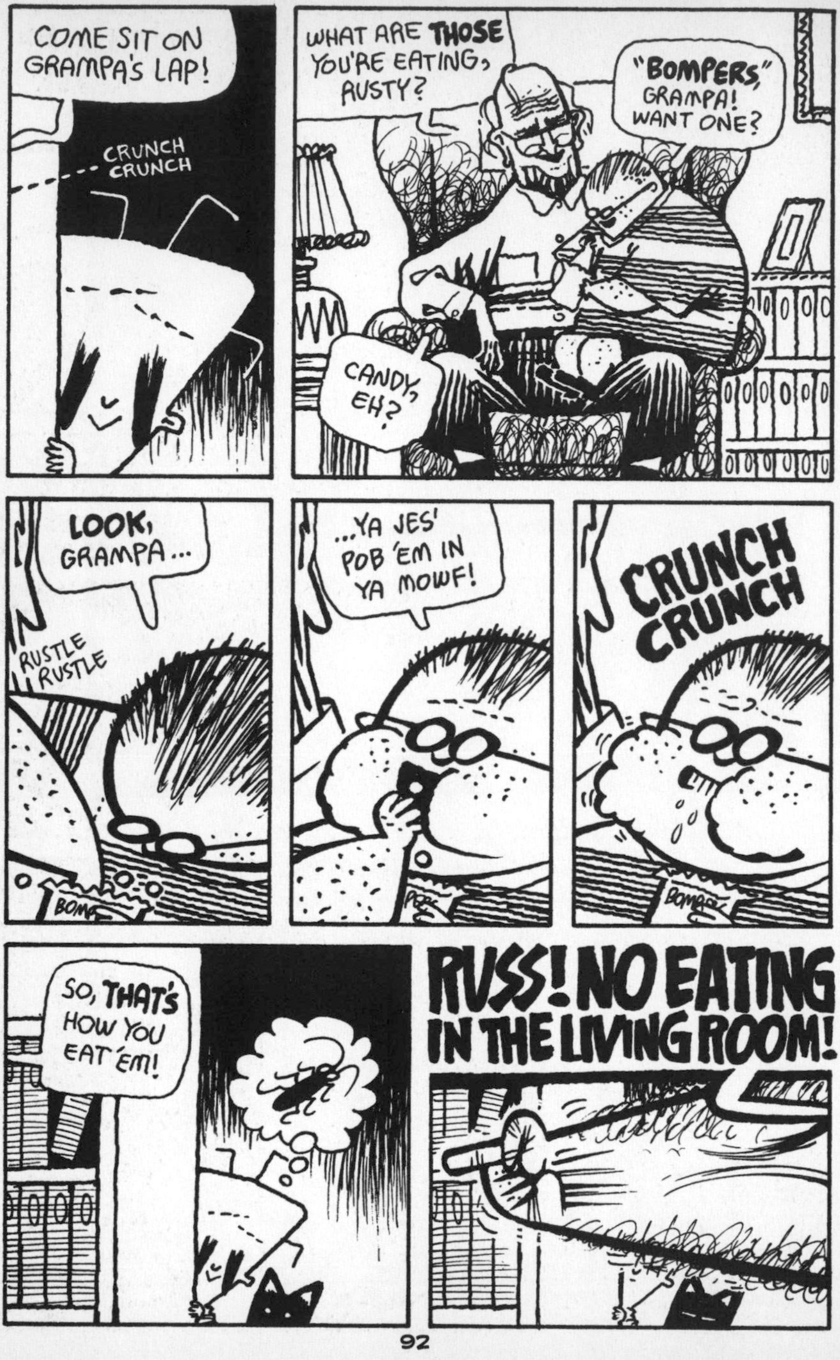

COME SIT ON GRAMPA'S LAP!
CRUNCH CRUNCH
WHAT ARE THOSE YOU'RE EATING, RUSTY?
"BOMPERS," GRAMPA! WANT ONE?
CANDY, EH?
LOOK, GRAMPA...
RUSTLE RUSTLE
...YA JES' POB 'EM IN YA MOWF!
CRUNCH CRUNCH
SO, THAT'S HOW YOU EAT 'EM!
RUSS! NO EATING IN THE LIVING ROOM!

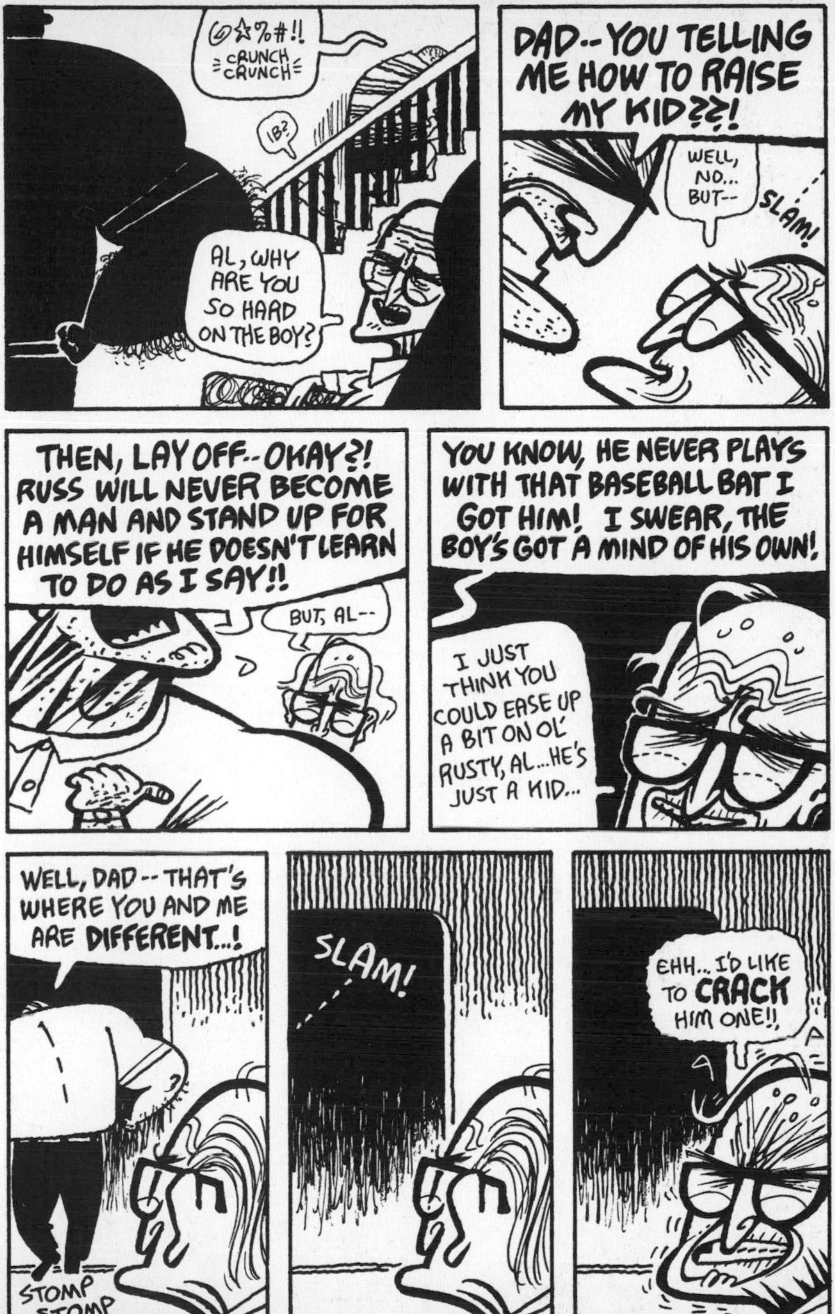

@☆%#!!
CRUNCH CRUNCH
IB?
AL, WHY ARE YOU SO HARD ON THE BOY?
DAD--YOU TELLING ME HOW TO RAISE MY KID??!
WELL, NO... BUT--
SLAM!
THEN, LAY OFF--OKAY?! RUSS WILL NEVER BECOME A MAN AND STAND UP FOR HIMSELF IF HE DOESN'T LEARN TO DO AS I SAY!!
BUT, AL--
YOU KNOW, HE NEVER PLAYS WITH THAT BASEBALL BAT I GOT HIM! I SWEAR, THE BOY'S GOT A MIND OF HIS OWN!
I JUST THINK YOU COULD EASE UP A BIT ON OL' RUSTY, AL...HE'S JUST A KID...
WELL, DAD -- THAT'S WHERE YOU AND ME ARE DIFFERENT...!
STOMP STOMP
SLAM!
EHH... I'D LIKE TO CRACK HIM ONE!!

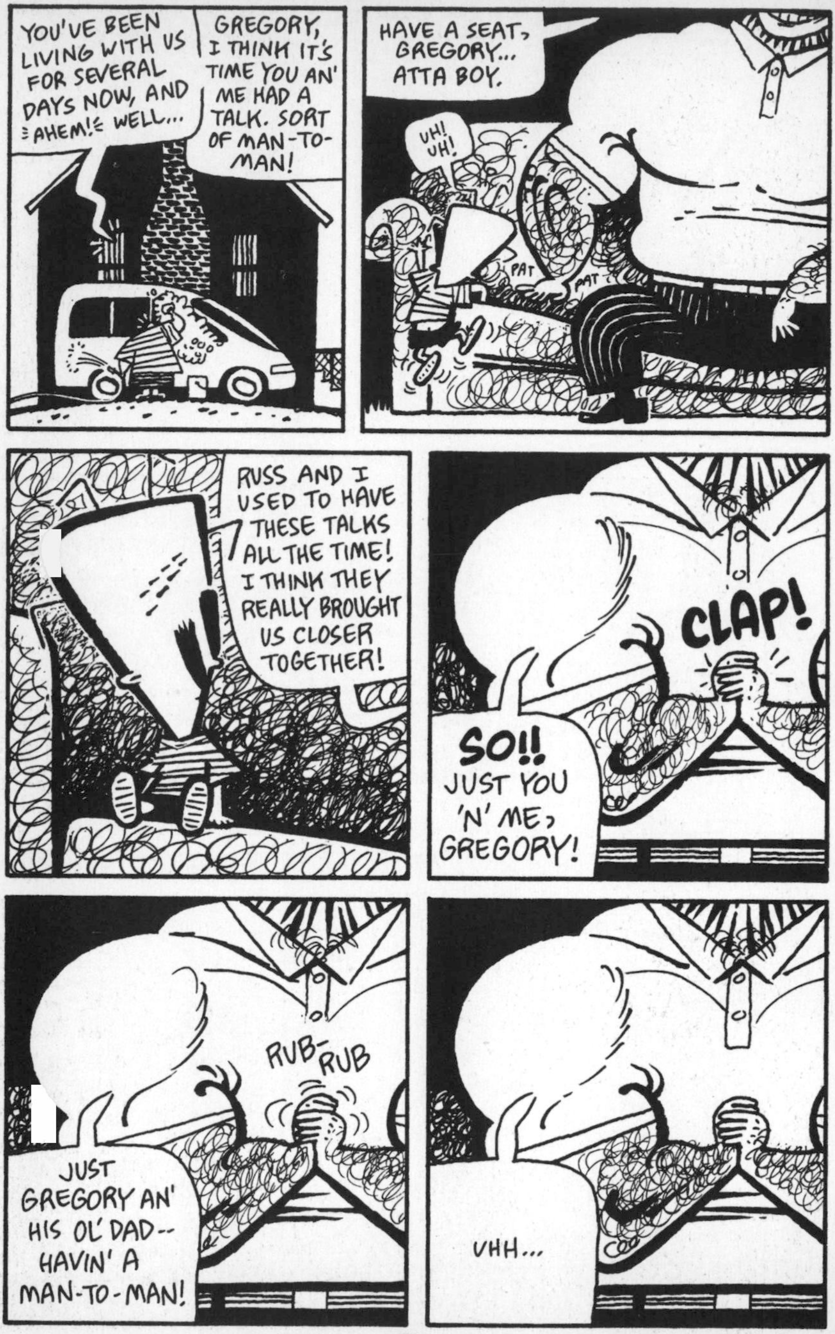
YOU'VE BEEN LIVING WITH US FOR SEVERAL DAYS NOW, AND ≡AHEM!≡ WELL...
GREGORY, I THINK IT'S TIME YOU AN' ME HAD A TALK. SORT OF MAN-TO-MAN!
HAVE A SEAT, GREGORY... ATTA BOY.
UH! UH!
PAT
PAT
RUSS AND I USED TO HAVE THESE TALKS ALL THE TIME! I THINK THEY REALLY BROUGHT US CLOSER TOGETHER!
CLAP!
SO!! JUST YOU 'N' ME, GREGORY!
RUB-RUB
JUST GREGORY AN' HIS OL' DAD-- HAVIN' A MAN-TO-MAN!
UHH...

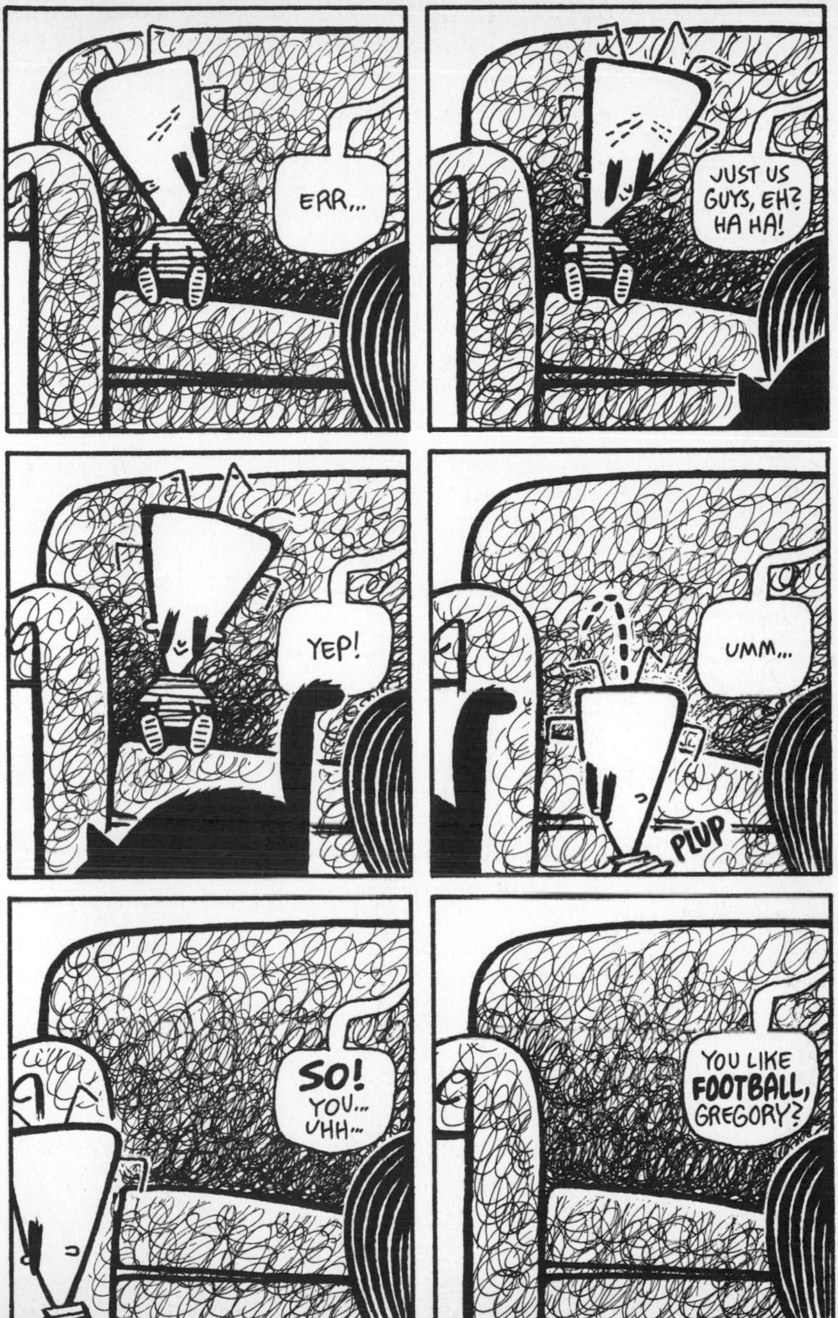
ERR,...
JUST US GUYS, EH? HA HA!
YEP!
UMM...
PLUP
SO! YOU... UHH...
YOU LIKE FOOTBALL, GREGORY?

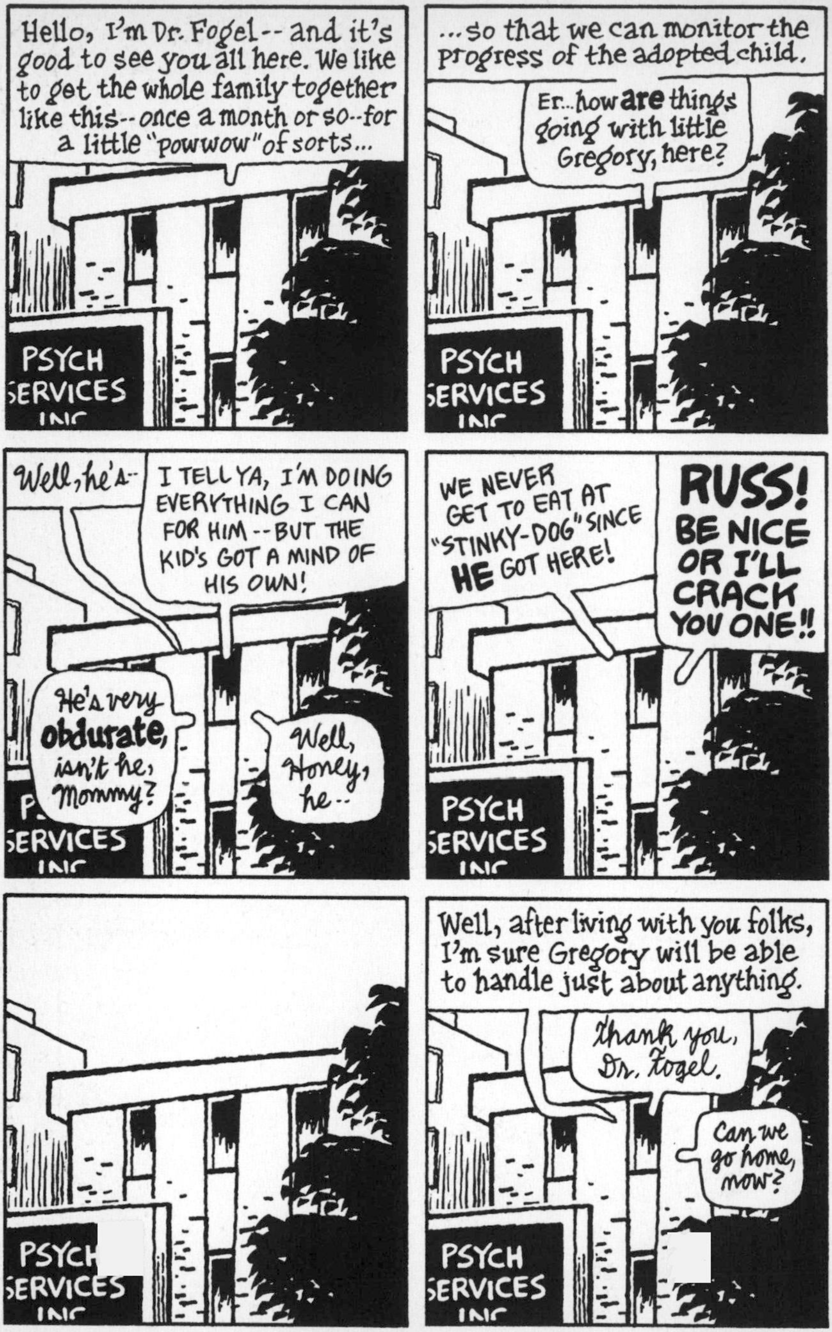
Hello, I'm Dr. Fogel -- and it's good to see you all here. We like to get the whole family together like this -- once a month or so -- for a little "powwow" of sorts...
PSYCH SERVICES INC
...so that we can monitor the progress of the adopted child.
Er...how **are** things going with little Gregory, here?
PSYCH SERVICES INC
Well, he's--
I TELL YA, I'M DOING EVERYTHING I CAN FOR HIM -- BUT THE KID'S GOT A MIND OF HIS OWN!
He's very **obdurate,** isn't he, Mommy?
Well, Honey, he--
SERVICES INC
WE NEVER GET TO EAT AT "STINKY-DOG" SINCE **HE** GOT HERE!
**RUSS! BE NICE OR I'LL CRACK YOU ONE!!**
PSYCH SERVICES INC
SERVICES INC
Well, after living with you folks, I'm sure Gregory will be able to handle just about anything.
Thank you, Dr. Fogel.
Can we go home, now?
PSYCH SERVICES INC

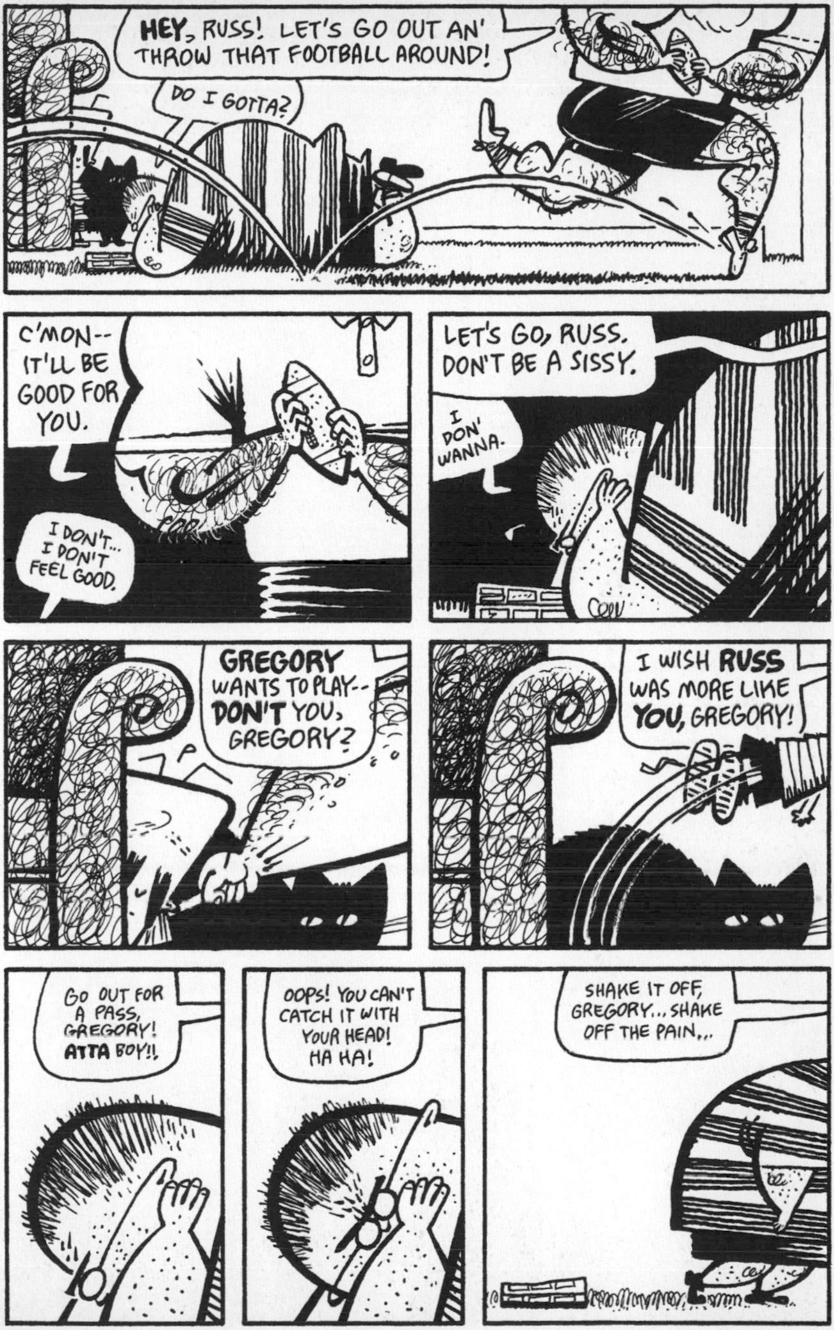
HEY, RUSS! LET'S GO OUT AN' THROW THAT FOOTBALL AROUND!
DO I GOTTA?
C'MON-- IT'LL BE GOOD FOR YOU.
I DON'T... I DON'T FEEL GOOD.
LET'S GO, RUSS. DON'T BE A SISSY.
I DON' WANNA.
GREGORY WANTS TO PLAY-- DON'T YOU, GREGORY?
I WISH RUSS WAS MORE LIKE YOU, GREGORY!
GO OUT FOR A PASS, GREGORY! ATTA BOY!!
OOPS! YOU CAN'T CATCH IT WITH YOUR HEAD! HA HA!
SHAKE IT OFF, GREGORY... SHAKE OFF THE PAIN...

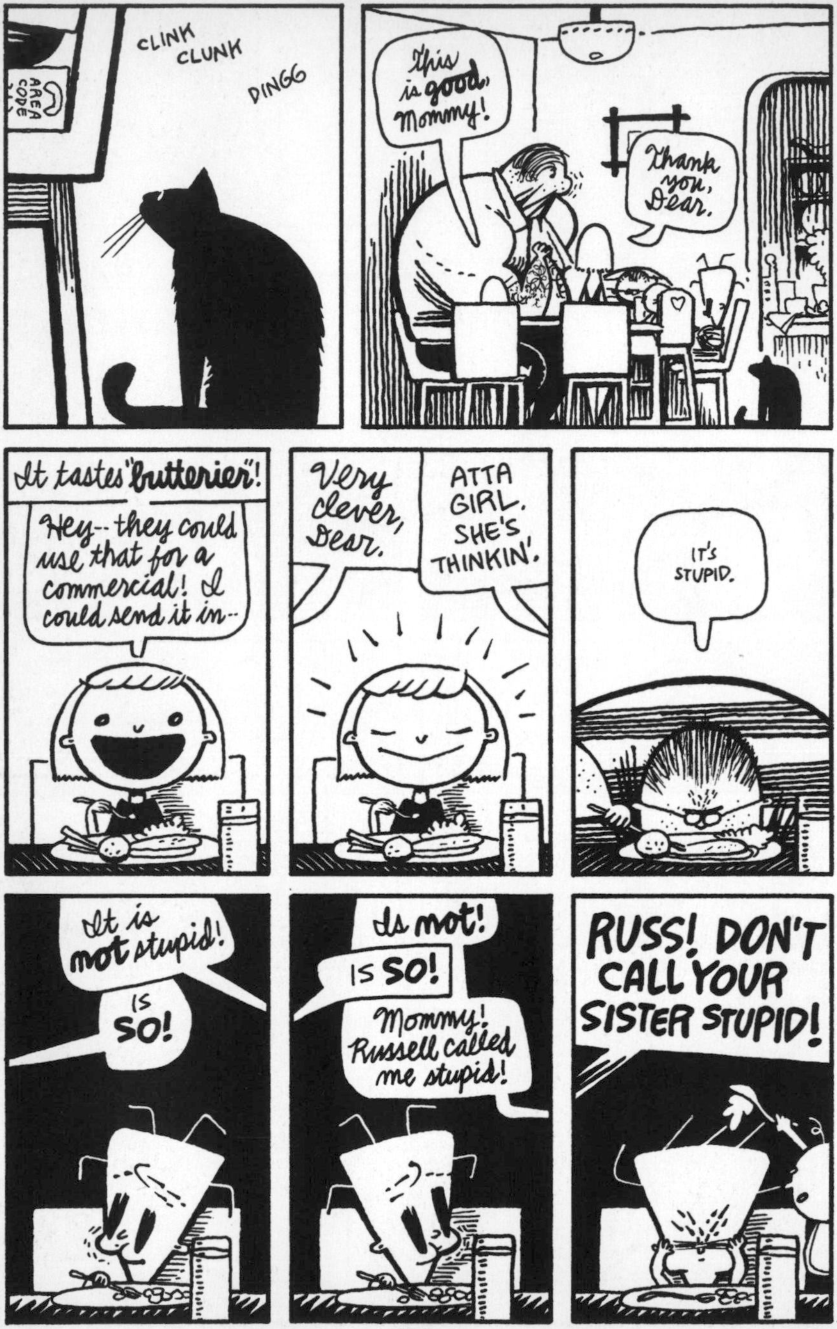
CLINK
CLUNK
DINGG
AREA CODE
This is good, Mommy!
Thank you, Dear.
It tastes "butterier"!
Hey-- they could use that for a commercial! I could send it in--
Very clever, Dear.
ATTA GIRL. SHE'S THINKIN'.
IT'S STUPID.
It is not stupid!
IS SO!
Is not!
IS SO!
Mommy! Russell called me stupid!
RUSS! DON'T CALL YOUR SISTER STUPID!

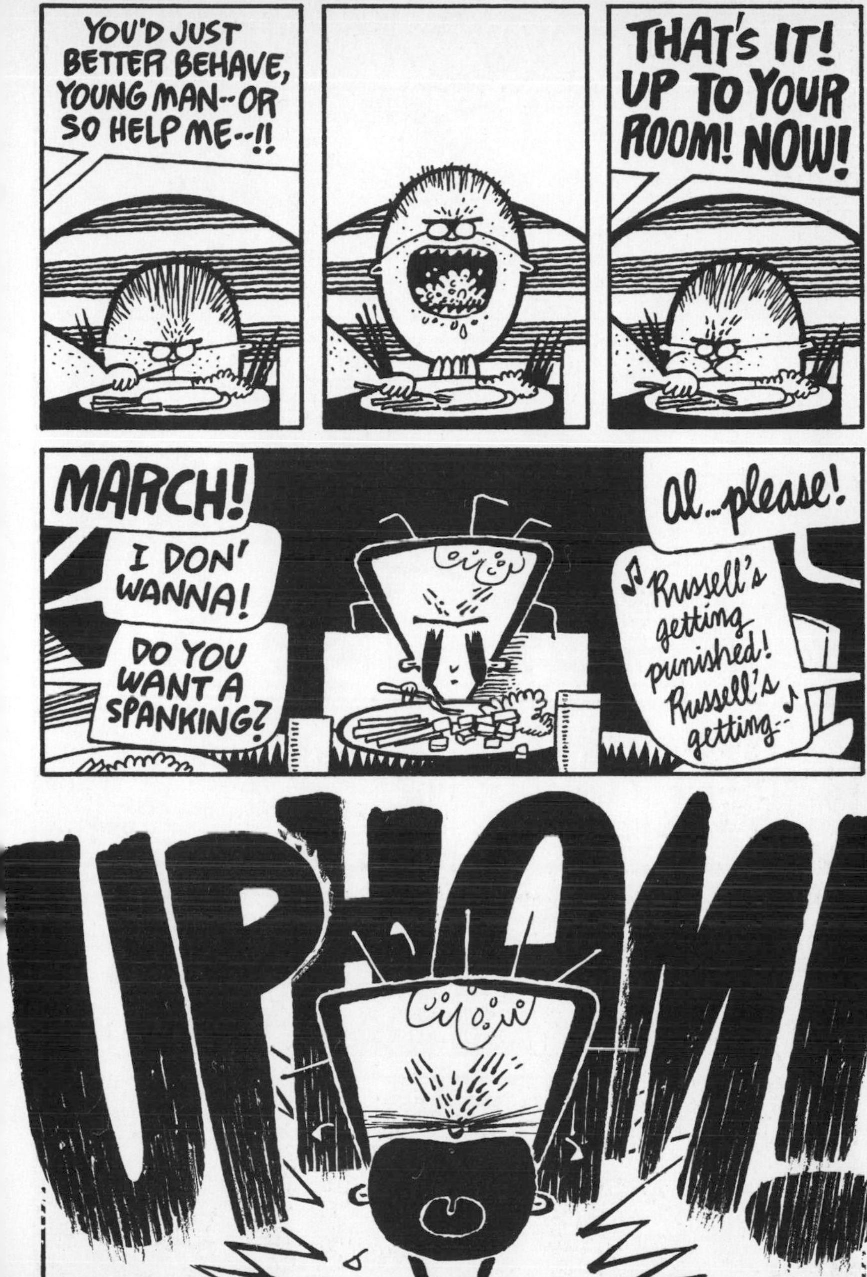
YOU'D JUST BETTER BEHAVE, YOUNG MAN--OR SO HELP ME--!!
THAT'S IT! UP TO YOUR ROOM! NOW!
MARCH!
I DON' WANNA!
DO YOU WANT A SPANKING?
Al...please!
♪ Russell's getting punished! Russell's getting-♪

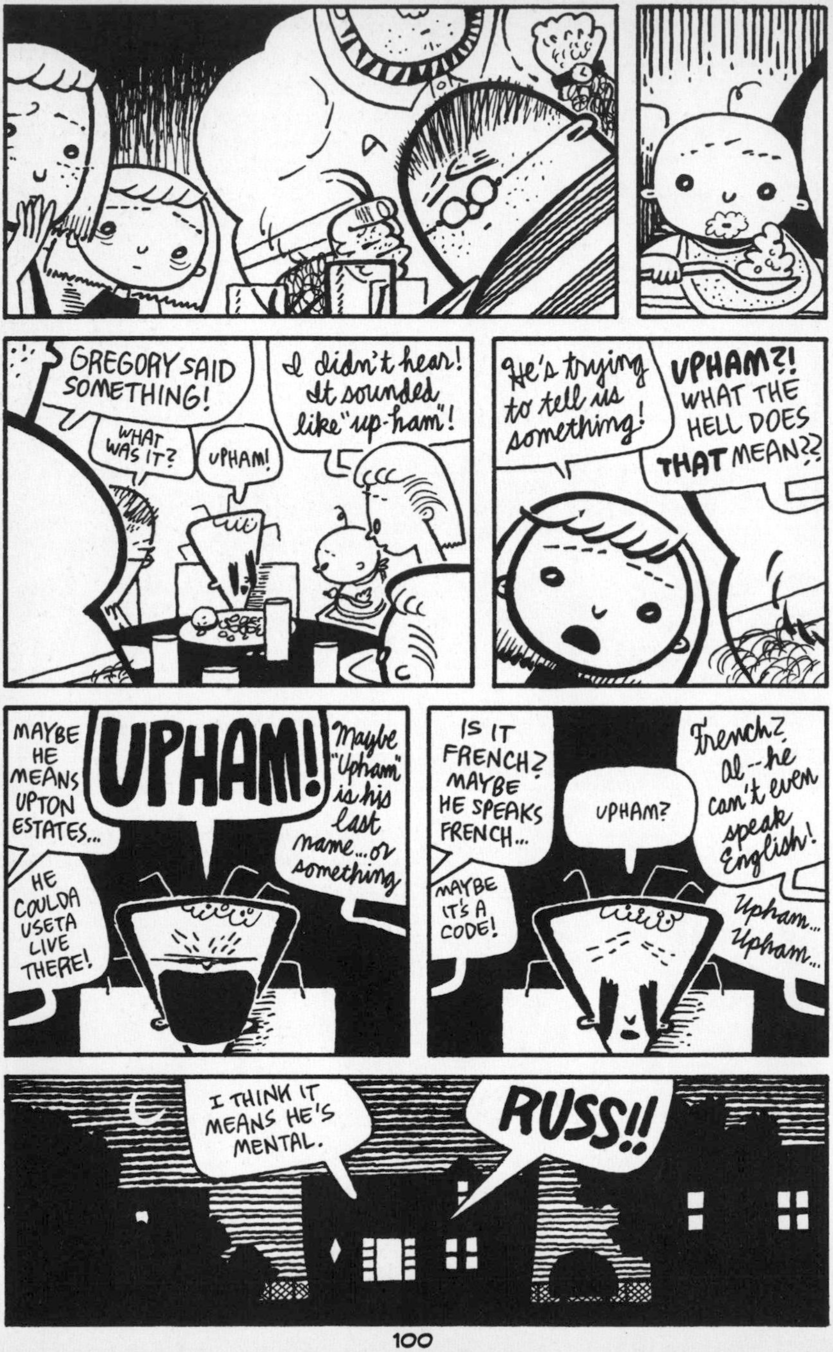
GREGORY SAID SOMETHING!
WHAT WAS IT?
UPHAM!
I didn't hear! It sounded like "up-ham"!
He's trying to tell us something!
UPHAM?! WHAT THE HELL DOES THAT MEAN??
MAYBE HE MEANS UPTON ESTATES...
UPHAM!
Maybe "Upham" is his last name... or something
HE COULDA USETA LIVE THERE!
IS IT FRENCH? MAYBE HE SPEAKS FRENCH...
UPHAM?
French? Al--he can't even speak English!
MAYBE IT'S A CODE!
Upham... Upham...
I THINK IT MEANS HE'S MENTAL.
RUSS!!

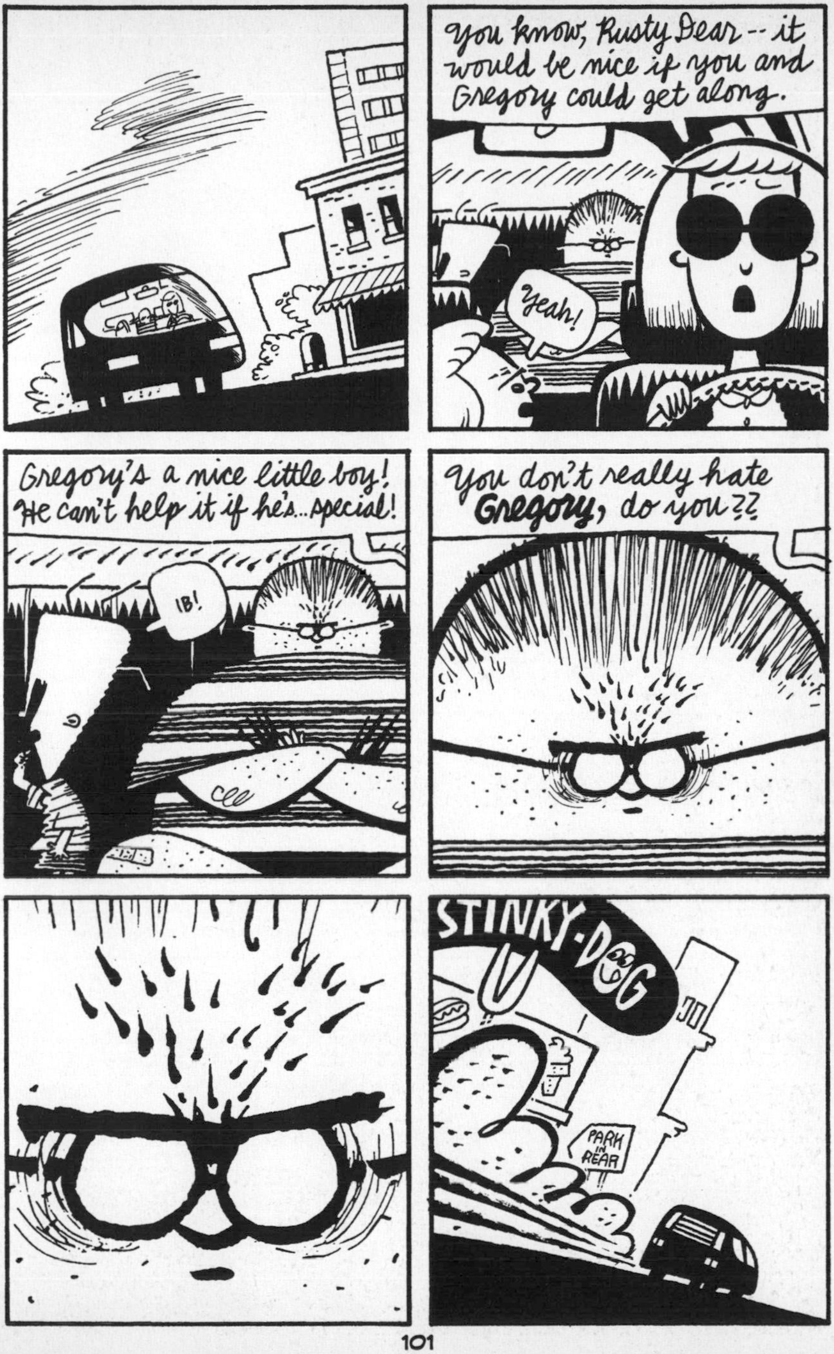
You know, Rusty Dear -- it would be nice if you and Gregory could get along.
Yeah!
Gregory's a nice little boy! He can't help it if he's...special!
IB!
You don't really hate **Gregory**, do you??
STINKY-DOG
PARK IN REAR

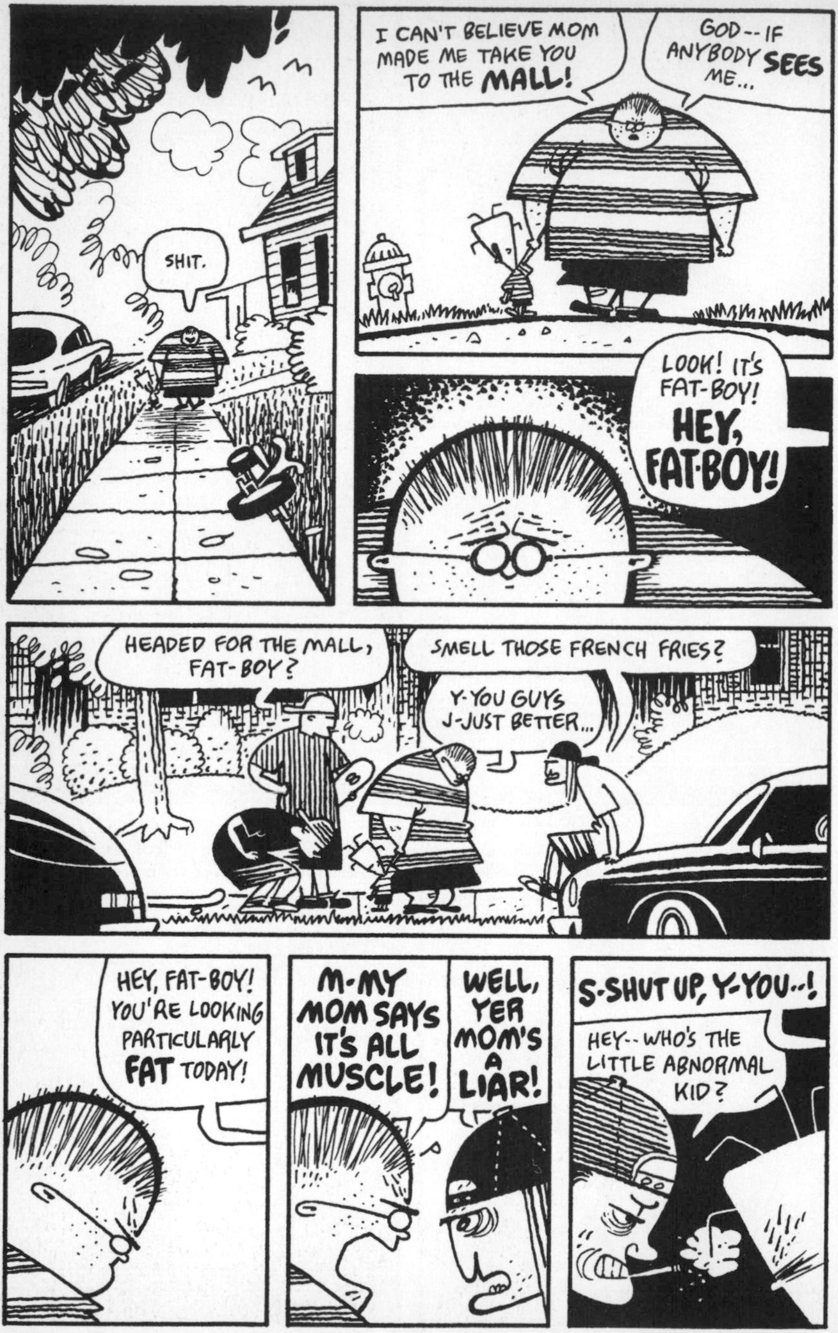
SHIT.
I CAN'T BELIEVE MOM MADE ME TAKE YOU TO THE MALL!
GOD-- IF ANYBODY SEES ME...
LOOK! IT'S FAT-BOY!
HEY, FAT-BOY!
HEADED FOR THE MALL, FAT-BOY?
SMELL THOSE FRENCH FRIES?
Y-YOU GUYS J-JUST BETTER...
HEY, FAT-BOY! YOU'RE LOOKING PARTICULARLY FAT TODAY!
M-MY MOM SAYS IT'S ALL MUSCLE!
WELL, YER MOM'S A LIAR!
S-SHUT UP, Y-YOU..!
HEY-- WHO'S THE LITTLE ABNORMAL KID?

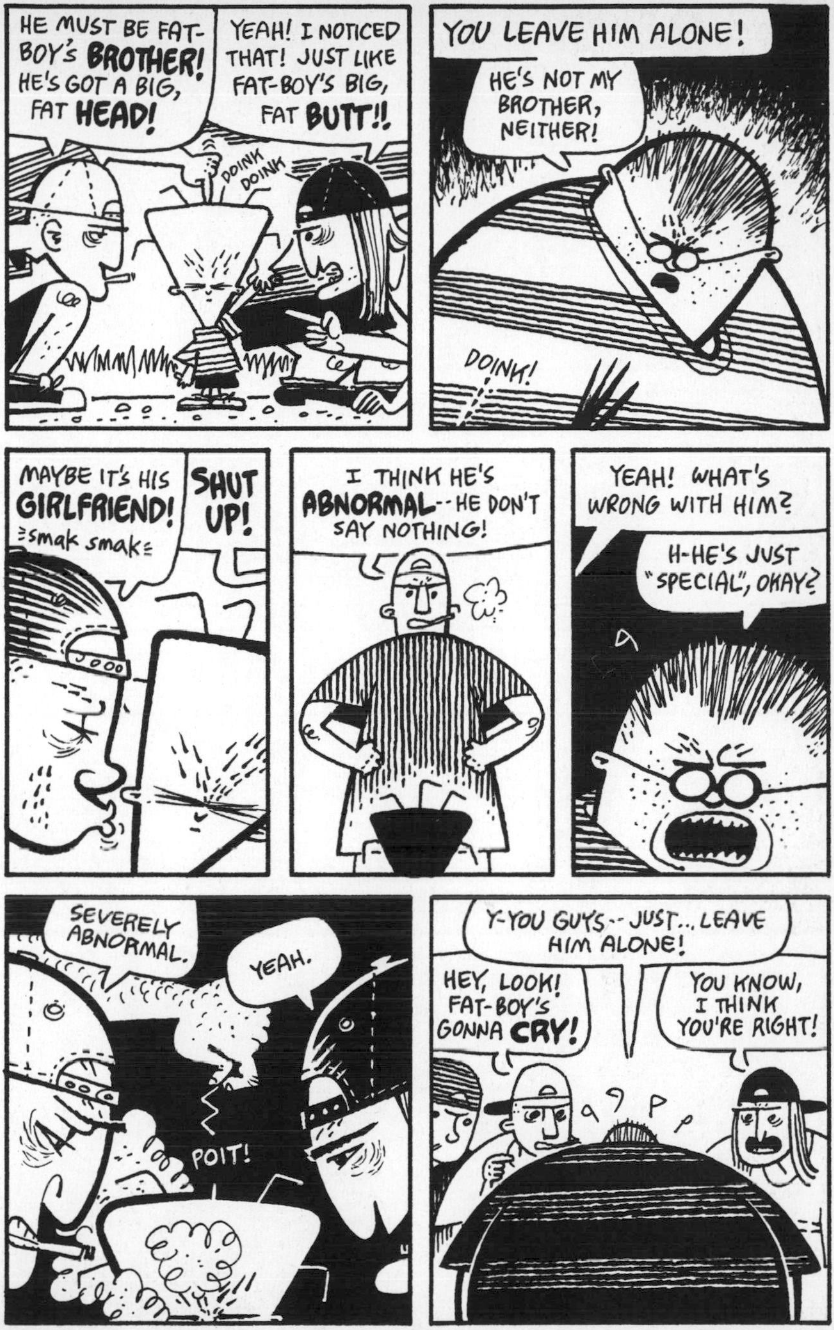
HE MUST BE FAT-BOY'S **BROTHER!** HE'S GOT A BIG, FAT **HEAD!**
YEAH! I NOTICED THAT! JUST LIKE FAT-BOY'S BIG, FAT **BUTT!!**
DOINK DOINK
YOU LEAVE HIM ALONE!
HE'S NOT MY BROTHER, NEITHER!
DOINK!
MAYBE IT'S HIS **GIRLFRIEND!**
smak smak
**SHUT UP!**
I THINK HE'S **ABNORMAL**-- HE DON'T SAY NOTHING!
YEAH! WHAT'S WRONG WITH HIM?
H-HE'S JUST "SPECIAL", OKAY?
SEVERELY ABNORMAL.
YEAH.
POIT!
Y-YOU GUYS -- JUST... LEAVE HIM ALONE!
HEY, LOOK! FAT-BOY'S GONNA **CRY!**
YOU KNOW, I THINK YOU'RE RIGHT!

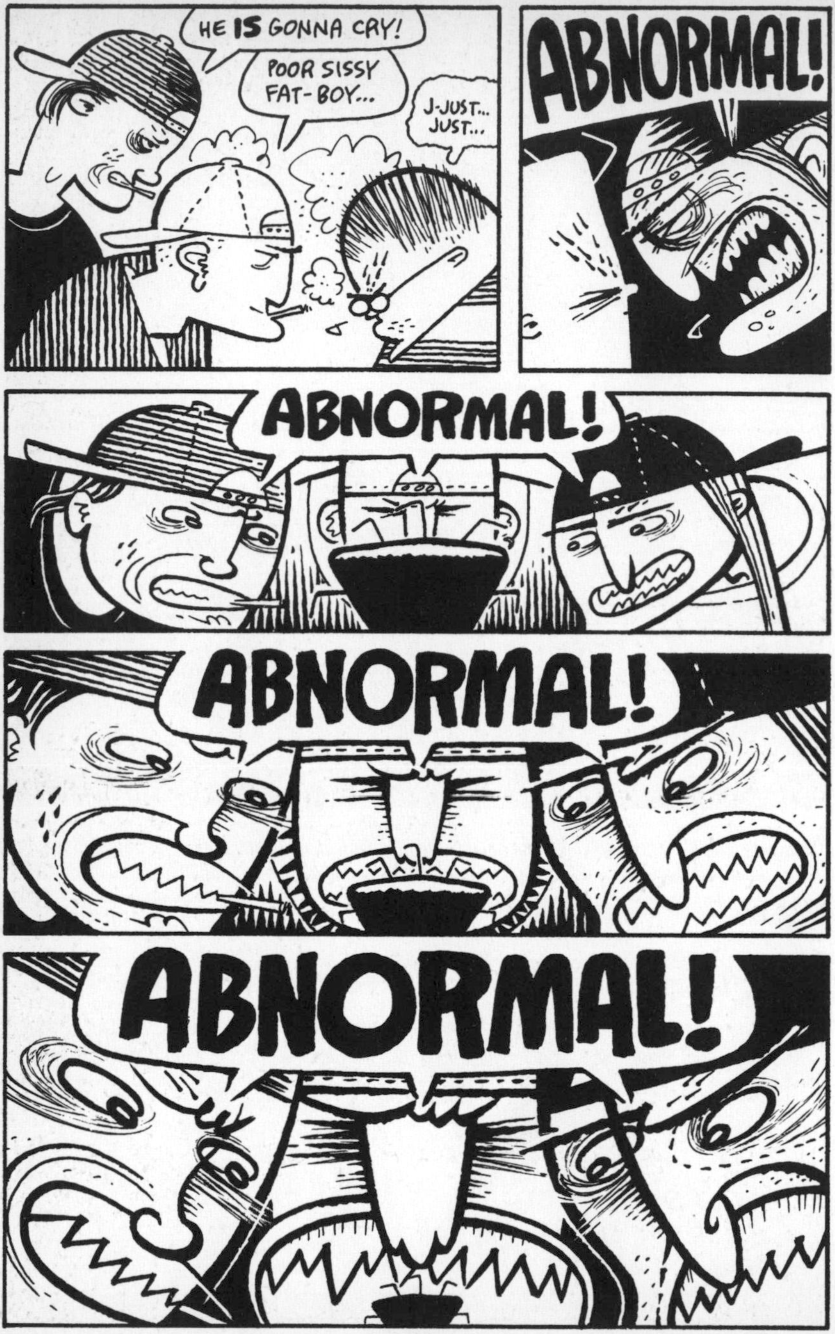
HE IS GONNA CRY!
POOR SISSY FAT-BOY...
J-JUST... JUST...
ABNORMAL!
ABNORMAL!
ABNORMAL!
ABNORMAL!

ABNORMAL.

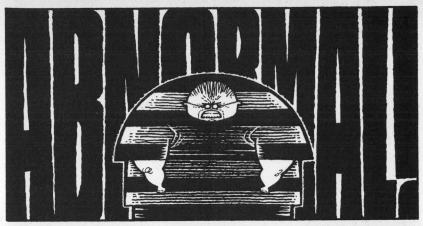

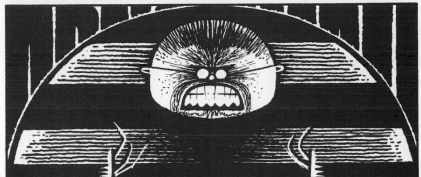

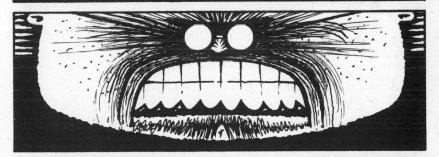

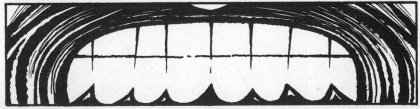

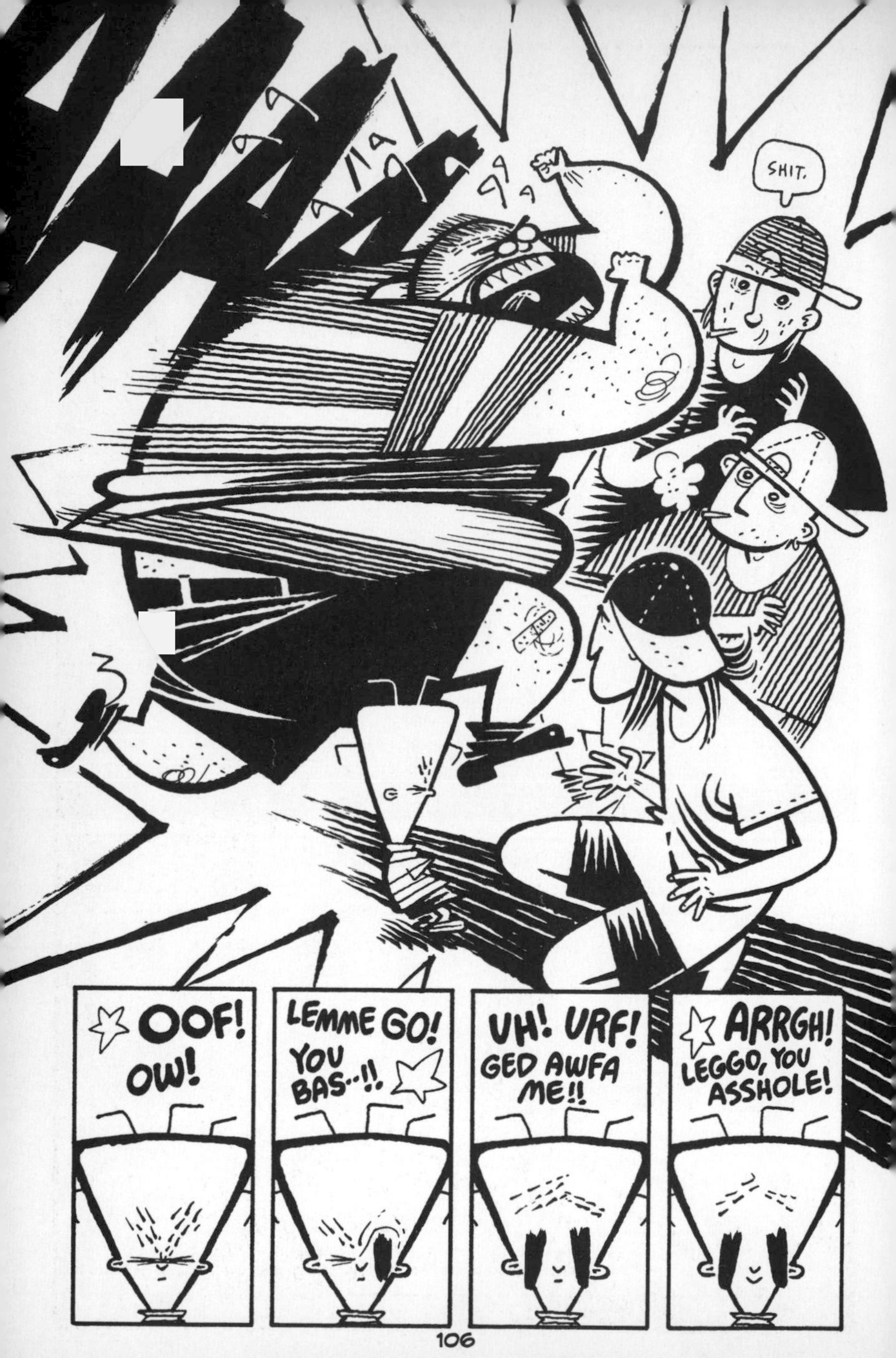
SHIT.
OOF!
OW!
LEMME GO!
YOU BAS-!!
UH! URF!
GED AWFA ME!!
ARRGH!
LEGGO, YOU ASSHOLE!

UH! UH! UH!
HELP ME, MAN! HE'S KICKIN'!
STUPID--
FAT-BOY!!
WUNK!
SNIF
P
HA HA HA!
UPHAM!

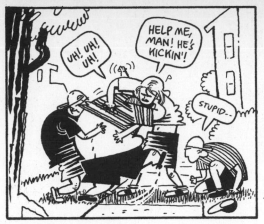

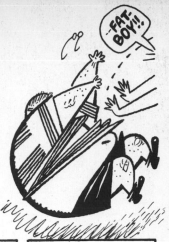

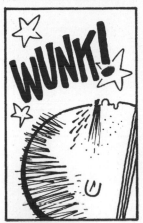

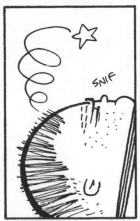

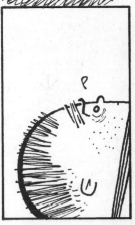

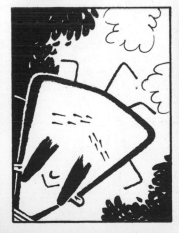

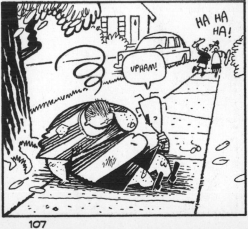

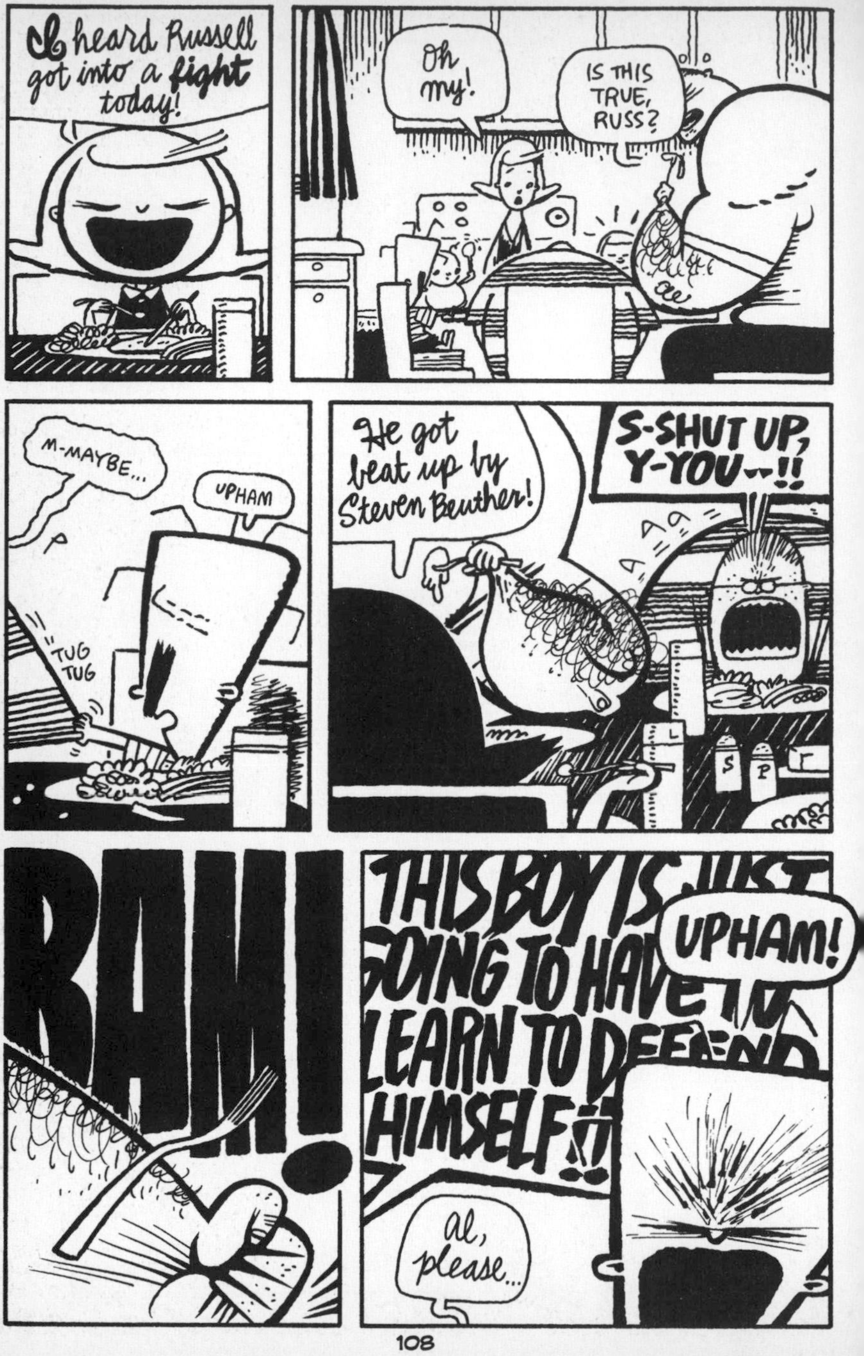
I heard Russell got into a **fight** today!
Oh my!
IS THIS TRUE, RUSS?
M-MAYBE...
UPHAM
TUG TUG
He got beat up by Steven Beuther!
S-SHUT UP, Y-YOU--!!
BAM!
THIS BOY IS
GOING TO HAVE
LEARN TO D
HIMSELF!!
UPHAM!
al, please...

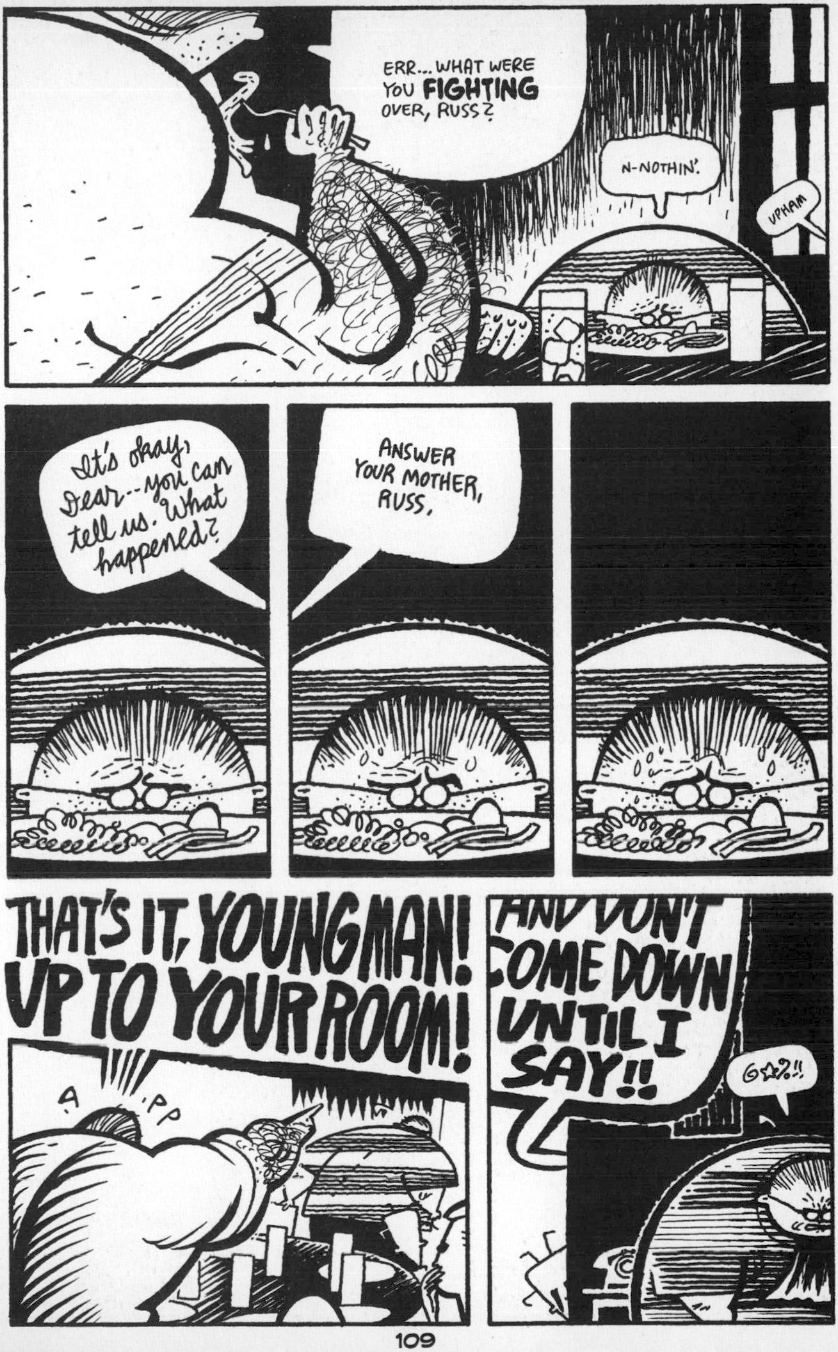
ERR... WHAT WERE YOU FIGHTING OVER, RUSS?
N-NOTHIN'.
UPHAM
It's okay, Dear... you can tell us. What happened?
ANSWER YOUR MOTHER, RUSS.
THAT'S IT, YOUNG MAN! UP TO YOUR ROOM!
AND DON'T COME DOWN UNTIL I SAY!!
G☆?%!!

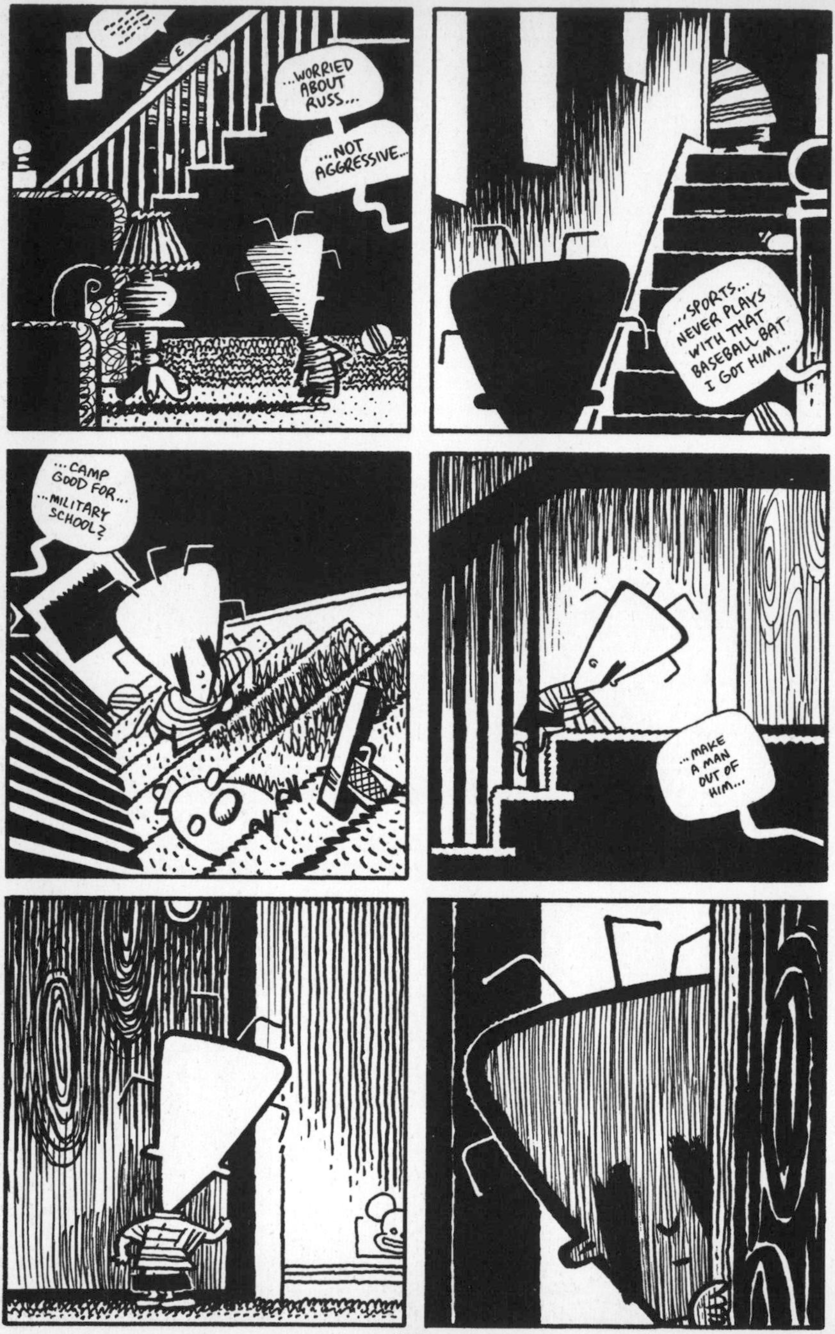
...WORRIED ABOUT RUSS...
...NOT AGGRESSIVE...
...SPORTS... NEVER PLAYS WITH THAT BASEBALL BAT I GOT HIM...
...CAMP GOOD FOR... ...MILITARY SCHOOL?
...MAKE A MAN OUT OF HIM...

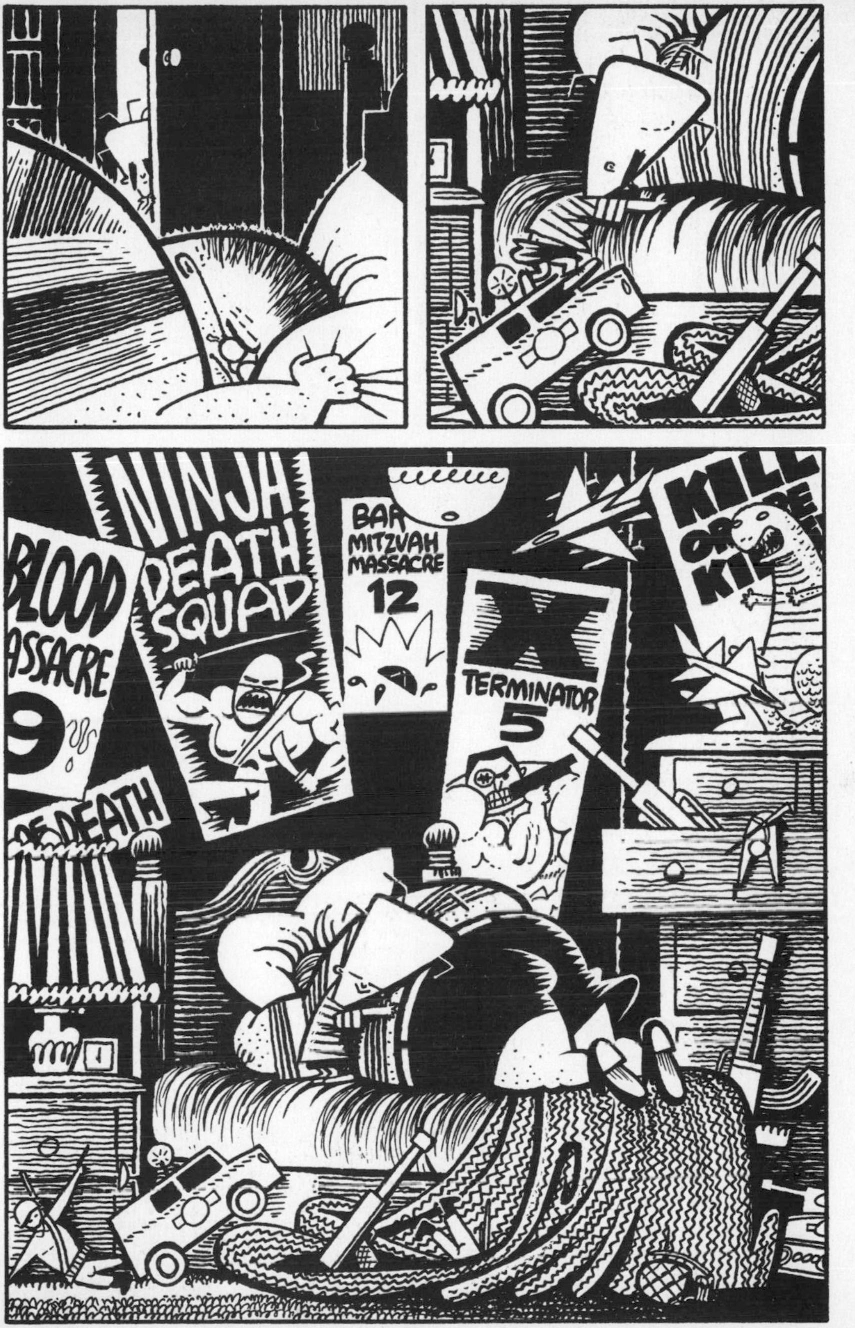

NINJA
DEATH SQUAD
BAR MITZVAH MASSACRE
12
BLOOD
ASSACRE
9
DEATH
X
TERMINATOR
5

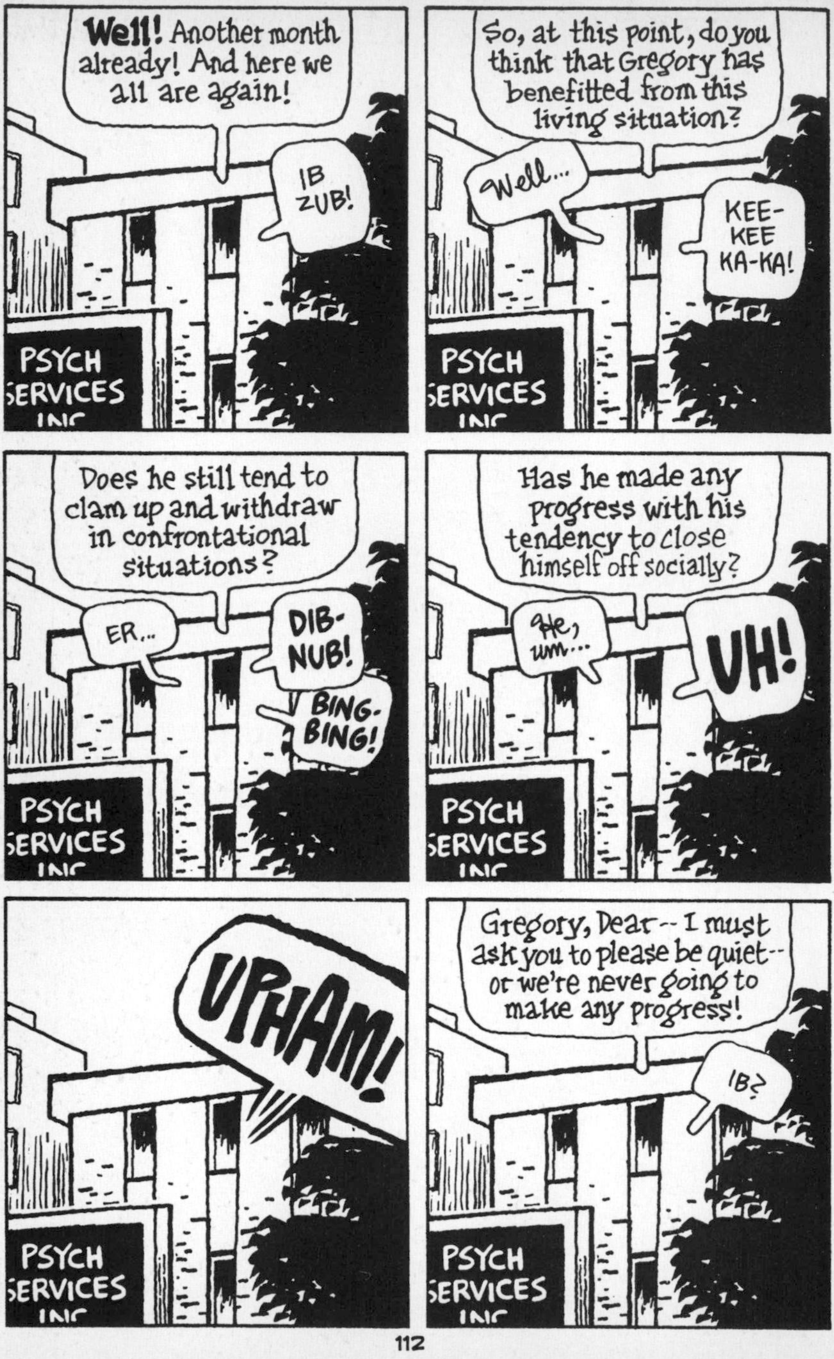
Well! Another month already! And here we all are again!
IB ZUB!
PSYCH SERVICES INC
So, at this point, do you think that Gregory has benefitted from this living situation?
Well...
KEE-KEE KA-KA!
PSYCH SERVICES INC
Does he still tend to clam up and withdraw in confrontational situations?
ER...
DIB-NUB!
BING-BING!
PSYCH SERVICES INC
Has he made any progress with his tendency to close himself off socially?
He, um...
UH!
PSYCH SERVICES INC
UPHAM!
PSYCH SERVICES INC
Gregory, Dear -- I must ask you to please be quiet -- or we're never going to make any progress!
IB?
PSYCH SERVICES INC

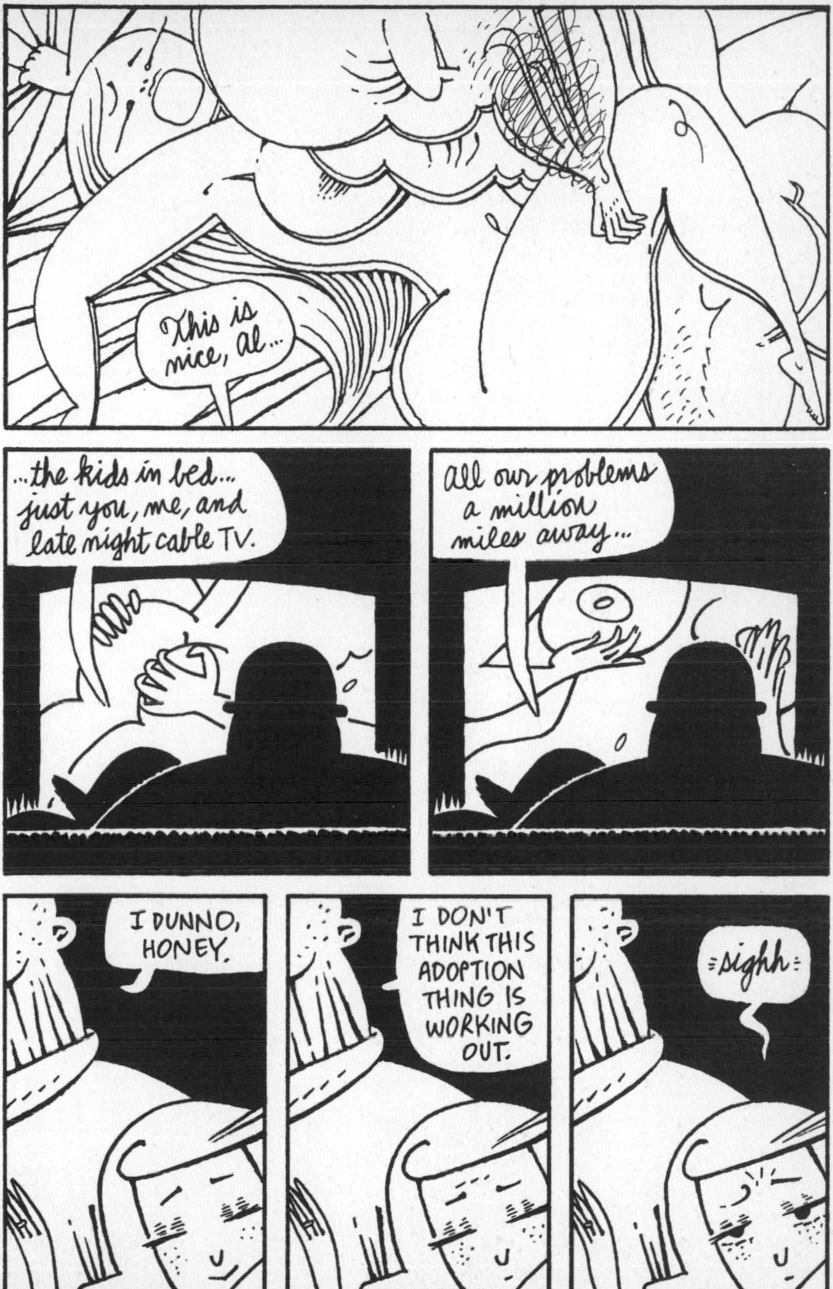
This is nice, Al...
...the kids in bed... just you, me, and late night cable TV.
All our problems a million miles away...
I DUNNO, HONEY.
I DON'T THINK THIS ADOPTION THING IS WORKING OUT.
sighh

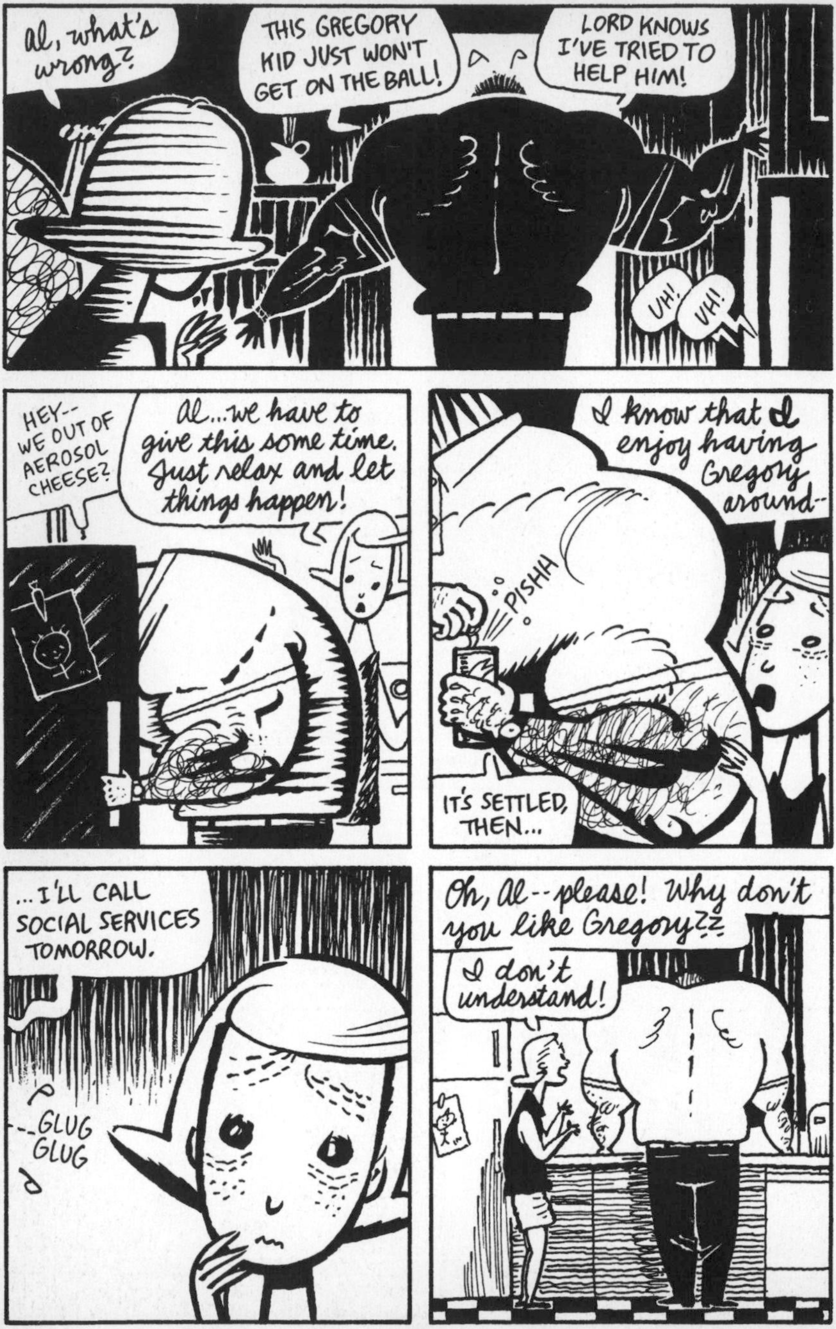
al, what's wrong?
THIS GREGORY KID JUST WON'T GET ON THE BALL!
LORD KNOWS I'VE TRIED TO HELP HIM!
UH!
UH!
HEY-- WE OUT OF AEROSOL CHEESE?
Al...we have to give this some time. Just relax and let things happen!
I know that I enjoy having Gregory around--
PISHH
IT'S SETTLED, THEN...
...I'LL CALL SOCIAL SERVICES TOMORROW.
--GLUG GLUG
Oh, Al--please! Why don't you like Gregory??
I don't understand!

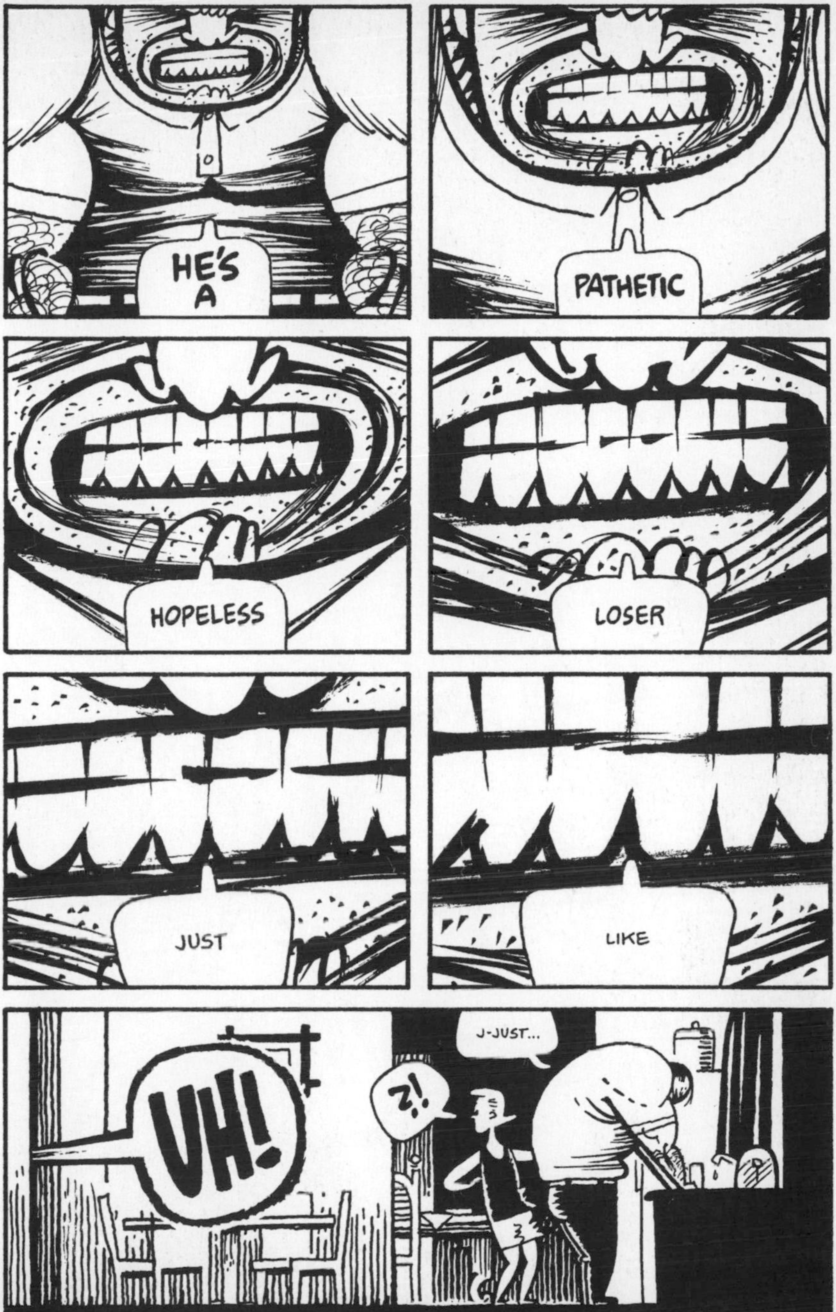
HE'S A
PATHETIC
HOPELESS
LOSER
JUST
LIKE
J-JUST...
?!
UH!

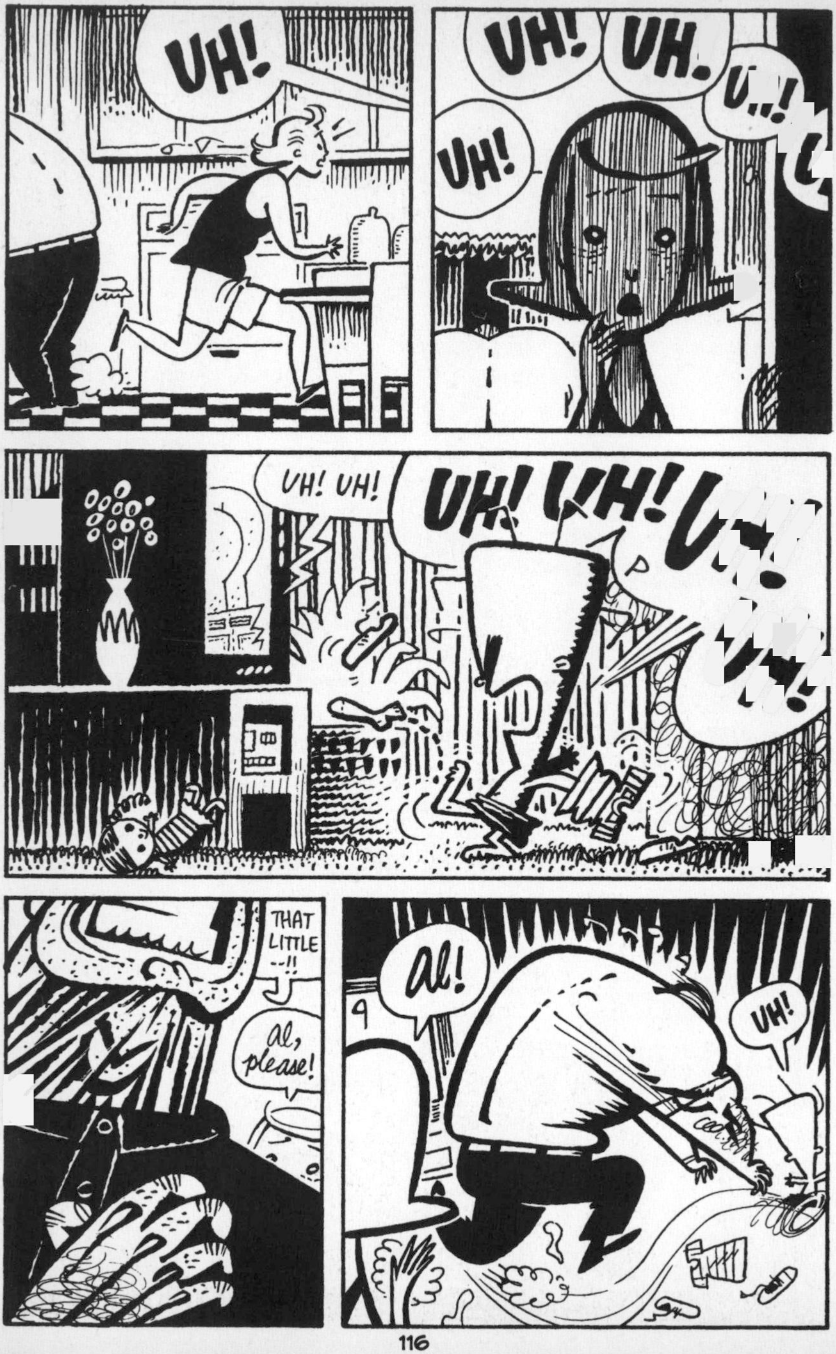
UH!
UH!
UH.
UH!
UH! UH!
UH! UH!
THAT LITTLE --!!
al, please!
al!
UH!

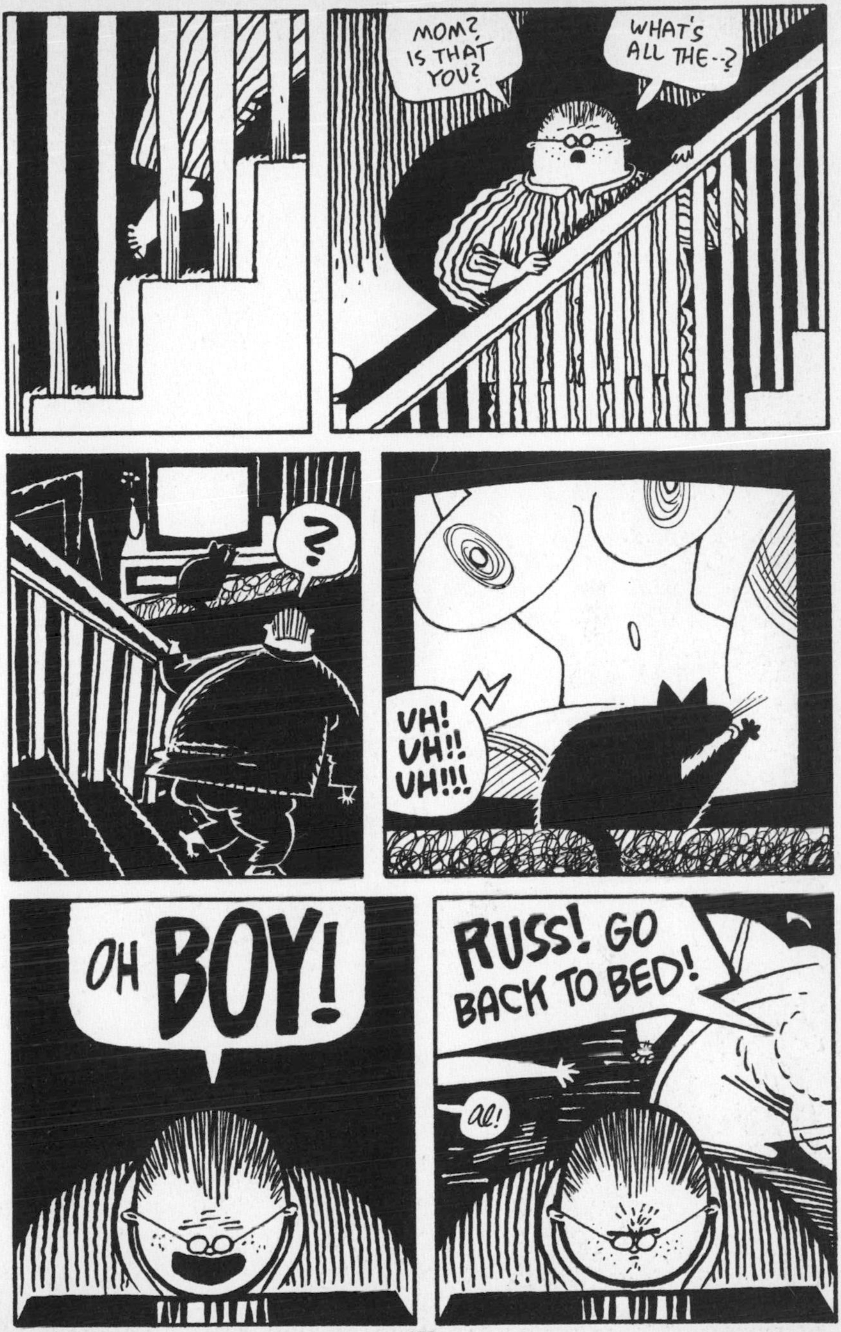
MOM? IS THAT YOU?
WHAT'S ALL THE--?
?
VH! VH!! VH!!!
OH BOY!
RUSS! GO BACK TO BED!
al!

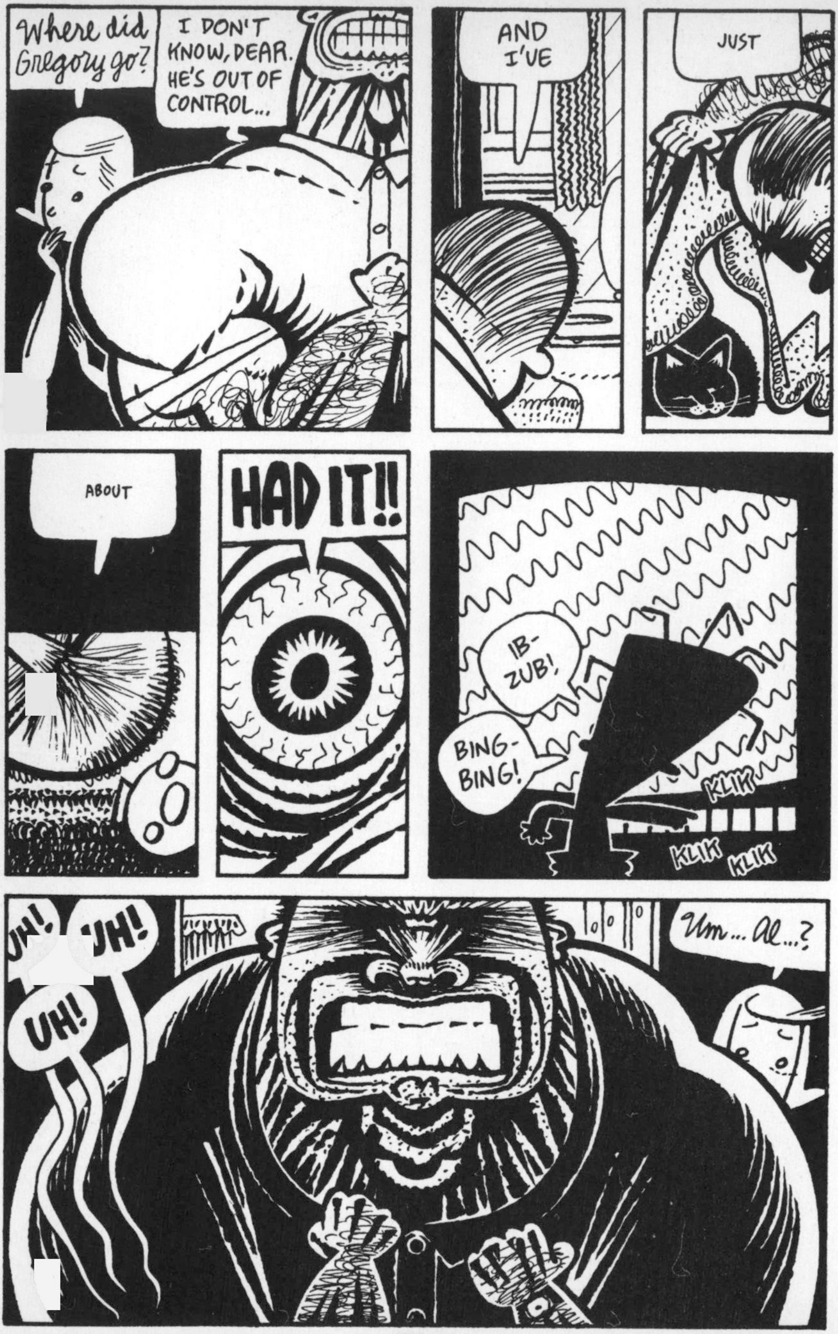
Where did Gregory go?
I DON'T KNOW, DEAR. HE'S OUT OF CONTROL...
AND I'VE
JUST
ABOUT
HAD IT!!
IB-ZUB!
BING-BING!
KLIK
KLIK
KLIK
UH!
UH!
UH!
Um... Al...?

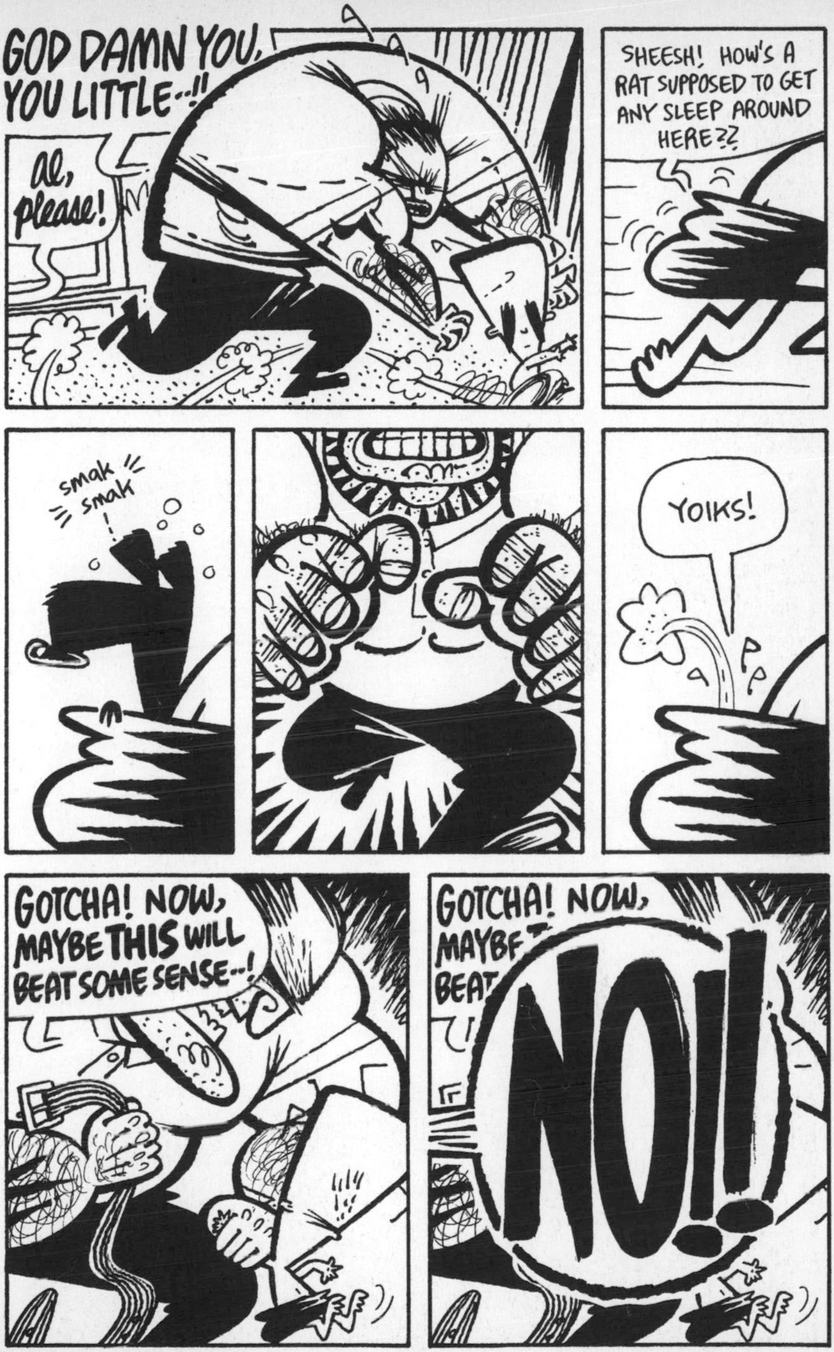
GOD DAMN YOU, YOU LITTLE--!!
al, please!
SHEESH! HOW'S A RAT SUPPOSED TO GET ANY SLEEP AROUND HERE??
smak smak !
YOIKS!
GOTCHA! NOW, MAYBE THIS WILL BEAT SOME SENSE--!
GOTCHA! NOW,
NO!!

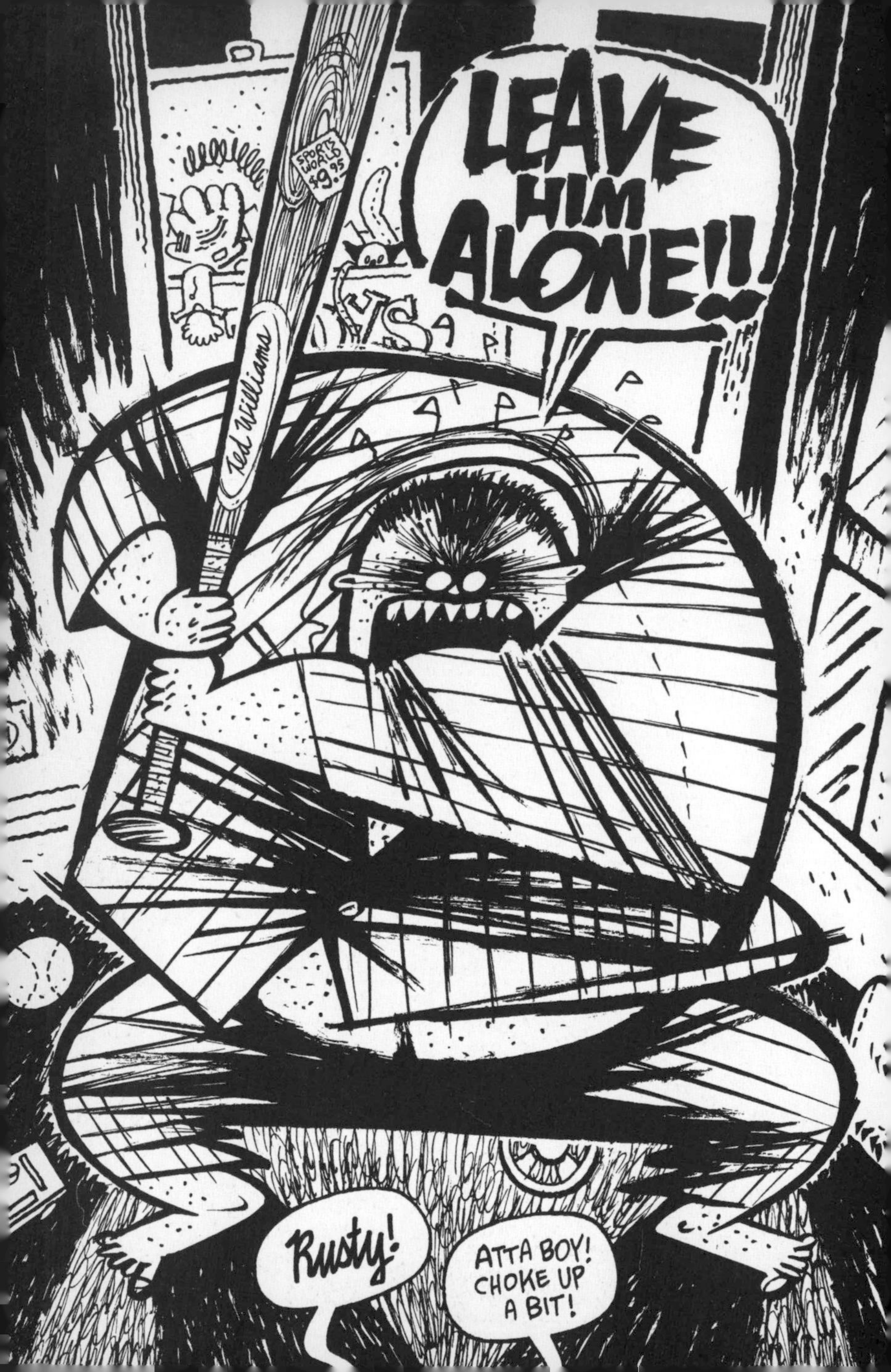

SPORTS WORLD $9.95
Ted Williams
LEAVE HIM ALONE!!
Rusty!
ATTA BOY! CHOKE UP A BIT!

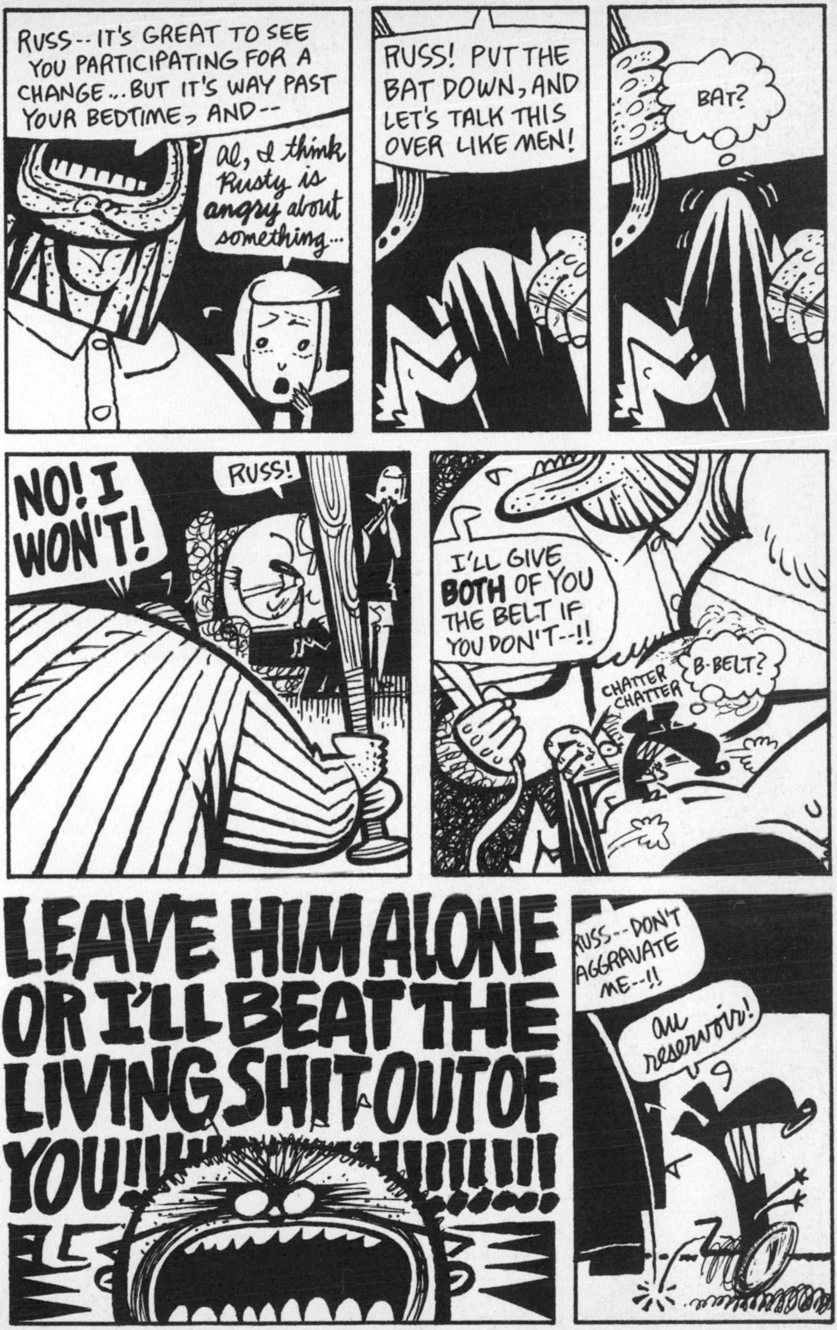
RUSS--IT'S GREAT TO SEE YOU PARTICIPATING FOR A CHANGE...BUT IT'S WAY PAST YOUR BEDTIME, AND--
Al, I think Rusty is angry about something...
RUSS! PUT THE BAT DOWN, AND LET'S TALK THIS OVER LIKE MEN!
BAT?
NO! I WON'T!
RUSS!
I'LL GIVE BOTH OF YOU THE BELT IF YOU DON'T--!!
CHATTER CHATTER
B-BELT?
LEAVE HIM ALONE OR I'LL BEAT THE LIVING SHIT OUT OF YOU!!!!!!!!!!!!!!!!!!
RUSS--DON'T AGGRAVATE ME--!!
au reservoir!

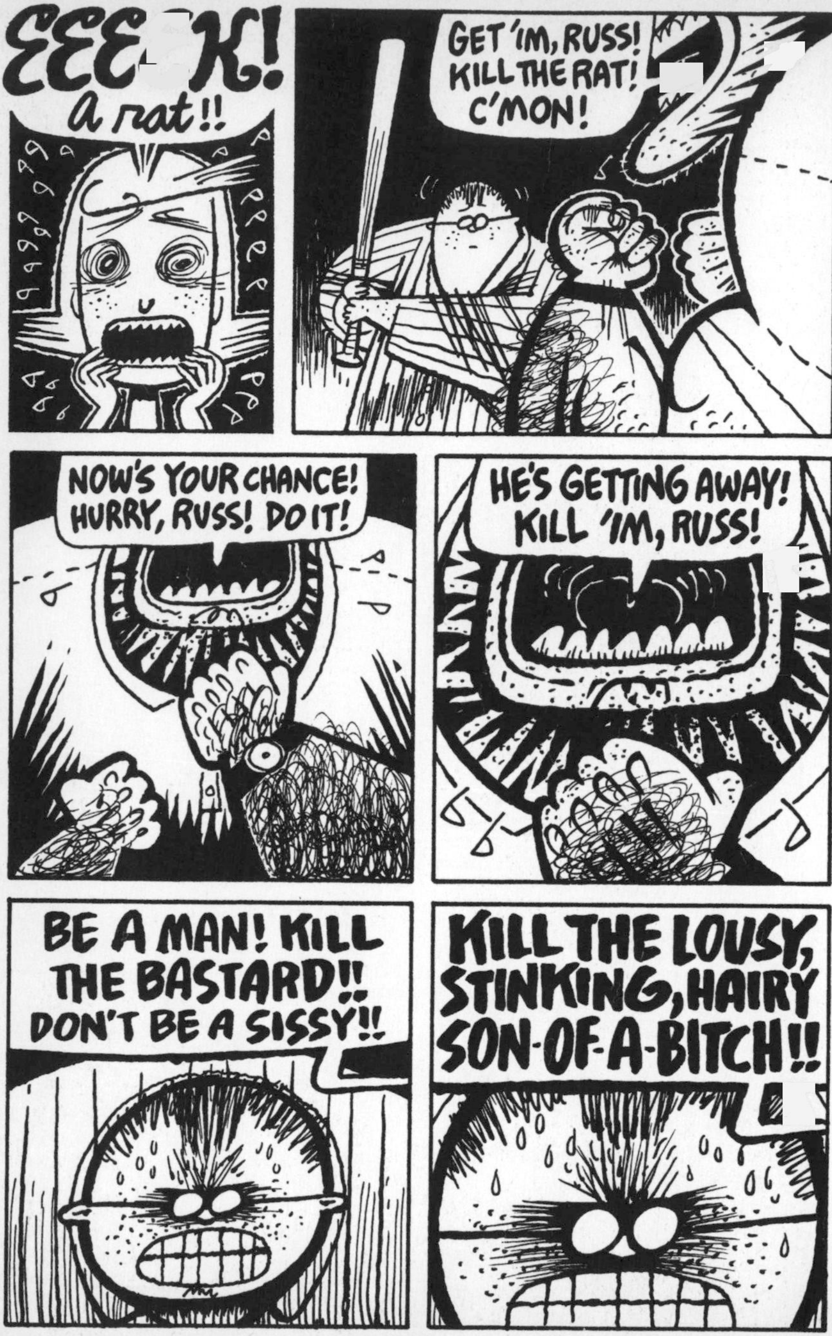
EEEK!
a rat!!
GET 'IM, RUSS! KILL THE RAT! C'MON!
NOW'S YOUR CHANCE! HURRY, RUSS! DO IT!
HE'S GETTING AWAY! KILL 'IM, RUSS!
BE A MAN! KILL THE BASTARD!! DON'T BE A SISSY!!
KILL THE LOUSY, STINKING, HAIRY SON-OF-A-BITCH!!

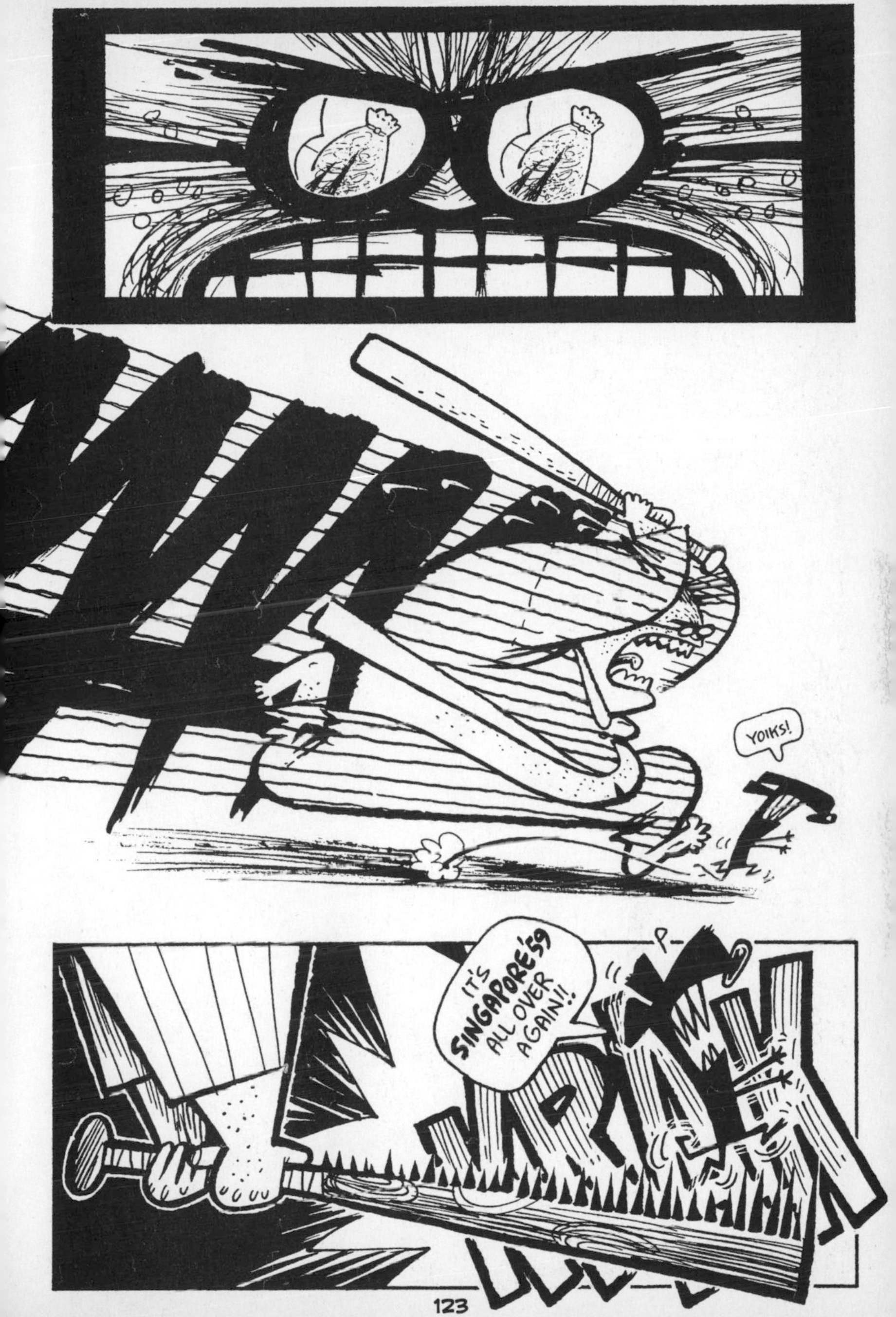
YOIKS!
IT'S SINGAPORE '59 ALL OVER AGAIN!!

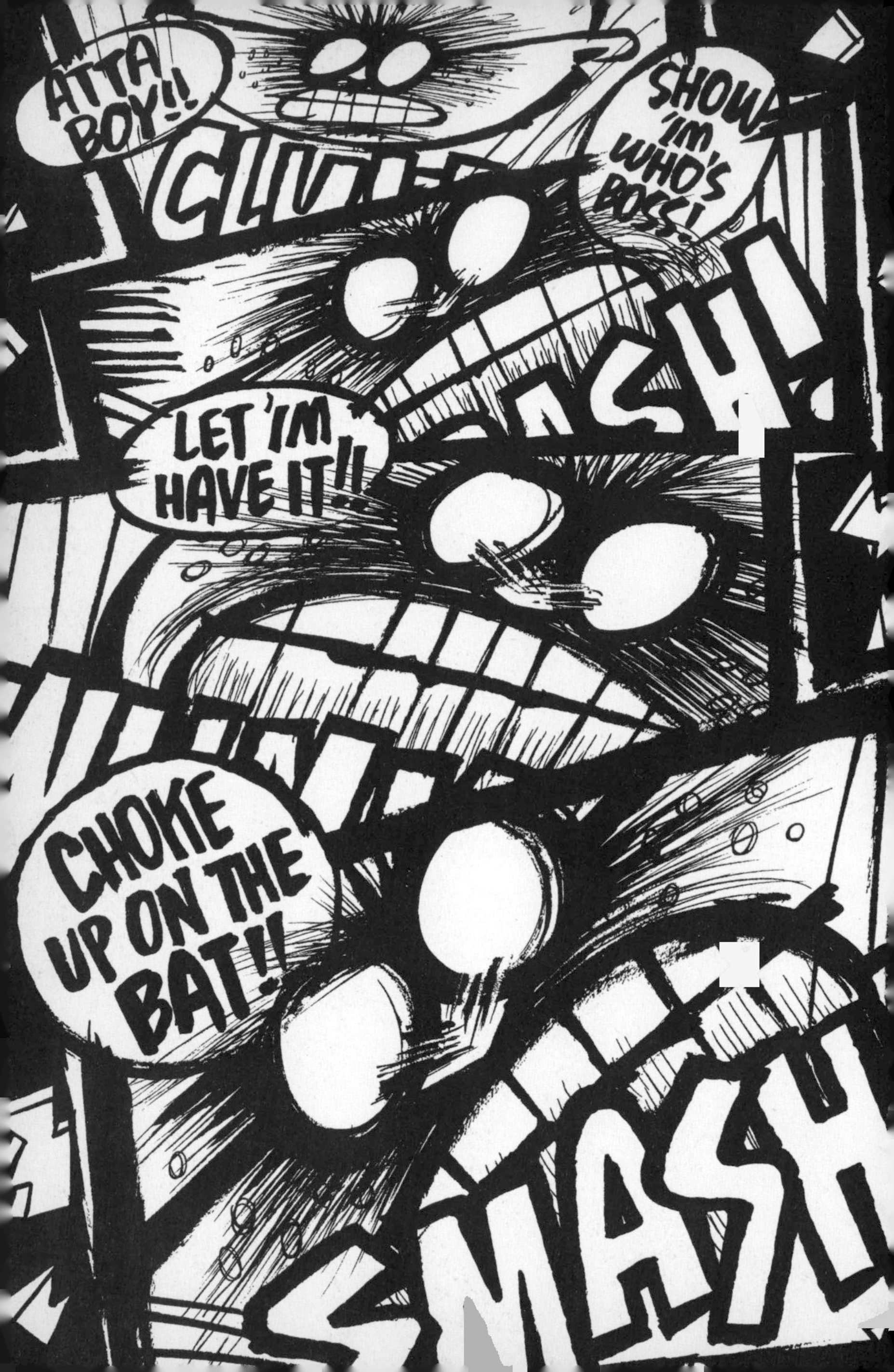
ATTA BOY!!
SHOW 'IM WHO'S BOSS!
LET 'IM HAVE IT!!
CHOKE UP ON THE BAT!!
SMASH

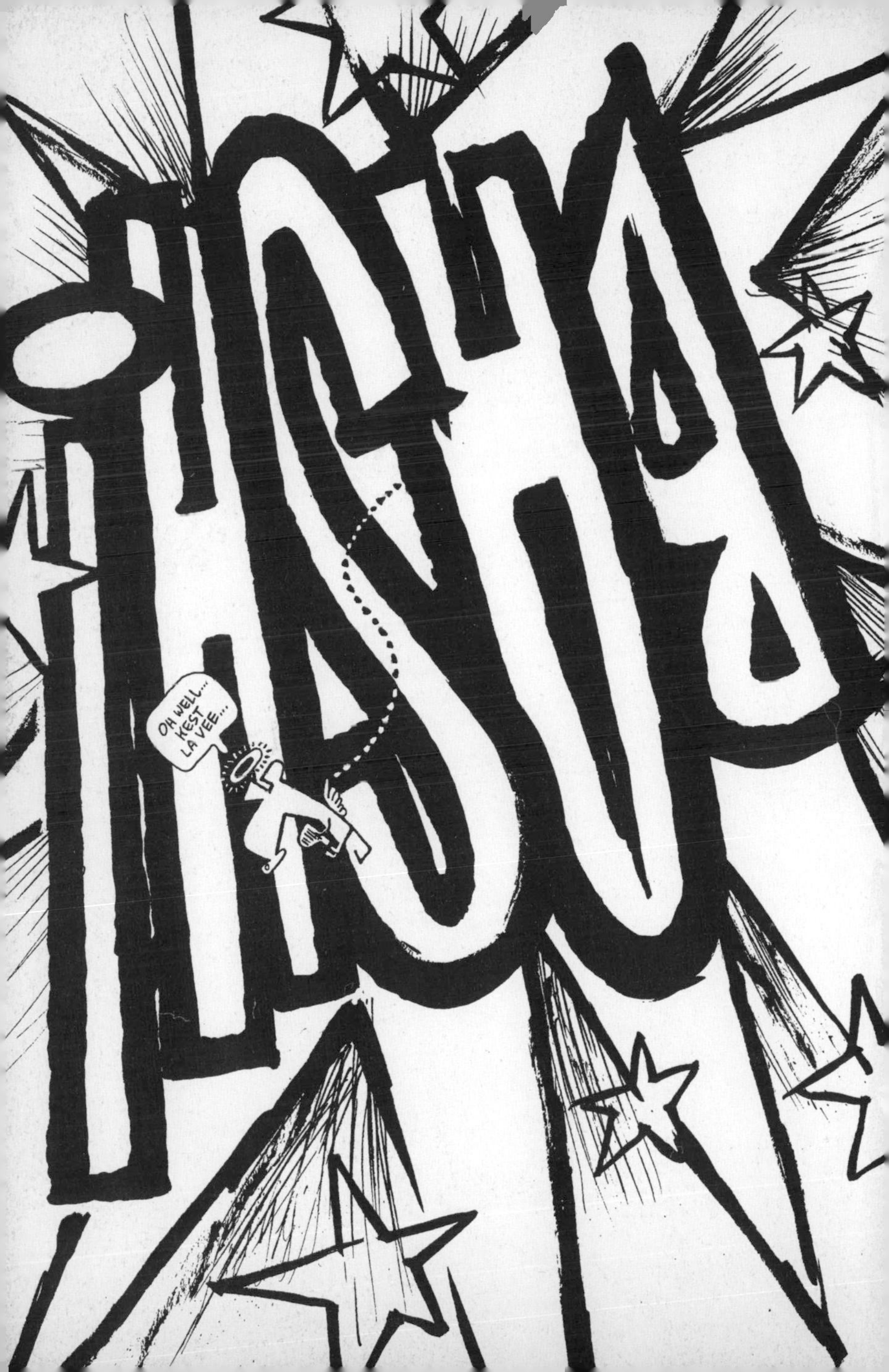
OH WELL... KEST LA VEE...

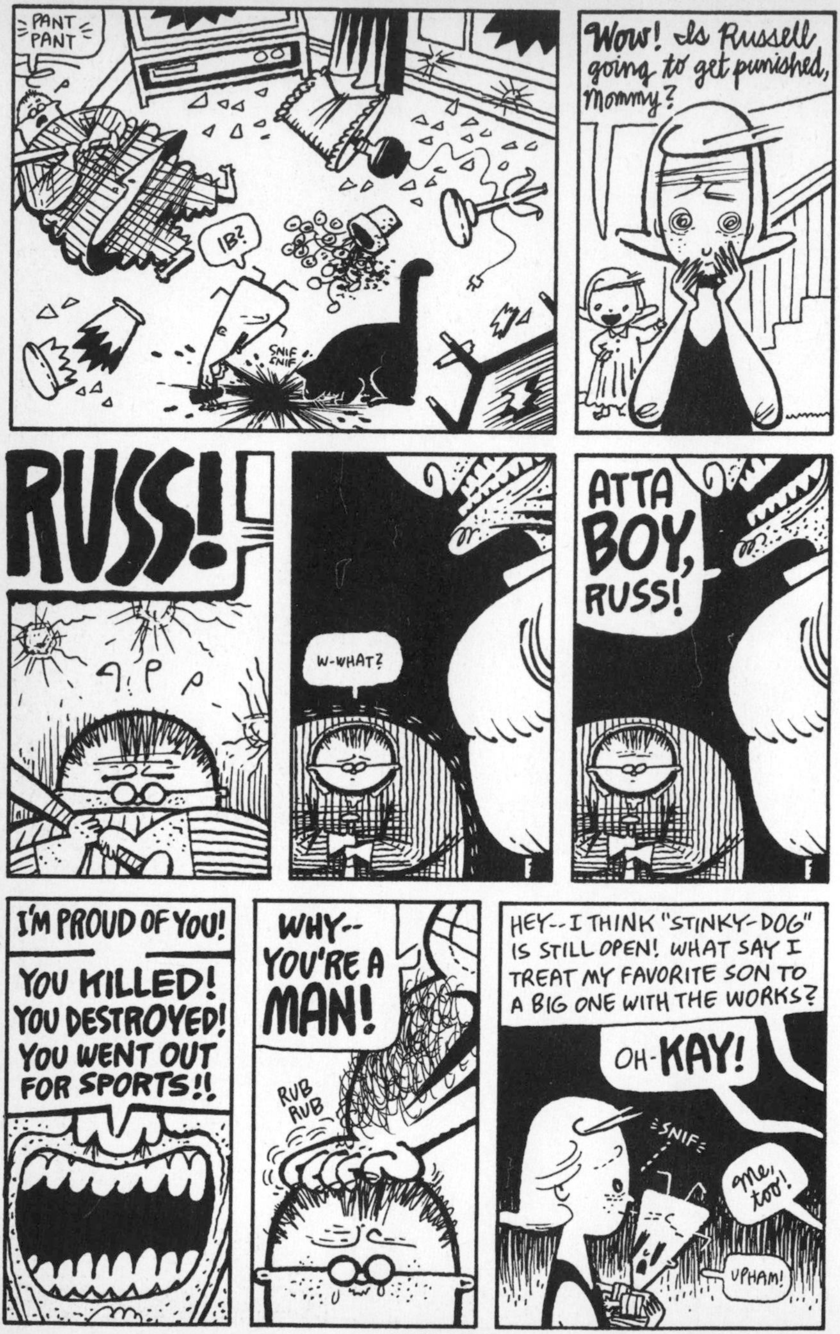

PANT PANT
IB?
SNIF SNIF
Wow! Is Russell going to get punished, Mommy?
RUSS!
W-WHAT?
ATTA BOY, RUSS!
I'M PROUD OF YOU!
YOU KILLED! YOU DESTROYED! YOU WENT OUT FOR SPORTS!!
WHY-- YOU'RE A MAN!
RUB RUB
HEY--I THINK "STINKY-DOG" IS STILL OPEN! WHAT SAY I TREAT MY FAVORITE SON TO A BIG ONE WITH THE WORKS?
OH-KAY!
SNIF
me, too!
UPHAM!

epilogue

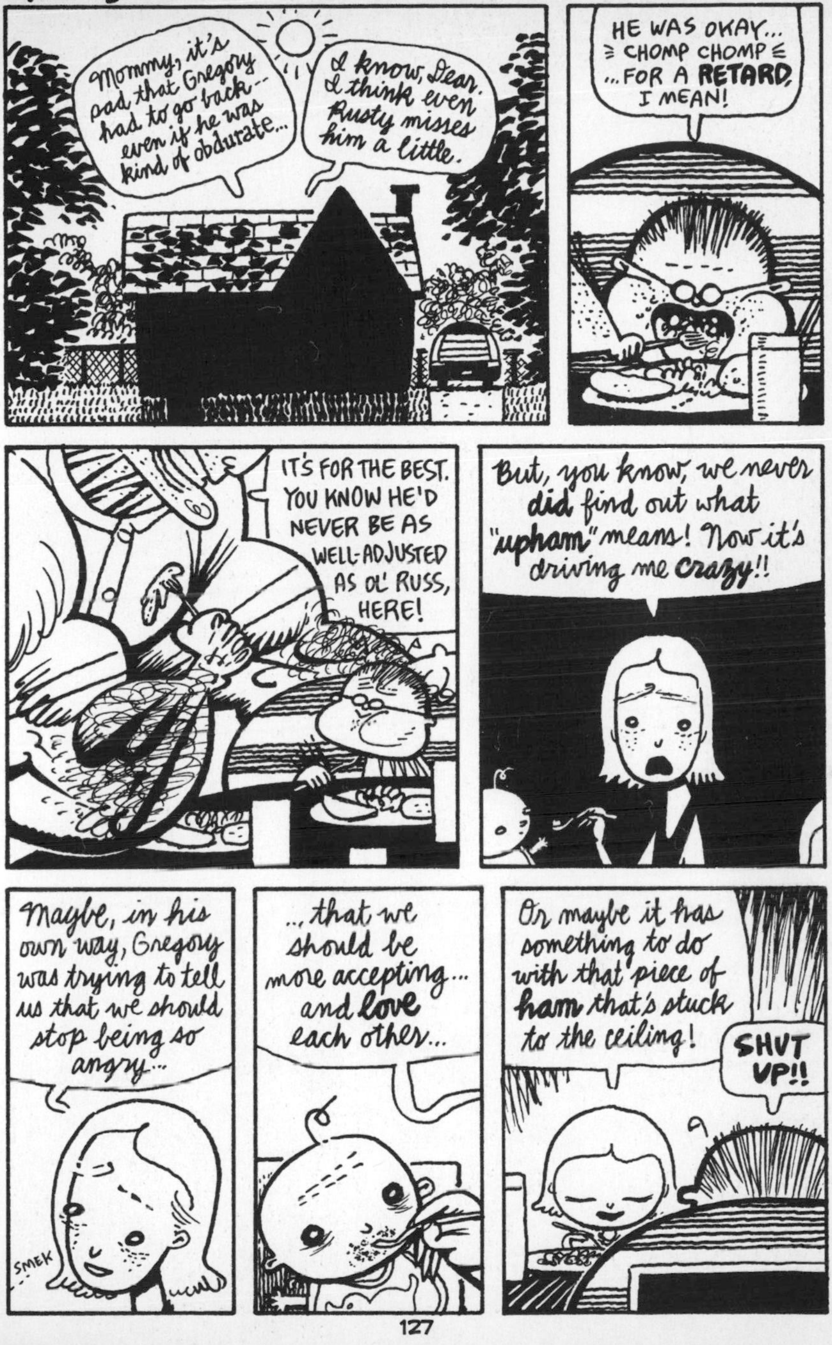
Mommy, it's sad that Gregory had to go back-- even if he was kind of obdurate...
I know, Dear. I think even Rusty misses him a little.
HE WAS OKAY... CHOMP CHOMP ...FOR A RETARD, I MEAN!
IT'S FOR THE BEST. YOU KNOW HE'D NEVER BE AS WELL-ADJUSTED AS OL' RUSS, HERE!
But, you know, we never did find out what "upham" means! Now it's driving me crazy!!
Maybe, in his own way, Gregory was trying to tell us that we should stop being so angry...
SMEK
...that we should be more accepting... and love each other...
Or maybe it has something to do with that piece of ham that's stuck to the ceiling!
SHUT UP!!

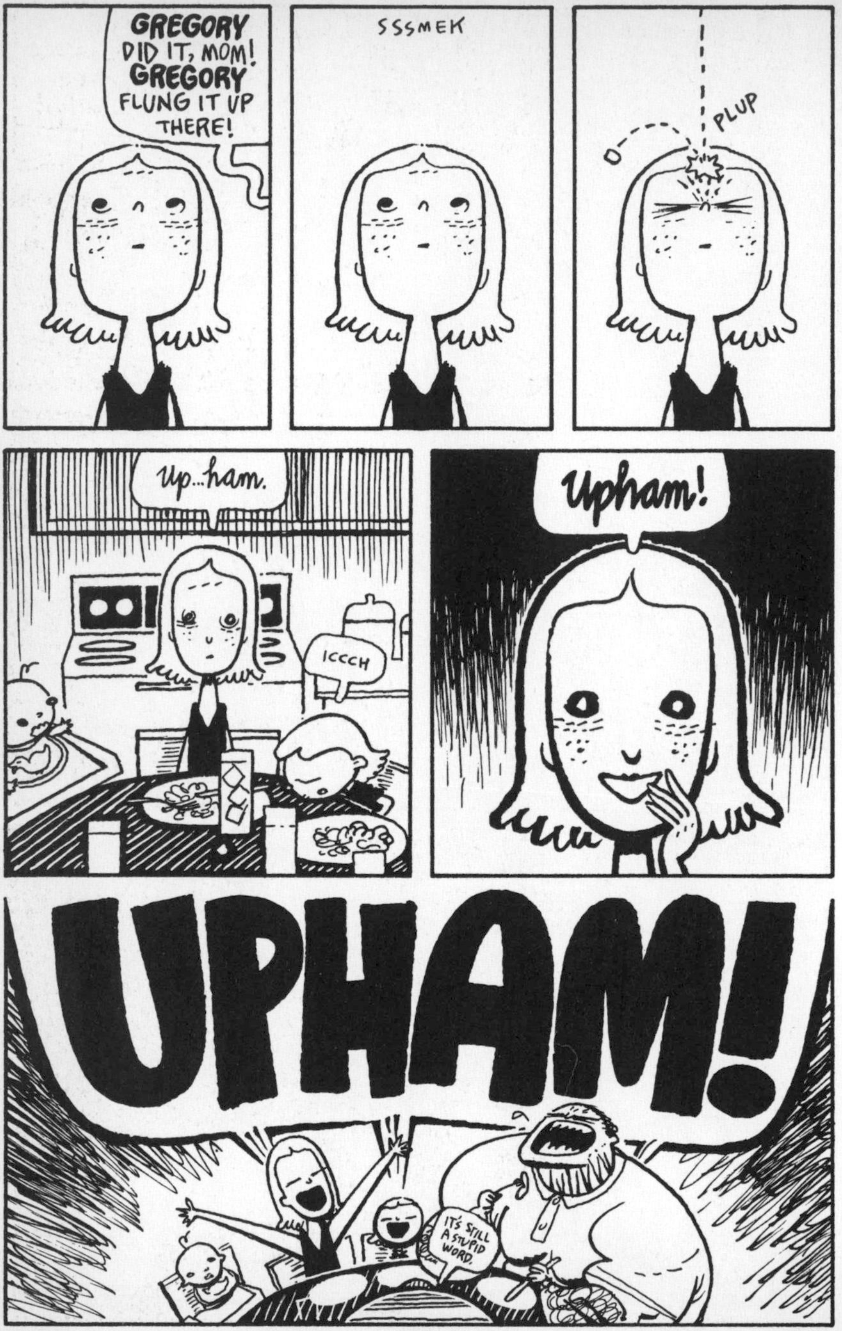

GREGORY DID IT, MOM! GREGORY FLUNG IT UP THERE!
SSSMEK
PLUP
Up...ham.
ICCCH
Upham!
UPHAM!
IT'S STILL A STUPID WORD.

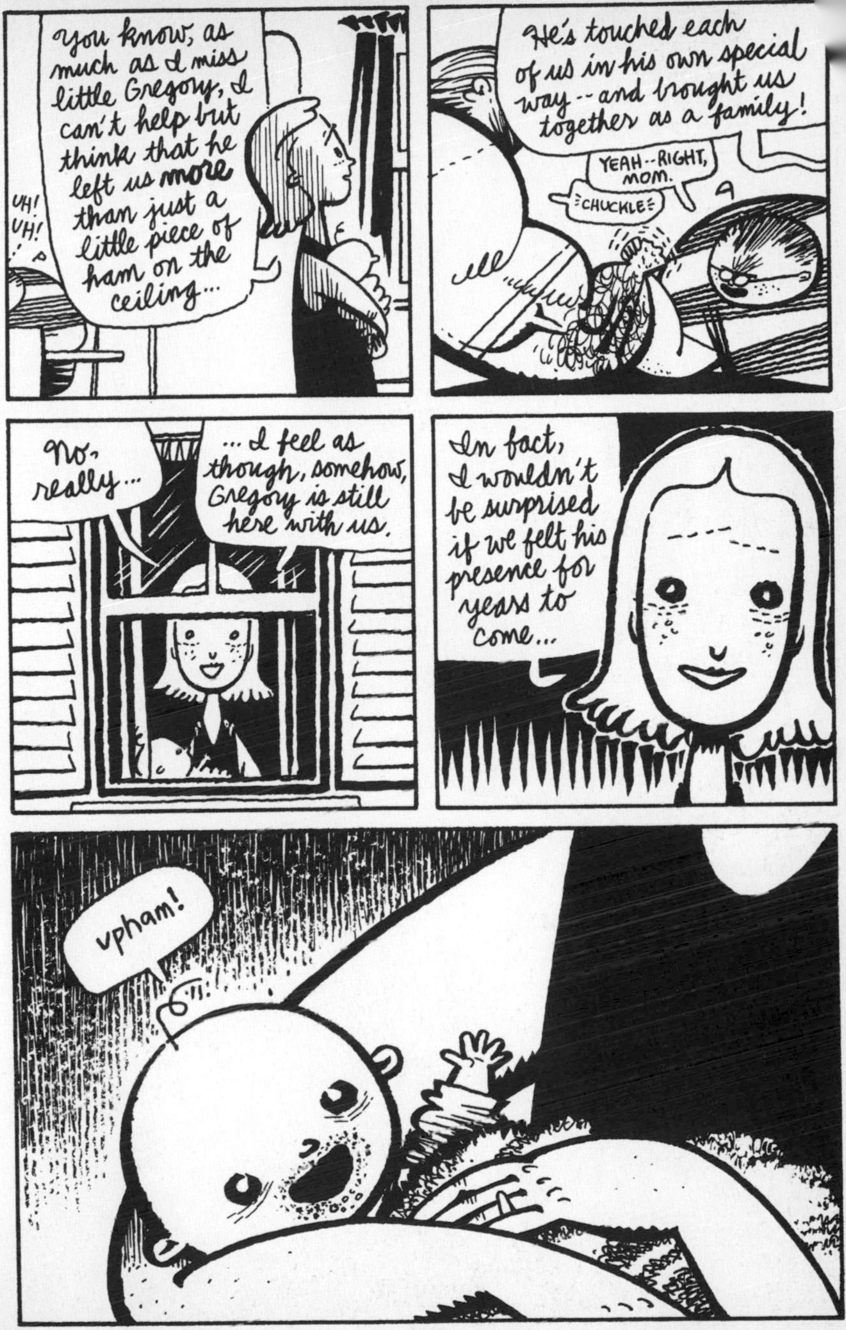
you know, as much as I miss little Gregory, I can't help but think that he left us **more** than just a little piece of ham on the ceiling...
UH! UH!
He's touched each of us in his own special way -- and brought us together as a family!
YEAH -- RIGHT, MOM.
CHUCKLE
No, really...
... I feel as though, somehow, Gregory is still here with us.
In fact, I wouldn't be surprised if we felt his presence for years to come...
vpham!

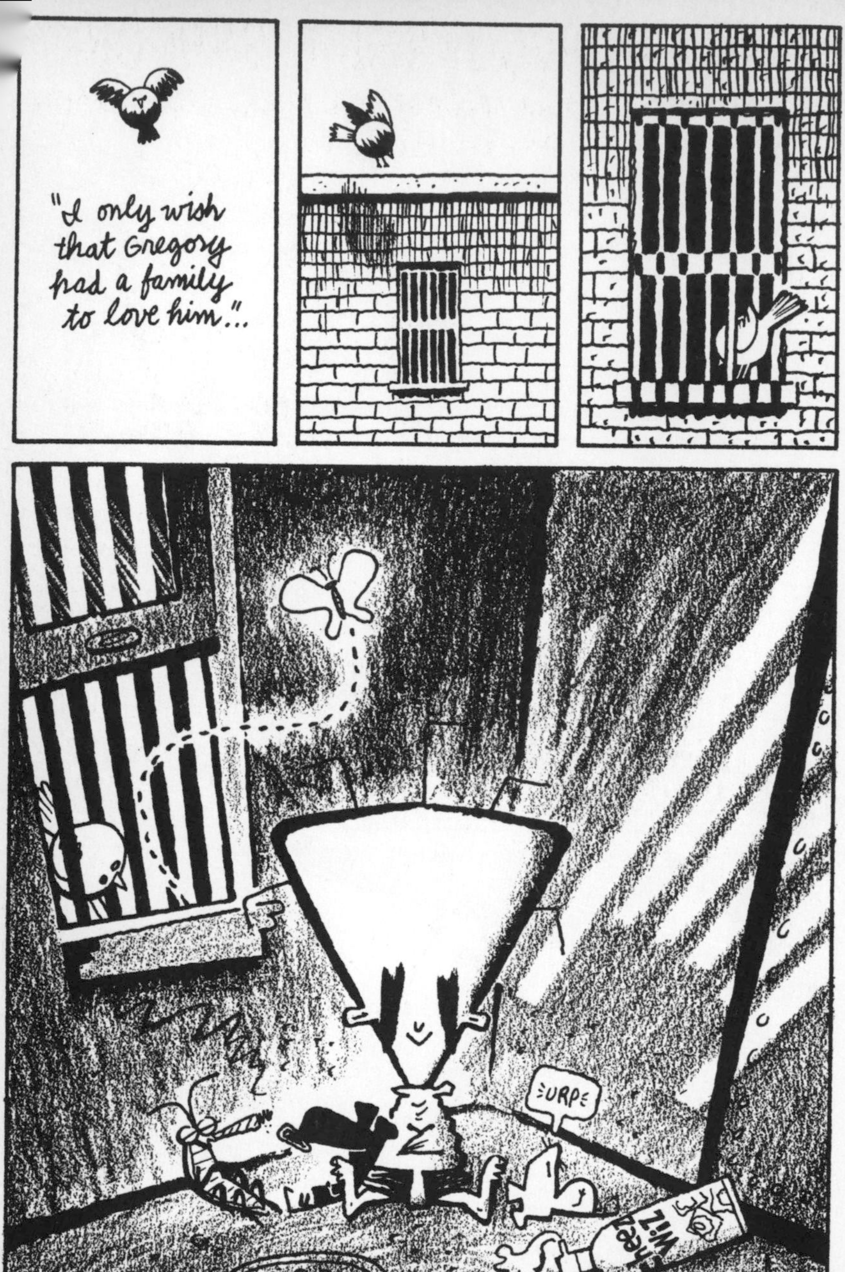
"I only wish that Gregory had a family to love him."...
URP
Cheez Wiz

# THE UNDISCOVERED GREGORY

## UNPUBLISHED STRIPS AND PROMOTIONAL PIECES FROM CREATOR

## Marc Hempel

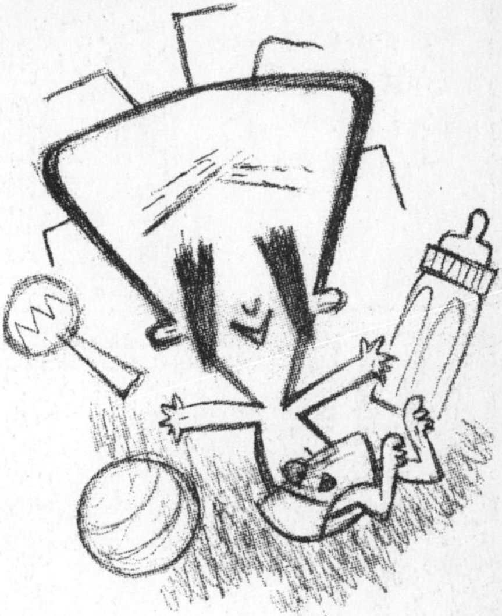

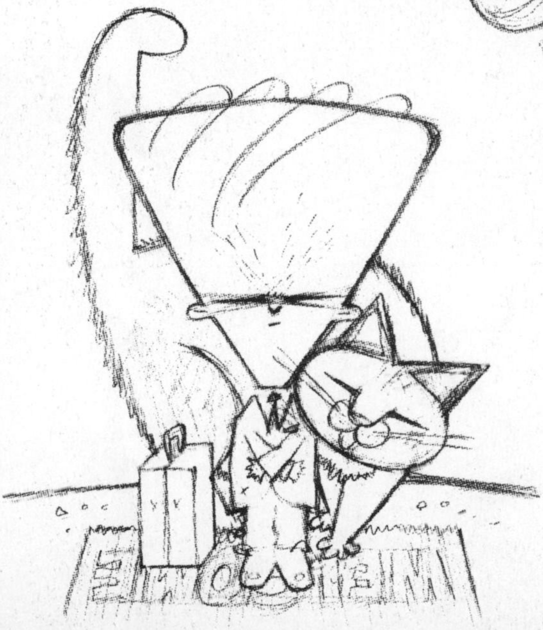

These two small drawings were intended to be used as promotional art for *Gregory IV: Fat Boy* (for an "adoption notice" that tied in with the storyline) — but they were nixed in favor of another piece. They are presented here in unfinished pencil form.

# he SHOW by MARC HEMPEL

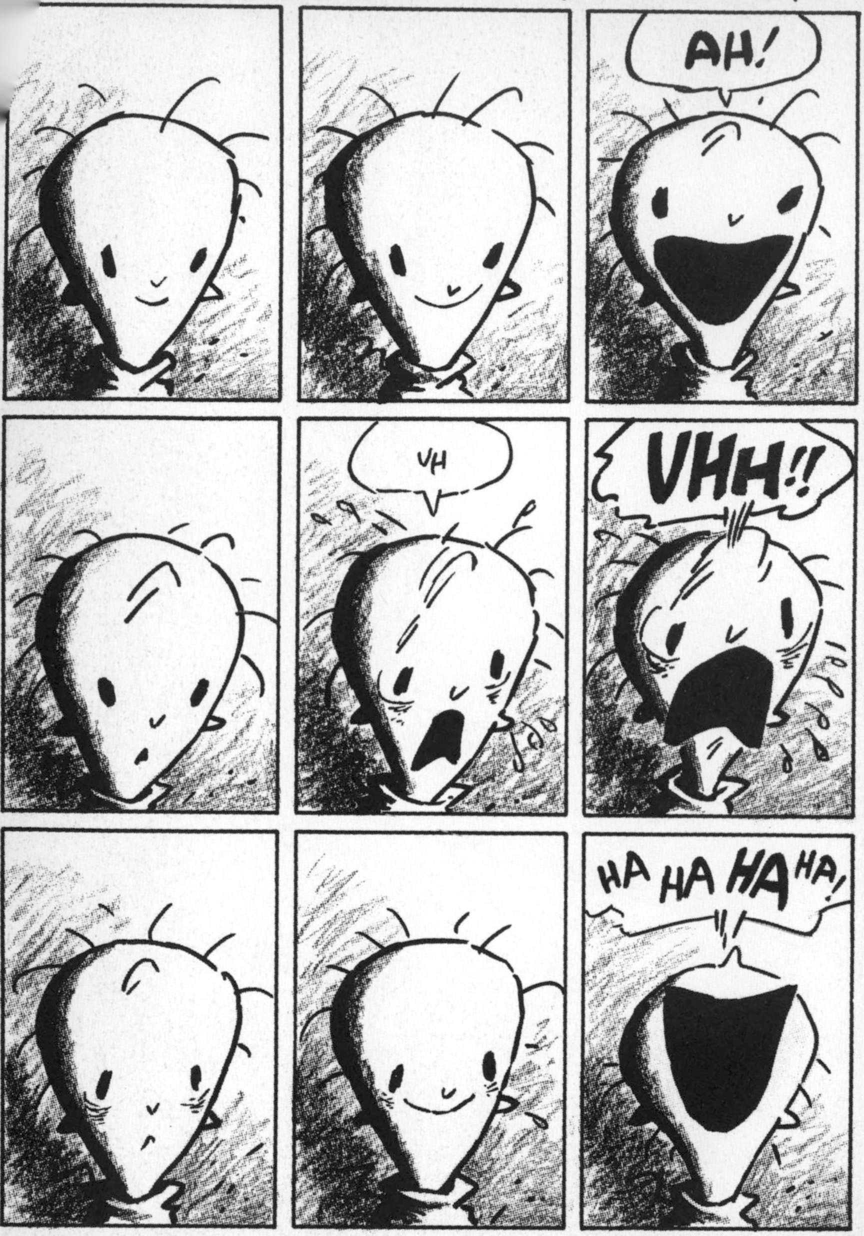

AH!
UH
UHH!!
HA HA HA HA!

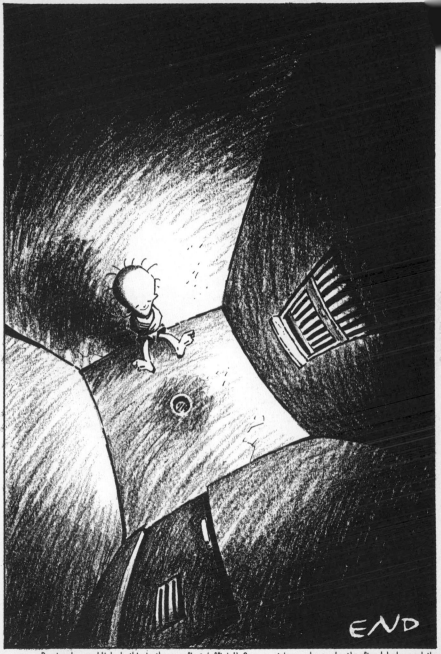

END

Previously unpublished, this is the very first (official) Gregory strip — drawn shortly after I had named the character and finalized his look. It was part of the original proposal that I sent to DC Comics in 1988.

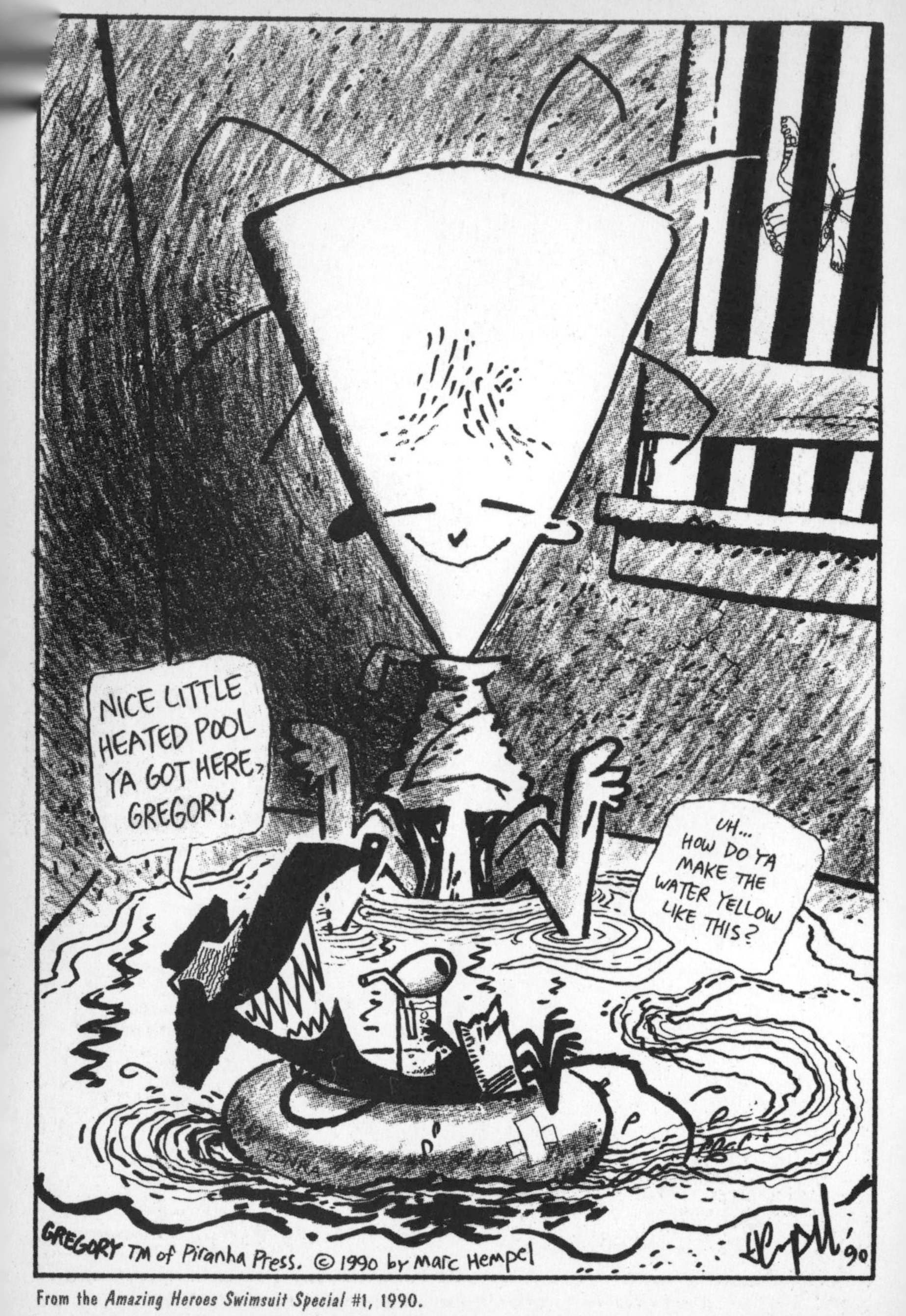
NICE LITTLE HEATED POOL YA GOT HERE, GREGORY.
UH... HOW DO YA MAKE THE WATER YELLOW LIKE THIS?
TONKA
GREGORY TM of Piranha Press. © 1990 by Marc Hempel
Hempel '90

From the *Amazing Heroes Swimsuit Special* #1, 1990.

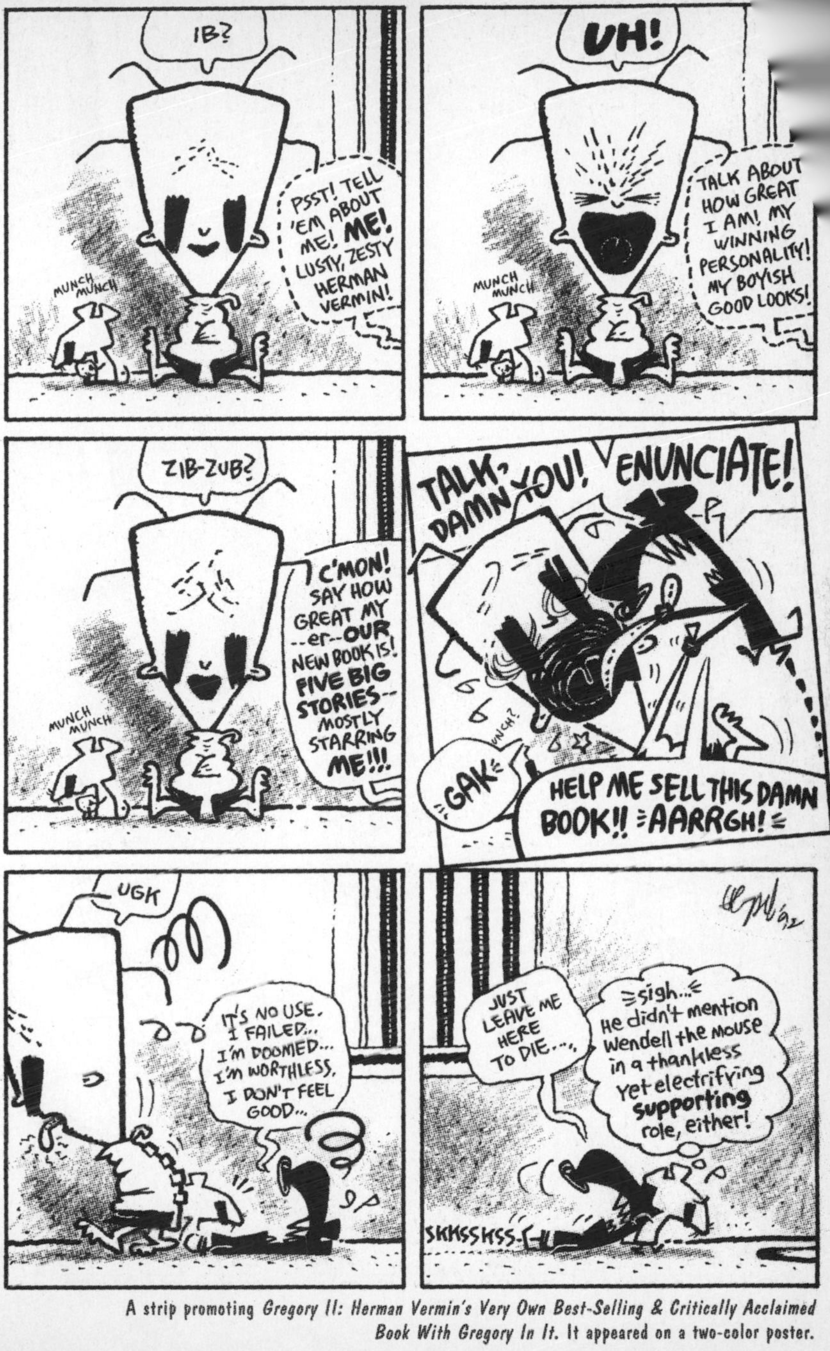
IB?
PSST! TELL 'EM ABOUT ME! ME! LUSTY, ZESTY HERMAN VERMIN!
MUNCH MUNCH
UH!
TALK ABOUT HOW GREAT I AM! MY WINNING PERSONALITY! MY BOYISH GOOD LOOKS!
MUNCH MUNCH
ZIB-ZUB?
C'MON! SAY HOW GREAT MY --er--OUR NEW BOOK IS! FIVE BIG STORIES--MOSTLY STARRING ME!!!
MUNCH MUNCH
TALK, DAMN YOU! ENUNCIATE!
GAK
HELP ME SELL THIS DAMN BOOK!! AARRGH!
UGK
IT'S NO USE. I FAILED... I'M DOOMED... I'M WORTHLESS. I DON'T FEEL GOOD...
JUST LEAVE ME HERE TO DIE...
sigh... He didn't mention Wendell the mouse in a thankless yet electrifying supporting role, either!
SKKSSKSS

A strip promoting *Gregory II: Herman Vermin's Very Own Best-Selling & Critically Acclaimed Book With Gregory In It*. It appeared on a two-color poster.

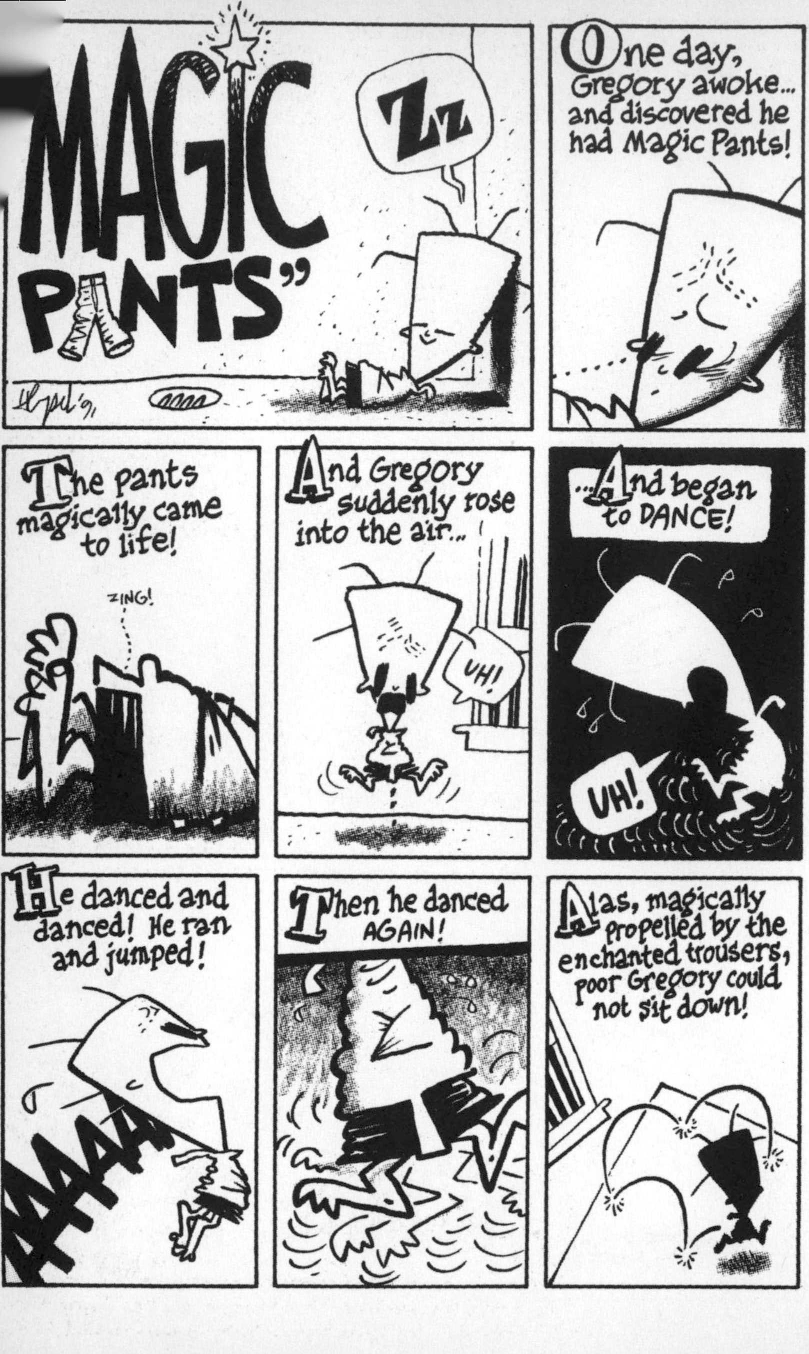
"MAGIC PANTS"
Zz
One day, Gregory awoke... and discovered he had Magic Pants!
The pants magically came to life!
ZING!
And Gregory suddenly rose into the air...
UH!
...And began to DANCE!
UH!
He danced and danced! He ran and jumped!
Then he danced AGAIN!
Alas, magically propelled by the enchanted trousers, poor Gregory could not sit down!

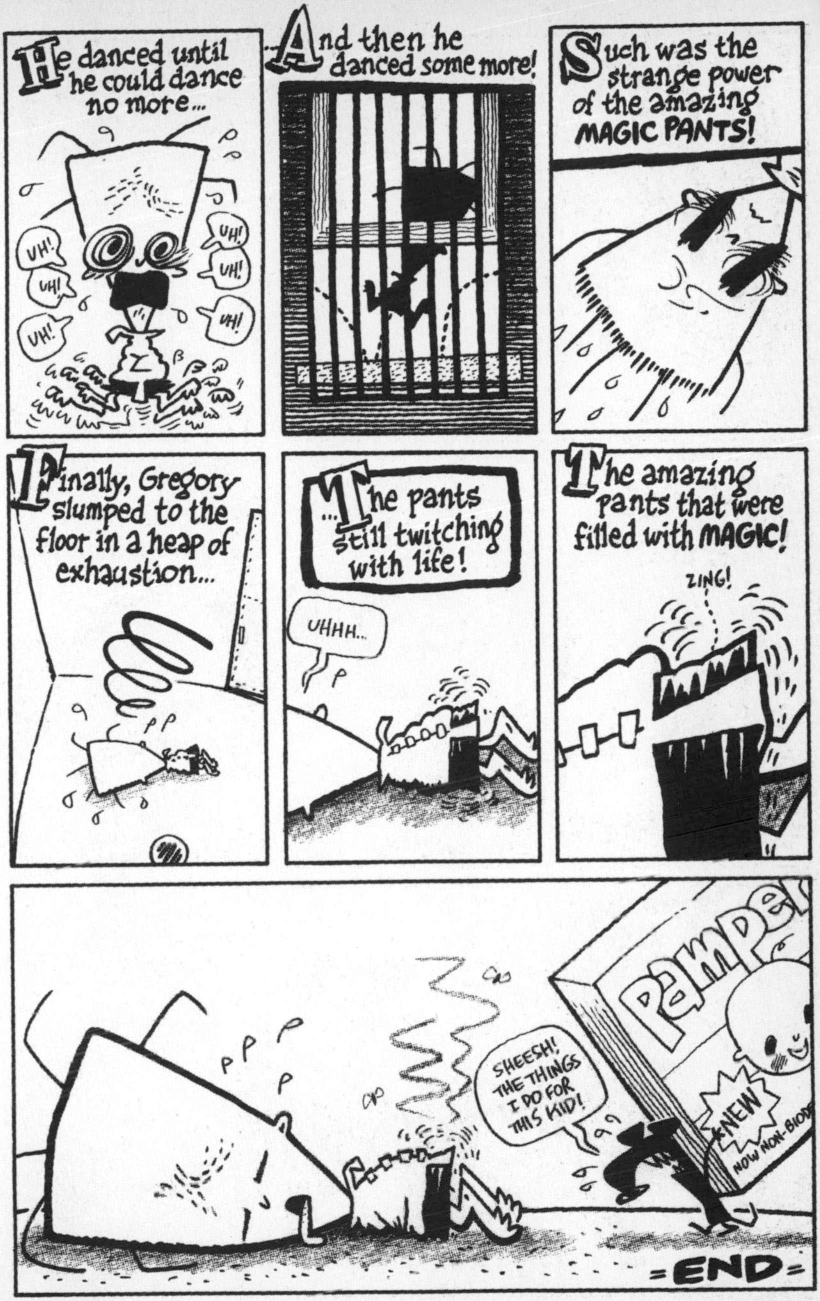
He danced until he could dance no more...
UH!
UH!
UH!
UH!
UH!
UH!
And then he danced some more!
Such was the strange power of the amazing MAGIC PANTS!
Finally, Gregory slumped to the floor in a heap of exhaustion...
...The pants still twitching with life!
UHHH...
The amazing pants that were filled with MAGIC!
ZING!
SHEESH! THE THINGS I DO FOR THIS KID!
NEW
=END=

Dated 1991, this unpublished strip was to appear in a later *Gregory* volume, but I felt that the ending needed more clarification (problem rectified, 2004).

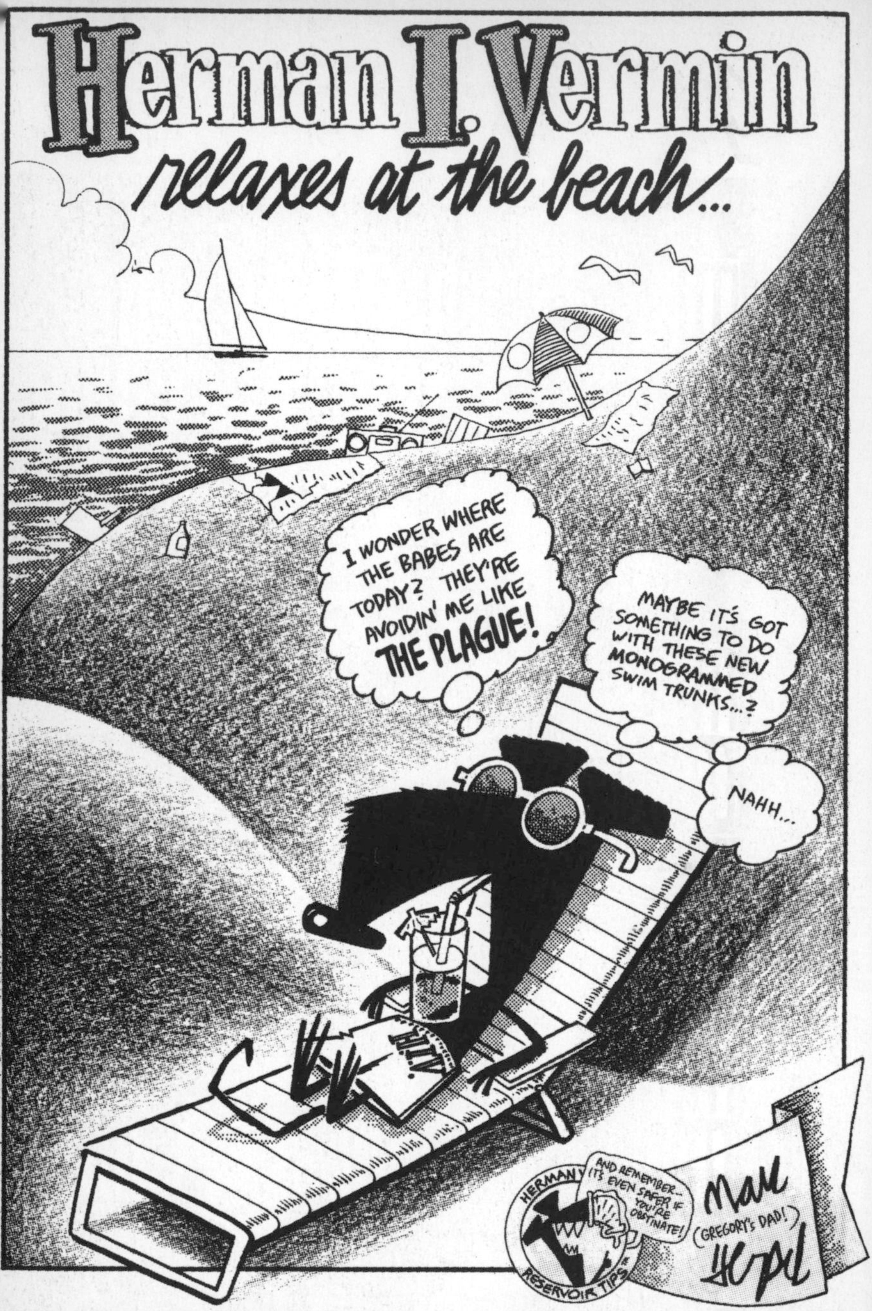
Herman I. Vermin
relaxes at the beach...
I WONDER WHERE THE BABES ARE TODAY? THEY'RE AVOIDIN' ME LIKE THE PLAGUE!
MAYBE IT'S GOT SOMETHING TO DO WITH THESE NEW MONOGRAMMED SWIM TRUNKS...?
NAHH...
HERMAN'S RESERVOIR TIPS
AND REMEMBER... IT'S EVEN SAFER IF YOU'RE OBSTINATE!
Marc (GREGORY'S DAD!) Hempel
GREGORY ©1992 by MARC HEMPEL. TM of PIRANHA PRESS.

From the *Amazing Heroes Swimsuit Special* #3, 1992.

# Gregory Learns a New Word

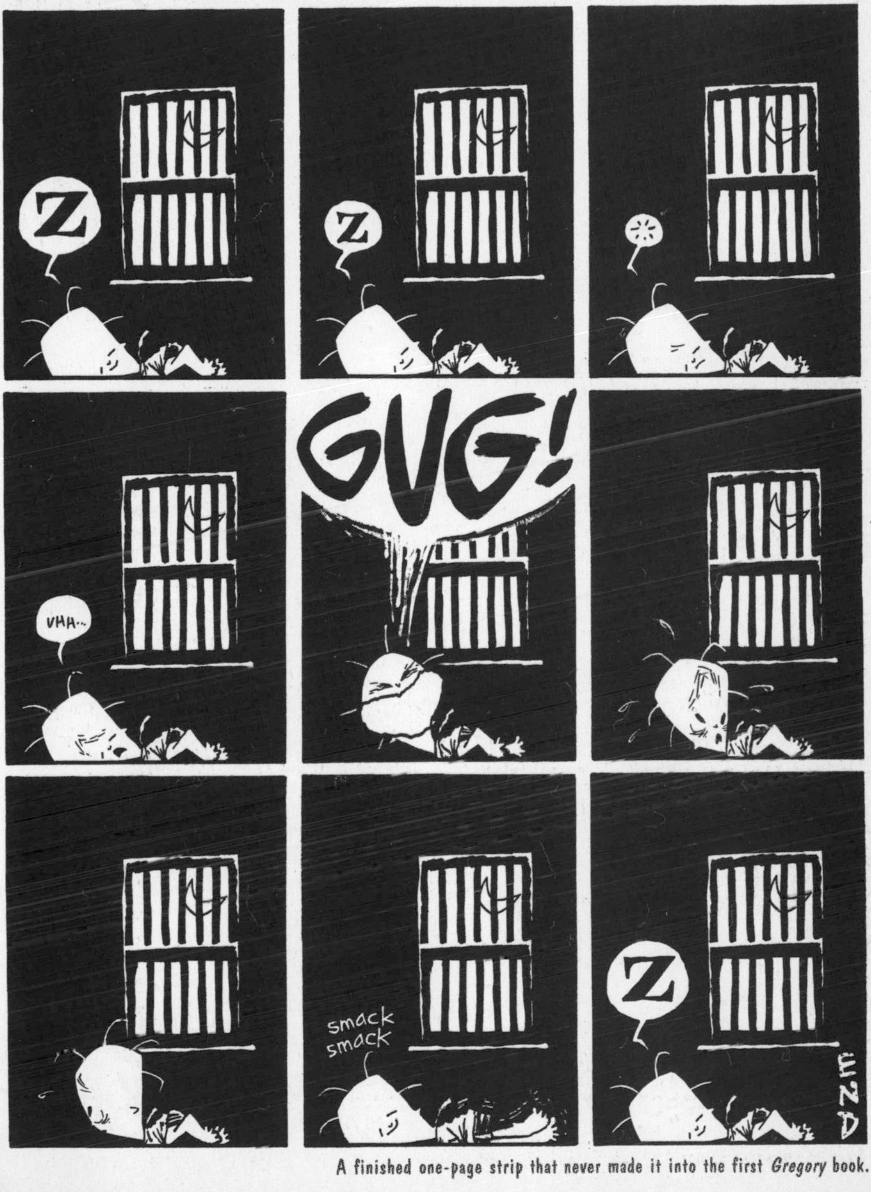
Z
Z
VHA...
GUG!
smack
smack
Z
EZD

A finished one-page strip that never made it into the first *Gregory* book.

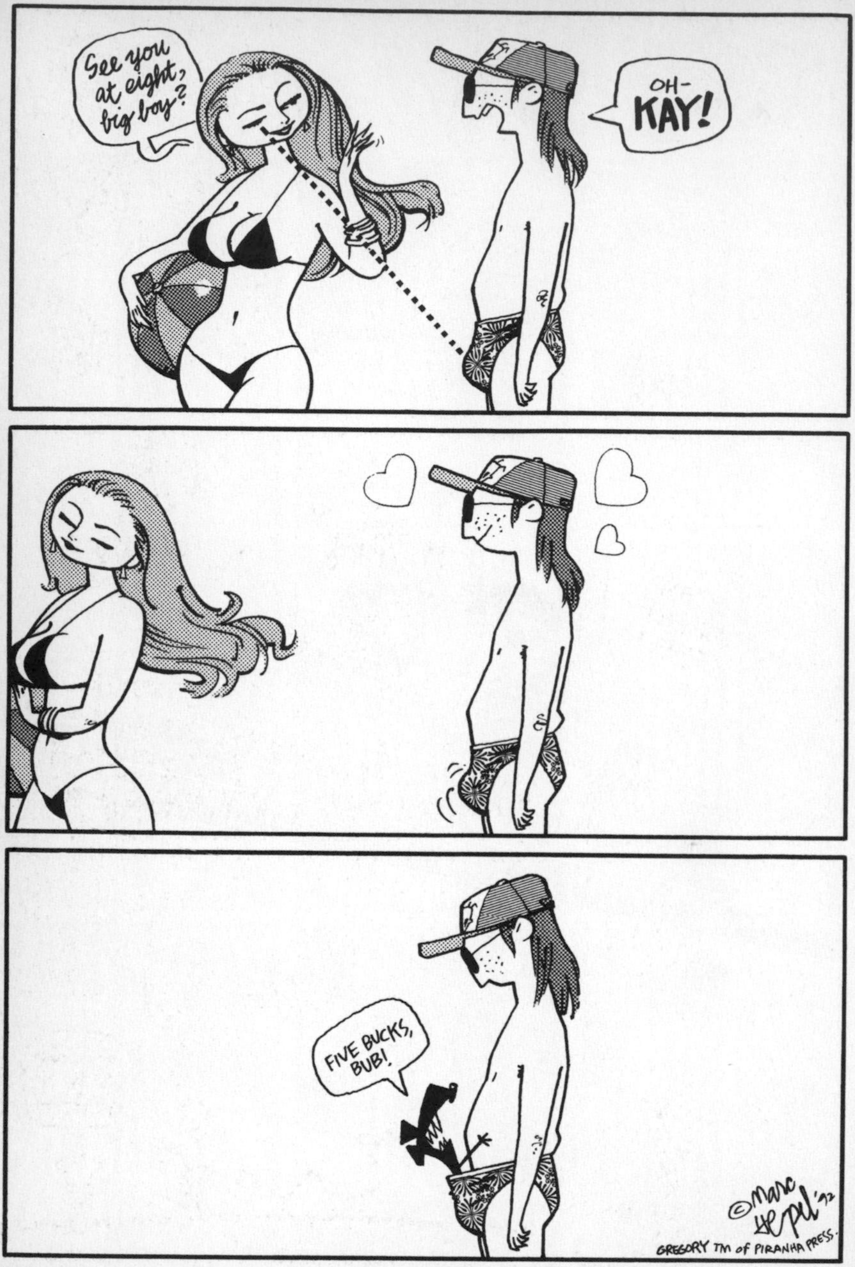
See you at eight, big boy?
OH-KAY!
FIVE BUCKS, BUB!
©Marc Hempel '92
GREGORY TM of PIRANHA PRESS.

From the *Amazing Heroes Swimsuit Special* #3, 1992. The original caption: "Gregory's pal, Herman Vermin (star of the almost-here *Gregory II*), searched long and hard for this summer job: a position as a private... well... something-or-other. And he moonlighted as a 'lice-guard!'"

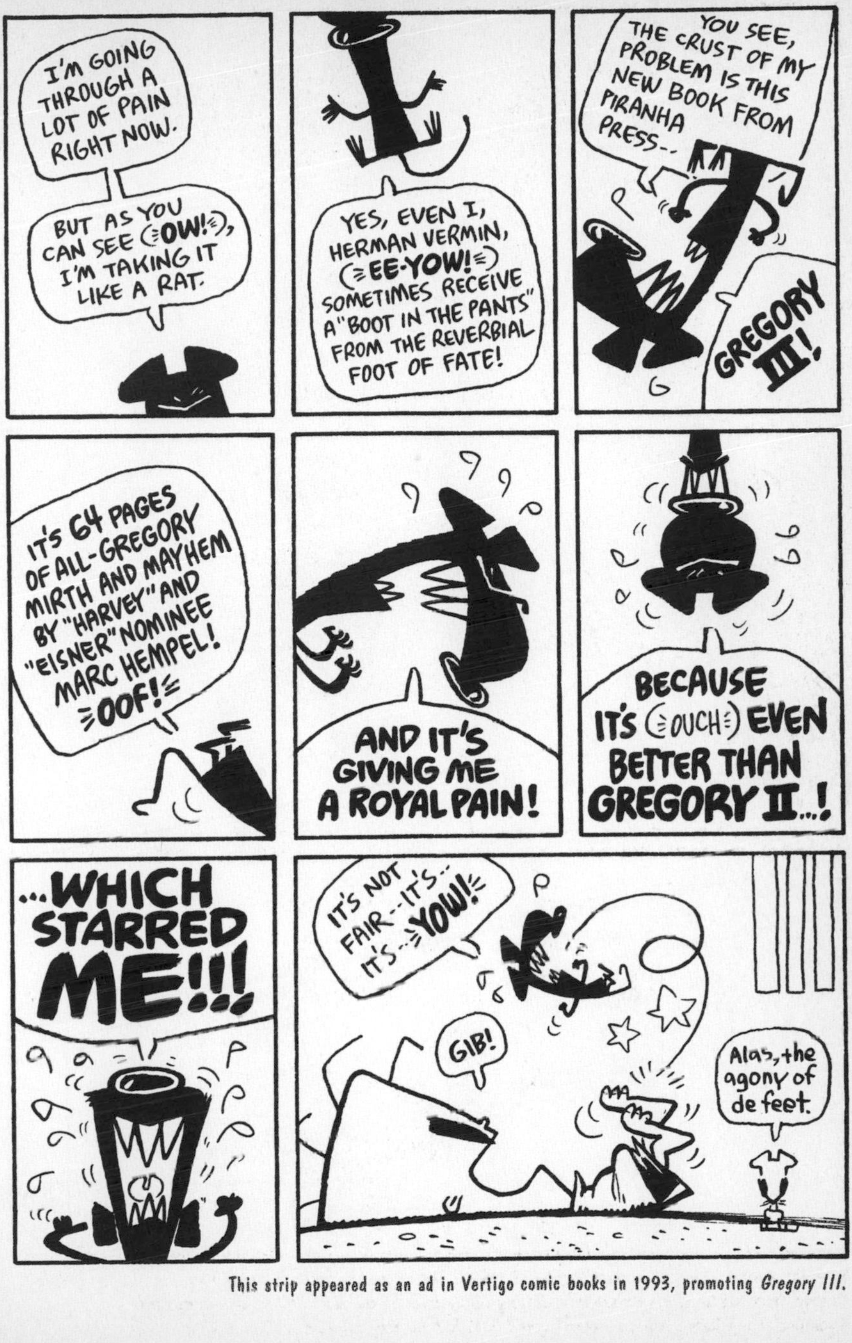
I'M GOING THROUGH A LOT OF PAIN RIGHT NOW.
BUT AS YOU CAN SEE (OW!), I'M TAKING IT LIKE A RAT.
YES, EVEN I, HERMAN VERMIN, (EE-YOW!) SOMETIMES RECEIVE A "BOOT IN THE PANTS" FROM THE REVERBIAL FOOT OF FATE!
YOU SEE, THE CRUST OF MY PROBLEM IS THIS NEW BOOK FROM PIRANHA PRESS--
GREGORY III!
IT'S 64 PAGES OF ALL-GREGORY MIRTH AND MAYHEM BY "HARVEY" AND "EISNER" NOMINEE MARC HEMPEL! OOF!
AND IT'S GIVING ME A ROYAL PAIN!
BECAUSE IT'S (OUCH) EVEN BETTER THAN GREGORY II...!
...WHICH STARRED ME!!!
IT'S NOT FAIR--IT'S.. IT'S.. YOW!
GIB!
Alas, the agony of de feet.

This strip appeared as an ad in Vertigo comic books in 1993, promoting *Gregory III*.

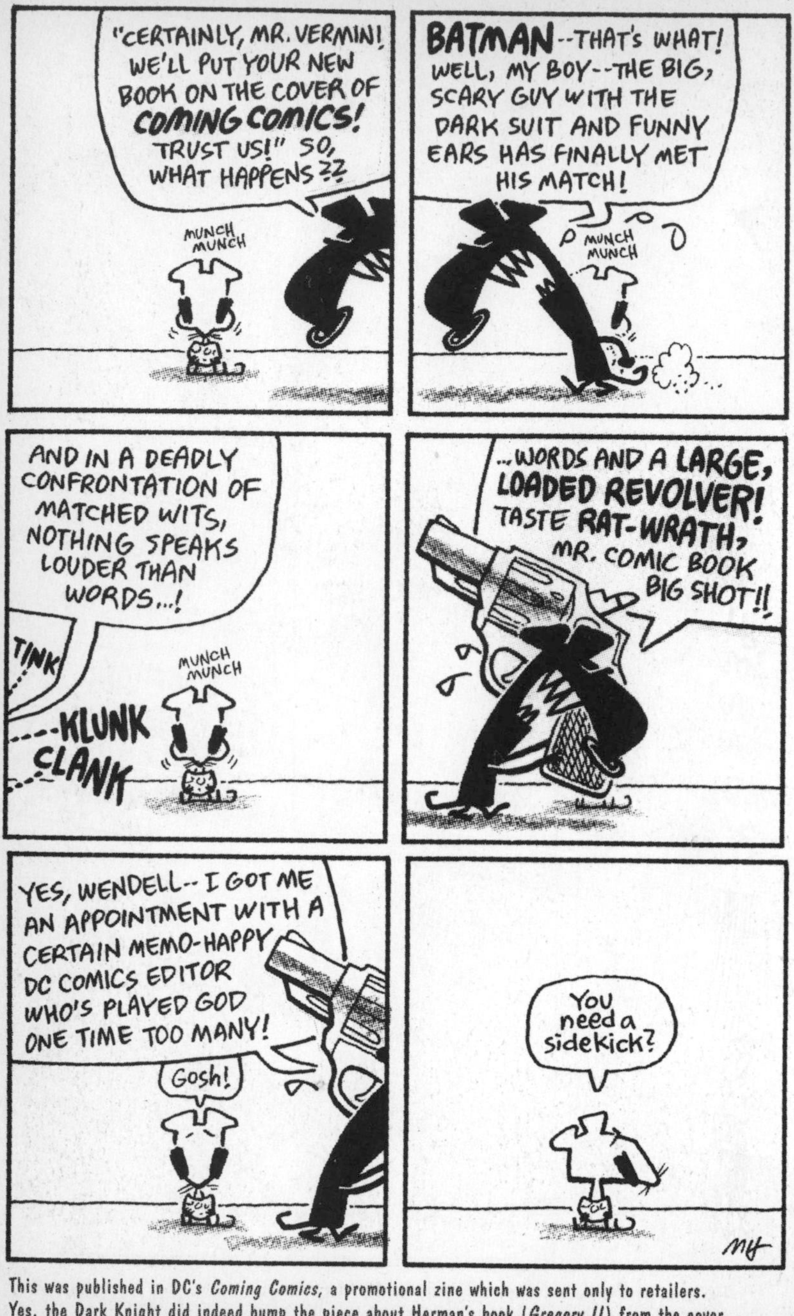
"CERTAINLY, MR. VERMIN! WE'LL PUT YOUR NEW BOOK ON THE COVER OF COMING COMICS! TRUST US!" SO, WHAT HAPPENS ??
MUNCH MUNCH
BATMAN--THAT'S WHAT! WELL, MY BOY--THE BIG, SCARY GUY WITH THE DARK SUIT AND FUNNY EARS HAS FINALLY MET HIS MATCH!
MUNCH MUNCH
AND IN A DEADLY CONFRONTATION OF MATCHED WITS, NOTHING SPEAKS LOUDER THAN WORDS...!
TINK
KLUNK
CLANK
MUNCH MUNCH
...WORDS AND A LARGE, LOADED REVOLVER! TASTE RAT-WRATH, MR. COMIC BOOK BIG SHOT!!
YES, WENDELL-- I GOT ME AN APPOINTMENT WITH A CERTAIN MEMO-HAPPY DC COMICS EDITOR WHO'S PLAYED GOD ONE TIME TOO MANY!
Gosh!
You need a sidekick?
MH

This was published in DC's *Coming Comics,* a promotional zine which was sent only to retailers. Yes, the Dark Knight did indeed bump the piece about Herman's book (*Gregory II*) from the cover. Strangely enough, the Batman book in question was titled... *Seduction of the Gun*!

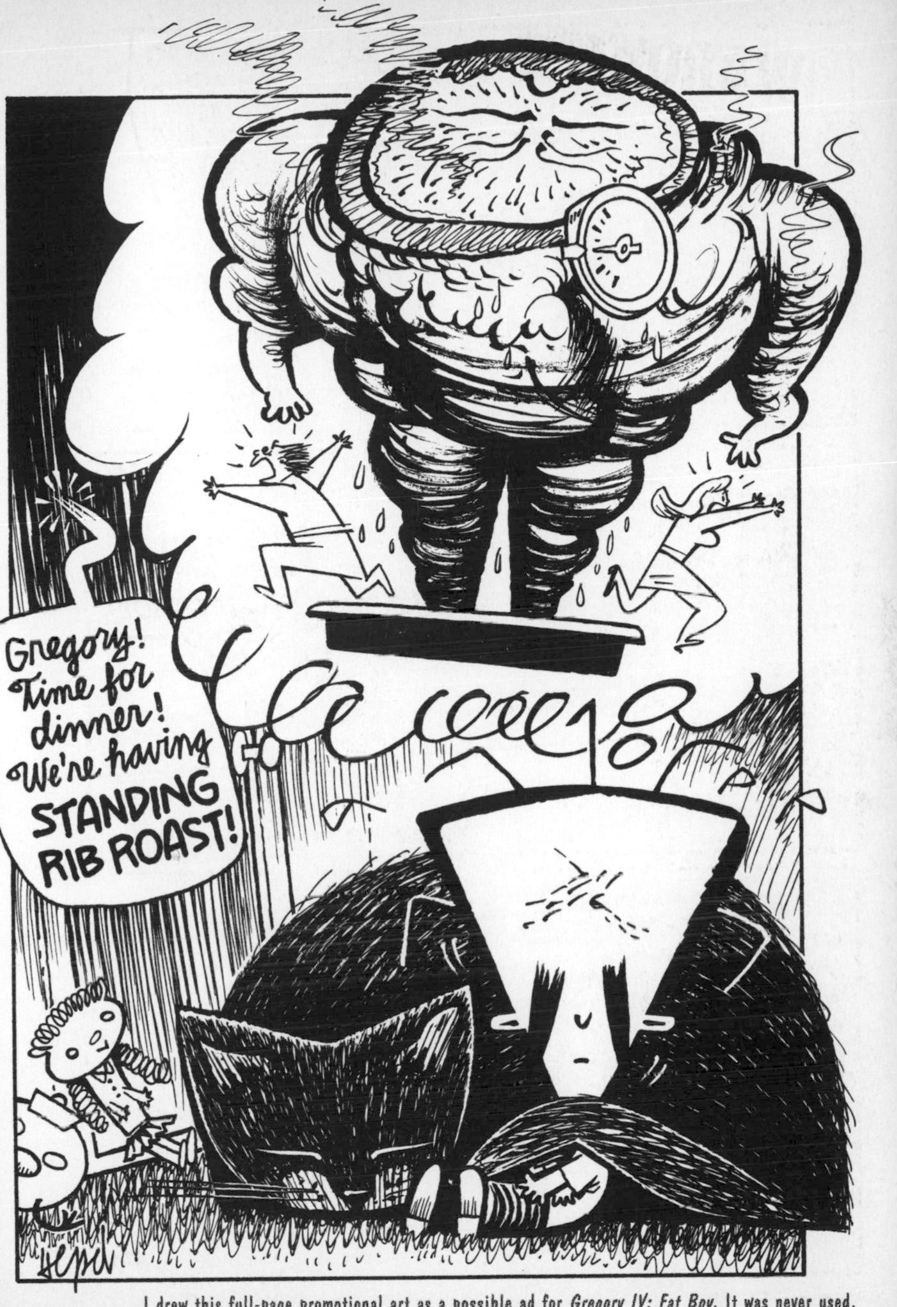
Gregory! Time for dinner! We're having STANDING RIB ROAST!

I drew this full-page promotional art as a possible ad for *Gregory IV: Fat Boy*. It was never used, but I always liked the piece. The drawing was only about 7/8 inked until this year, when I finally finished it.

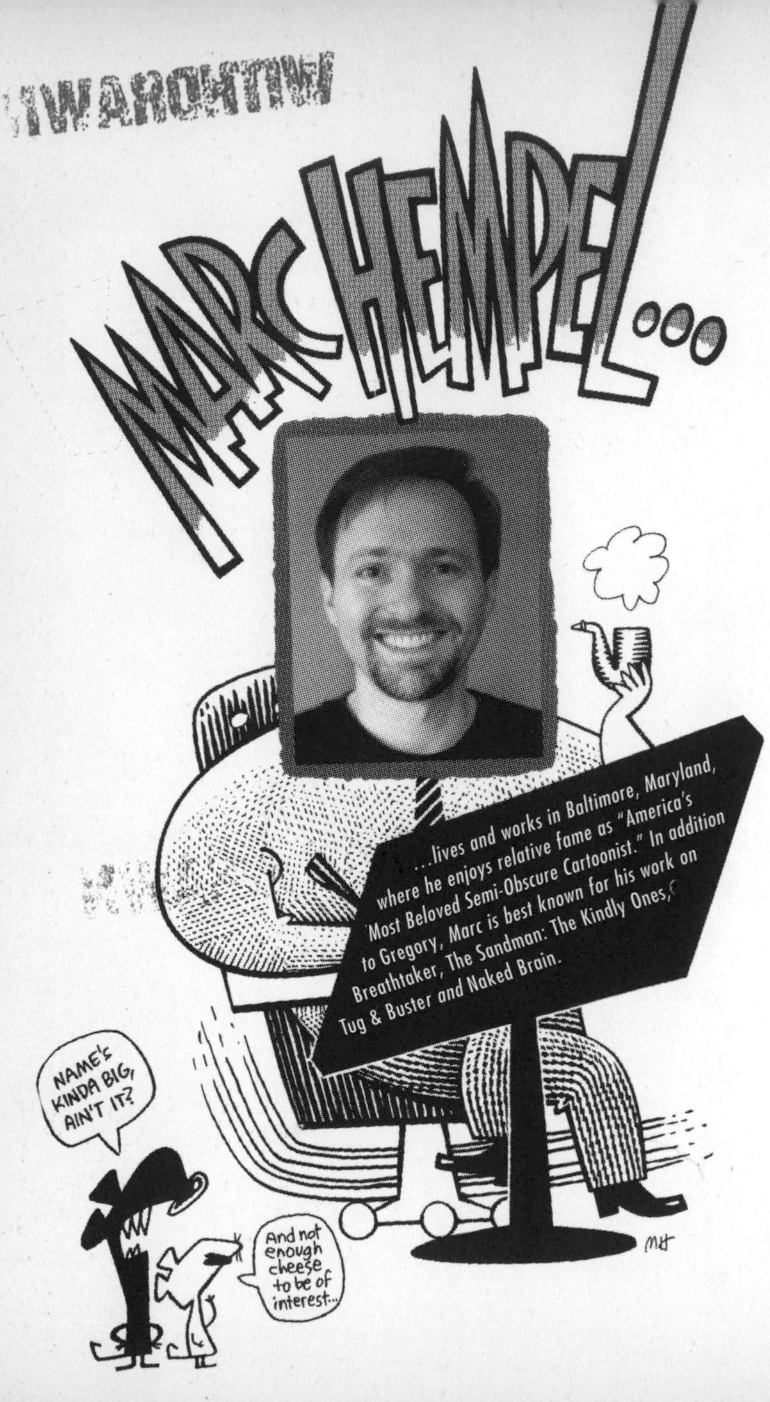
MARC HEMPEL...
...lives and works in Baltimore, Maryland, where he enjoys relative fame as "America's Most Beloved Semi-Obscure Cartoonist." In addition to Gregory, Marc is best known for his work on Breathtaker, The Sandman: The Kindly Ones, Tug & Buster and Naked Brain.
NAME'S KINDA BIG, AIN'T IT?
And not enough cheese to be of interest...
MH